AF250991

PLEASURES

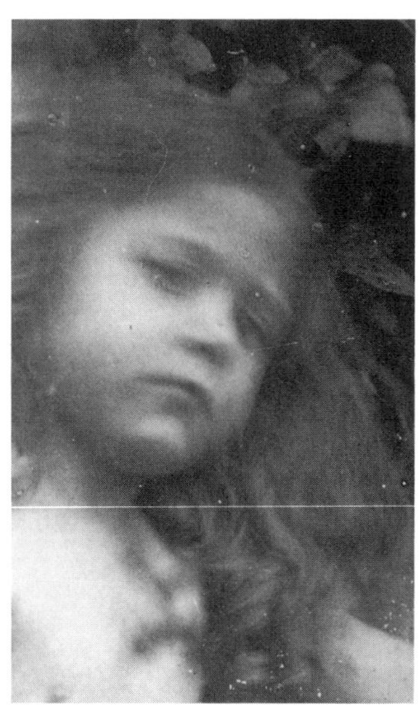

DUKE UNIVERSITY PRESS

Durham 1995

TAKEN

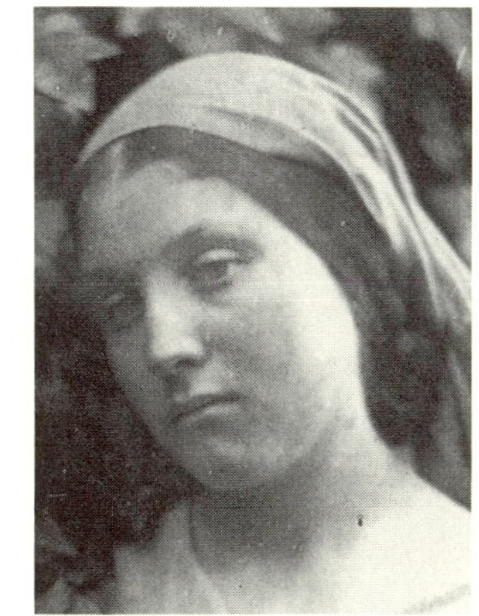

CAROL MAVOR

Performances

of

Sexuality

and

Loss

in

Victorian

Photographs

Second printing, 1996

© 1995 Duke University Press

All rights reserved

Printed in the United States

of America on acid-free paper ∞

Typeset in Perpetua

by Keystone Typesetting, Inc.

Library of Congress Cataloging-

in-Publication Data appear on the

last printed page of this book.

FOR GRANDMA

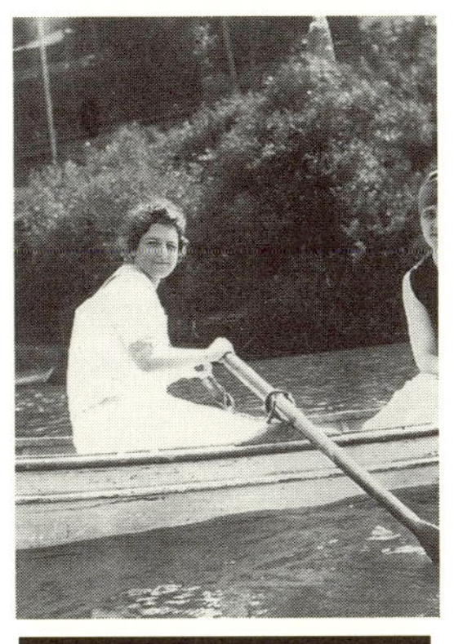

CONTENTS

LIST OF ILLUSTRATIONS

Figures

1. Lewis Carroll, *Edith, Lorina and Alice Liddell*, 1859
2. J. M. Barrie, *Peter, George and Jack Davies in a Wheelbarrow*, c. 1897
3. Lewis Carroll, *Portrait of Evelyn Hatch*, c. 1878
4. John Everett Millais, *Cherry Ripe*, 1880
5. Frederick Leighton, *Actaea, Nymph of the Shore*, 1868
6. Lawrence Alma-Tadema, *The Sculptor's Model*, 1877
7. Julia Margaret Cameron, *Spring*, 1865
8. Julia Margaret Cameron, *Florence/Study of St. John the Baptist*, 1872
9. Lewis Carroll, *Agnes Grace Weld as Little Red Riding Hood*, 1857
10. Henry Peach Robinson, from the *Little Red Riding Hood* series, 1858
11. Lewis Carroll, *Irene MacDonald*, 1863
12. Lewis Carroll, *Alice Liddell as a Beggar-Child*, c. 1858
13. Lewis Carroll, *Coates*, 1857
14. *Florence and Eliza Holder*, c. 1876
15. *Florence Holder*, c. 1876
16. Southwares and Hawes, *Photograph of a Dead Child*, 1865
17. Mary Cassatt, *Mother About to Wash Her Sleepy Child*, 1880
18. Julia Kristeva, page from the English translation of "Stabat Mater," 1986
19. The Munby Box, c. 1970
20. Howl, Hannah as a lady, 1874
21. Hannah as a chimney sweep, 1862
22. James Stodart, Hannah as Magdalene, 1864

Plates

ACKNOWLEDGMENTS

I want to begin by thanking Helene Moglen, a special teacher, scholar, and friend, who has always been there for me and still is. She gave me the gift of confidence. Thanks to Page duBois for telling me about the body, about Lacan, and for showing me some wonderful possibilities of how to be. And thanks again to Page for telling me that I had to start a writing group. Thank you Della, Jane, and Joy for saying yes to every Friday. Della Pollock enabled me to see performance again (and again), in ways that I never imagined. Joy Kasson's integrity and insistence on clarity enriched my approach to not only writing but also reading. Jane Blocker asked all the right questions, without hesitation, and has helped me to see the end. All three have been astute and enthusiastic readers of this book, and I will always be grateful to them. Thanks to elin o'Hara slavick for loving photographs with me, for opening my eyes, and for never being able to wait. Thanks to Amy Ruth Buchanan for loving photographs with me and for never backing down, intellectually or personally. Thanks to Hayden White for Roland Barthes and for asking all those hard questions a long time ago. Thanks to Stephen Heath for muddling Victorian sexuality for me, as it should be, for opening up the doors of Cambridge to me, and for the spring duck. Thanks to Patricia Patterson for telling me about utopias and color.

I owe many thanks to individuals and research programs at the University of North Carolina, Chapel Hill. I have had the joy of working with a number of wonderful graduate and undergraduate students in various seminars on Victorian culture; many of them have patiently and enthusiastically listened to the ideas presented in this book and have helped me to work through theoretical problems. I want to thank in particular Kelly Baum, Jo DeDecker, Joe Lucchesi, Fiona Ragheb, Jenny Shippen, and Anna Snoderly. I want to thank Professors Arthur Marks and Mary Sturgeon for granting me research leaves while each served as Chair of the Art Department. I received invaluable funding and time as a Fellow at the Institute for Arts and Humanities and as a Chapman Faculty Fellow. A much appreciated Junior Faculty Development Grant gave me a summer to work on this project. Several University Research Council grants made the pictures possible. Jennifer Olmsted served as a terrific research assistant as this book came to a close; her combination of professionalism and wit was always appreciated. Lindsay Fulenwider and Pam Andrews have helped in many kind and generous ways, and I am especially grateful to Peggy Quinn for cheerfully helping with financial details.

Many curators, librarians, photographers, lending coordinators, scholars, and lending institutions have helped to bring the book's pictures together: John Marais, John Smith, Diana Chardin, and the Trinity College Library, Cambridge; Debbie Ireland, Pam Roberts and the Royal Photographic Society of Great Britain; Jacklyn Burns and the J. Paul Getty Museum, Malibu, California; Andrea Inselmann, Ann Paterra and the Harry Ransom Humanities Research Center, the University of Texas at Austin; Janice Madhu and the International Museum of Photography at George Eastman House; John Kirkham and the Barnardo Photographic Archive; Sarah Shuttleworth and the Bodleian Library, University of Oxford; Sally Mann, Lisa Newlin, and Houk Friedman, New York; Kit Palmer and Great Ormond Street Children's Hospital, London; the National Gallery of Canada, Ottawa; Christ Church, Oxford; the Los Angeles County Museum of Art; the Fine Arts Museums of San Francisco; The Rosenbach Museum and Library; Christie's Images; Andrew Birkin; and Laurel Bradley.

I am especially grateful to Ken Wissoker for patiently waiting (with just the right amount of nudging) and then for making it go. He has somehow managed to be straightforward and gentle at the same time; he is one of my kindest friends and a smart and sensitive editor.

Love and thanks to my mother and father.

Love and thanks to Oliver, who learned how to walk in Cambridge. And to Ambrose, who was still inside when it all began.

And finally, where thanks would never be enough, love (all kinds of it) to Kevin.

PLEASURES TAKEN

PLEASURES TAKEN

INTRODUCTION

Pictures

and

Conversations

Alice was beginning to get very tired of sitting by her sister on the bank, and of having nothing to do: once or twice she had peeped into the book her sister was reading, but it had no pictures or conversations in it, "and what is the use of a book," thought Alice, "without pictures or conversations. —LEWIS CARROLL, *Alice's Adventures in Wonderland*

Like Alice, I am very fond of pictures and conversations. In fact, my earliest work on Lewis Carroll was a series of performances (conversations, really) within an elaborate installation space that featured walls filled with colored-pencil pictures—floors littered with large, painted cut-outs of anthropomorphic animals—and even a miniature house that the viewer could walk into (with some difficulty). The pinkened walls of the house were lined with Carroll's photographs of girl-children (framed in gold), which I, like Carroll, had fetishized. During the performances, I always played an impish professor (a portmanteau of Alice and Carroll the Oxford don), filled with Alice and malice, as I lectured (punished?) the audience on the real Alice (Alice Pleasance Liddell) and her role, not only as muse but also as author.[1] My Alice conversations (which were as one-sided as Humpty Dumpty's lectures to Alice—"The question is which is to be master—that's all") insisted on two basic points: one, that children have a sexuality that is as complex as anyone's; and two, that their sexuality deserves recognition, respect, and scrutiny.[2] One chapter in this book, "Dream-Rushes: Lewis Carroll's Photographs of Little Girls," focuses on these issues. My performances grew into that chapter, and that chapter, like Alice, grew and grew until it became this book. And as Alice once said, when "she found her head pressing against the ceiling, and had to stoop to save her neck from being broken": "That's quite enough—I hope."[3]

I have always been interested in the "cult of the child" (as part of a larger framework that concerns my own gender bias toward the "cult of the little girl"). Girldom reached new heights during my own plastic, pink, glittery youth: I wore elaborate dresses every day until I was twelve; I visited Disneyland very regularly from the time I was two (I was particularly taken with Tinkerbell's impressive role throughout the park, despite, or because of, her miniature state—I have always disagreed with Alice's assertion that "three inches is such a wretched height to be"); my parents have a wealth of souvenirs from my girlhood including a valuable storehouse in their garage of early Barbies (Midges, Kens, Francies, Tutties, Todds) saved from my fabulous childhood; in short, I attached myself to every girl-child product that I could get my girl-hands on.[4]

After growing up, going to college, and completing a series of Disney-gone-wackier performances and installations (that reflected my early days of consumer bliss), it was the filmmaker Jean-Pierre Gorin who suggested that I turn back the pages to the origins of childhood madness: the work of Lewis Carroll. It was a wonderful and smart idea. After all, when Carroll first told the Alice story, while gliding down a river on a boat with Alice Liddell and her sisters Lorina and Edith and the Reverend Robinson Duckworth, nurserydom and all of its products were being produced as never before.[5] Once published, *Alice's Adventures in Wonderland* sold like hotcakes and gave rise to the sequel, *Through the Looking-Glass.* Alice products, such as the Alice Postage Stamp Case and the Looking-Glass Tin, were mass produced alongside fashions inspired by literature, such as flouncy dresses and mobcaps spurred on by Kate Greenaway books.

For the Victorians, the charm of buying childhood grew out of an active imagination that envisioned one's early years as a lost utopia: a bower to retreat to, a secret garden that every middle-class person could enter through children's books and other child-centered products. The material culture of Victorian childhood produced souvenirs of a time and place that never was—a true Neverland. The evolving commodity culture, fecund with useful and not-so-useful, pretty and bizarre things, was also providing a kind of vulgarity that the middle class took pleasure in shunning. Of course, they often shunned it by purchasing even more of its vulgar products and promoting a myth of historical decline or even degeneracy to shadow the often flickering official optimism of an undimmed future. As a consequence, they turned resolutely to the past as a kind of moral obligation, either the medieval past (as did William Morris, who managed to materialize his medieval fantasies into sunflower wallpaper, handmade furniture, and beautiful uncorseted woman with unpinned hair) or, because that might seem a bit far removed and laborious, their own pasts, their prettied-up, overdressed childhoods—which were as real as Morris's world was medieval.

And "we other Victorians" (of the twentieth century) have continued the tradition of infantilizing history by recharming our past.[6] We have remade the Victorians themselves into lost, innocent children: through BBC television shows such as "Upstairs, Downstairs" (even the maids had a wonderful life); through recent films, such as those by the Merchant-Ivory team, which always seem sort-of Victorian, even if they do make it into the twentieth century (in that special Laura Ashley way in which "the past is free from wear and tear"); through magazines with titles like *Victoria;* and of course through the ubiquitous Victoria's Secret, where you can buy reproduction postcards of Pre-Raphaelite paintings and audio tapes of the classical music they play for you while you try on your padded and pearled bras and lacy, lacy panties . . . a mise-en-scène of fabricated Victorian sex as high culture.[7] (Never mind that it was typical for Victorian women to wear long-legged, cotton drawers or knickerbockers. Never mind that it all takes place at a mall.)

And unlike any era before, we have photographic records of Alice, of Carroll, of the fashions of the time, of Queen Victoria herself: photography was invented hand-in-hand with our modern conception of childhood. The child and the photograph were commodified, fetishized, developed alongside each other: they were laminated and framed as one.[8] By the middle of the nineteenth century, the carte de visite had been invented (which enabled prints to be mass-produced easily and inexpensively), and "the traditional forms of children's artifacts had disappeared . . . to be replaced by completely new and different artifacts. The crib, high chair, swing, and perambulator all served as barriers between the child and the adult world."[9] Interestingly enough, both our image of childhood and the photograph (mythically) keep time still, innocent, untouched. For the Victorians and *still* for ourselves, wooden toys, children's tales by Carroll and his friend George MacDonald, Pears' gentle soap, handknit woolen jackets with pewter buttons—things that were and are far less precious to children than to the adults who demand them—preserved and preserve an impossible childhood sealed with utopian wax. Similarly, as Peter Wollen has told us, photography preserves fragments of the past "like flies in amber."[10]

Yet recent critical theory has playfully contradicted the more obvious static nature of the photograph by reading it as *also* performative. Roland Barthes, Victor Burgin, Henry Sayre, and Peggy Phelan are but a few of those who have participated in a discourse that understands photography as representing a complex *movement* from presence to absence. For only with photography (as opposed to painting or sculpture) is one assured of the fact that what was once before the artist / camera—its referent—was there and is no longer there.[11] Yet the photograph (fictitiously) registers it as right before your eyes: as simulacrum.

Roland Barthes poetically describes the photograph's particularly in-dexical relationship as being like "those pairs of fish (sharks, I think, according to Michelet) which navigate in convoy, as though united by an eternal coitus," or like that "class of laminated objects whose two leaves cannot be separated without destroying them both: the windowpane and the landscape, and why not: Good and Evil, desire and its object: dualities we can conceive but not perceive."[12] As a result, we perform that move-ment from presence to absence that the missing referent fixes and unfixes in its emulsion.

But the photograph's analogical relationship with its referent does not stop there: it extends into our fantasies of our identities and histories. The "reality of an object" in a photograph, like the smell and taste of Proust's madeleine cakes, triggers our own memories, our own stories. For Barthes, it once was a "slender ribbon of braided gold," a particular necklace worn by a woman in a James Van der Zee photograph from 1926.[13] The necklace, which might easily go unnoticed by others, looked just like the one that Barthes "had seen worn by someone" in his "own family, and which, once she died, remained shut up in a family box of old jewelry."[14] Barthes tells the story of the original owner of this necklace: a sister of his father's; never married; lived with her mother as an old maid; lived a dreary life that always saddens him when he thinks of her. We all do this sometimes—and only with certain photographs, which are somehow magically right for us. We perform a dialogue with these special photo-graphs (and it usually has nothing to do with the original intentions behind the taking of the picture). What is no longer there performs upon us and we perform upon it. It bereaves us and we bereave it.

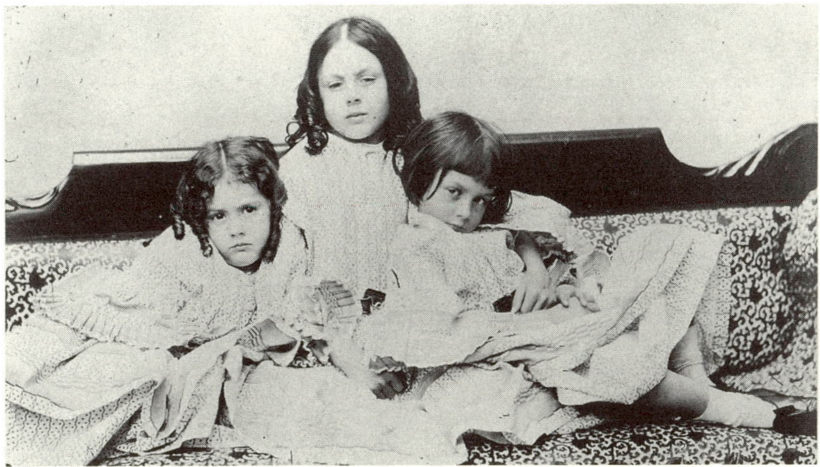

Figure 1. Lewis Carroll, *Edith, Lorina and Alice Liddell*, 1859.
(Gernsheim Collection, Harry Ransom Humanities Research Center,
The University of Texas at Austin)

Interestingly enough, the most meaningful (performative) photograph in *Camera Lucida* (for Barthes) is one of his mother as a little girl: the famous Winter Garden Photograph. The image of his mother was taken when she was five; the year was 1898. For Barthes, this "just image of his mother"—"of the mother-as-child"—"constituted the figure of a sovereign *innocence*."[15] What James Kincaid has written about J. M. Barrie, the author of *Peter Pan,* could easily have been written in regards to Barthes: "There is no doubt that the image of his mother as a girl meant much to him, at least in the way of material he could plunder for stories."[16] After all, Wendy was a little mother who flew back to Neverland two times to do Peter's spring cleaning, but she eventually had too many growing pains (despite her efforts not to grow) and grew too much for Peter's liking, so she never saw him again—until Peter flew to pick up her daughter, Jane, for spring cleanings. Then Jane grew too much, so she too never saw him again—until Peter flew to pick up her daughter, Margaret, for spring cleanings: "When Margaret grows up she will have a daughter, who is to be Peter's mother in turn; and so it will go on, so long as children are gay and innocent and heartless."[17] We have flown back to the place where we began: the photograph, the child.

Both the photograph and childhood accept their shape and their poignancy from death. If there were no death, why would childhood hold its

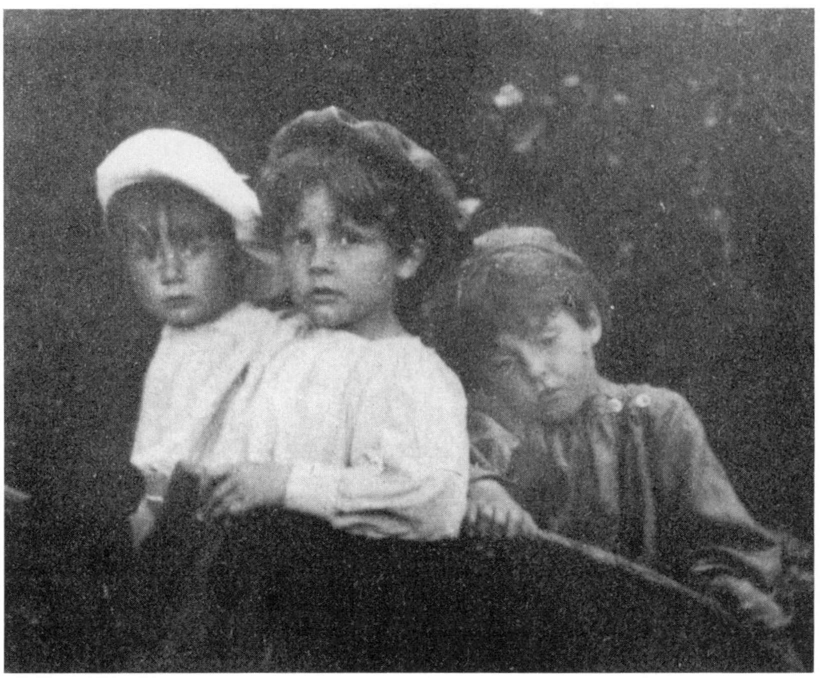

Figure 2. J. M. Barrie, *Peter, George and Jack Davies in a Wheelbarrow*,
c.1897. (Great Ormond Street Children's Hospital,
London and Andrew Birkin)

appeal? If there were no death, why would our desire to photograph and to preserve lost moments be so urgent? "All children, except one, grow up," wrote Barrie on the first page of *Peter and Wendy*.[18] Regarding the Davies boys, who inspired the story and upon whose ears the Neverland stories were christened, Barrie comments: "They had a long summer day, and I turned round twice and now they are off to school."[19] As Kincaid morosely reminds us, children "grow up with the speed of darkness."[20] Only the camera can keep up with the velocity of children. Is it any wonder that Alice, Lorina, and Edith Liddell and George, Jack, and Peter Davies have been relentlessly preserved by Carroll and Barrie (not only in ink but also) in emulsion? (figs. 1 and 2) Their pictures are no more and no less than a keepsake of a golden splash.

CHAPTER I

Dream-Rushes: Lewis Carroll's Photographs of Little Girls

On March twenty-fifth, 1863, Lewis Carroll (Charles Lutwidge Dodgson, 1832–98) composed a list of 107 names—girls "photographed or to be photographed." The girls are grouped under their Christian names, all the Alices together, all the Agneses together, and all the Beatrices together, all in alphabetical order. He also notes many of their dates of birth (that telltale sign of a girl's true girlishness). Carroll's is a poem of girlhood that rolls off the tongue, like a catalog of Victorian flowers. His prose from the twenty-fifth of March is not unlike one of Humbert Humbert's most cherished poems, Lolita's class list, a poem that Humbert took the pains to memorize by heart:

> A poem, a poem, forsooth! So strange and sweet was it to discover this "Haze, Dolores" (she!) [Lolita's full name] in its special bower of names, with its bodyguard of roses—a fairy princess between her two maids of honor. I am trying to analyze the spine-thrill of delight that it gives me, this name among all of the others. What is it that excites me almost to tears (hot, opalescent, thick tears that poets and lovers shed)? What is it? The tender anonymity of this name with the formal veil ("Dolores") and that abstract transposition of first name and surname, which is like a pair of new pale gloves or a mask?[1]

Very few critics have been willing to touch the little girls Carroll photographed. The subject makes them understandably uneasy. When they do touch upon the topic of his curious photographs, they tend to read not the pictures themselves, or the situation of the girl of the period, but rather Carroll. They want to make it clear that Carroll was not a Humbert Humbert.

Helmut Gernsheim, for instance, who was the first to seriously acknowledge the pictures as important to the history of photography and who has written the definitive book on Carroll's photographs, clearly seeks to minimize conflict when confronting the troubling images: "Beautiful little girls had a strange fascination for Lewis Carroll. This curious relationship, . . . may be described as innocent love."[2] Similarly, Morton Cohen, the man responsible for publishing the long-lost nude photographs taken by Carroll, argues that Carroll was "drawn *naturally* to them; he revelled in their unaffected innocence, their unsophisticated, unsocialized simplicity; he worshiped their fresh, pure unspoiled beauty" and was "far from being James Joyce's 'Lewd Carroll' or having anything in common with Vladimir Nabokov's Humbert Humbert."[3]

Cohen's emphasis on purity, innocence, and simplicity is peculiar when one considers what Carroll suggested about childhood in his own letters and diaries and in the *Alice* books themselves. Many of Carroll's letters revel in the sadistic desires of children, as Carroll-as-child takes sides with all of the girl-children of the world, battering his auditor with questions as only children (usually) do.[4] Likewise, Alice may try to be polite in Wonderland, but she is downright rude when she goes through the Looking Glass, and Carroll even refers to Alice as "Malice" in a letter to one of his child-friends. James Kincaid points out the maliciousness of children and the impossibility of valuing innocence: "[In the *Alice* books] there is often present a deeper and more ironic view that questions the value of human innocence altogether and sees the sophisticated and sad corruption of adults as preferable to the cruel selfishness of children."[5] The success of Kincaid's useful analysis is not all that surprising; the literary texts on Carroll are generally more satisfactory than those that focus on the photographs. Although the difference between the critical texts is partly due to different emphases within respective disciplines and factions, it is also a matter of confronting the nonfictional Alices—the real Alice Pleasance Liddell and all of her successors. Critics such as Cohen try to veil the obvious sexuality that Carroll captured on the photographic plates. Even more than the stories, the pictures "question the value of human innocence"—both Carroll's and his models'.

Cohen argues that Carroll was not of the stern evangelical tradition that informed the rearing of many children but, rather, inherited his approach to the child from romantic forebears, who "assumed that the child came into this world innocent and pure."[6] For Carroll (according to Cohen), the child, especially the female child, was divine, pure, good. Moments of Cohen's analysis are convincing, but he is unreasonably insistent upon washing out any contradictions. At the heart of the argument is not Carroll but Cohen's own desire to form a general theory of Carroll's sexuality. Cohen is interested in presenting Carroll as "repressed" by Victorian culture, and therefore innocent: "Only as a repressed human being could he have lived his paradoxical life and worshipped the young girls with a clear, Christian conscience."[7] What Cohen fails to see is how he in turn is repressed by our own society, and how this repression governs his reading of Carroll.

Confronted by the taboo combination of child and sexuality, such critics refuse to "see." In Foucauldian terms, participants in the tradition of modern sexual discourse feel the need to discuss sex in a way "that would not derive from morality alone but from rationality."[8] Thus while Carroll himself could lead a double-double life as photographer and clergyman, mathematician / logician and author of nonsense, Cohen forms a *rational* discourse that blocks our way to confronting the contradictions that the pictures play out. In the discussion of evangelical versus romantic, the difficulty actually lives with the depiction of the girls; like most observers of Carroll's pictures, Cohen renders the models as silent and even invisible, solving Carroll's problem by denying the children's sexuality. In Cohen's words, "Victorian parents who shared Dodgson's views allowed their innocent offspring to romp about in warm weather without any clothes on, particularly at the seaside, and were quite accustomed to seeing nude 'sexless' children used as objects of decoration in book illustrations and greeting cards."[9] The telltale words here are "used," "objects," and "decoration." (And is there no difference between playing on the beach and sitting nude before a man and his lens in his studio?) But the larger question still remains: Why do we have to insist that children have no sexuality? In pronouncing Carroll's romanticism, Cohen reveals himself to be a latter-day evangelical, trying to protect his own children (his life's work on Carroll) from falling into evil ways. Ironically, whereas Cohen remarks critically of evangelical children that they "could hardly be thought to have any freedom . . . these children had to be transmogrified from wicked things into beings of goodness and godliness," Cohen's "children" also lack the freedom of displaying sexuality.[10]

The word "sexuality," indeed, was born at the dawn of the nineteenth century (in 1800) and originally referred only to biology; it was crystallized into its current meaning in 1879, when J. Matthews Duncan used the term to mean (as defined in the *Oxford English Dictionary*) a "possession of sexual powers, or capability of sexual feelings."[11] Duncan reminded his readers that "in removing the ovaries you do not necessarily destroy sexuality in a woman"—a distinction between sexuality and reproduction that Sigmund Freud also drew (in "The Sexual Life of Human Beings"), this time with specific references to children:[12]

> To suppose that children have no sexual life—sexual excitations and needs and a kind of satisfaction—but suddenly acquire it between the ages of twelve and fourteen, would (quite apart from any observations) be as improbable, and indeed senseless, biologically as to suppose that they brought no genitals with them into the world and only grew them at the time of puberty. What *does* awaken in them at this time is the reproductive function, which makes use for its purposes of physical and mental material already present. You are committing the error of confusing sexuality and reproduction and by doing so you are blocking your path to an understanding of sexuality.[13]

Problematic as Freud's readings are, and problematic as it is to use his work in any kind of historical analysis (particularly one outside of his own period and culture), he nonetheless remains useful to a discussion like the one at hand—in part, as art historian Griselda Pollock has pointed out, because he gave us a language in which to talk about sexuality.[14] In particular, we may use this language to talk about sexuality's connection to theories of difference, which, as we shall see, become especially relevant to Carroll's photographs of little girls. Freud not only accelerated the discourse on male and female sexual difference but also acknowledged both that children are sexual and that they are sexual in a way different from adults. According to him, childhood sexuality is an "instinct" that has been tamed by the time we reach adulthood. To be sure, Freud is essentializing children, and he exacerbates this problem (again in "The Sexual Life of Human Beings") when he equates the child's sexuality with that of the "primitive," the "pervert," and so on. But what is salvageable for our purposes is that Freud alerts us to the ways in which we have been educated into thinking that children are pure, asexual, and innocent, and to how "anyone who describes them otherwise can be charged with being an infamous blasphemer against the tender and sacred feelings of mankind."[15] I am proposing to be blasphemous: to acknowledge the sexuality of children (and of the Victorian girl at that) while making every attempt *not* to project our oppressive desires onto their bodies—an impossible goal, of course.

Venus of Oxford

Carroll's first reference to photographing a nude child is in a diary entry dated May 21, 1867: "Mrs. L. brought Beatrice, and I took a photograph of the two; and several of Beatrice alone, 'sans habilement [*sic*].' "[16] Beatrice Hatch was one of Carroll's favorite models, along with her sister Evelyn; both were at ease in what Carroll has referred to as their "primitive dress." Of the four nude images that have been rediscovered, we are most surprised by the image of Evelyn Hatch (c. 1878, fig. 3).[17] She catches our eye and confronts us with her own gaze (not unlike Manet's *Olympia,* 1863) as she lies before us sprawled as a tiny odalisque. As child-woman, posed like a courtesan, Evelyn reminds us also of Titian's *Venus of Urbino* (1538)—not only in her pose but also in the treatment of the photograph, which gives it its Venetianesque quality. It is a portmanteau of a "real" photograph and layers of opalescent colors. Precious Evelyn has been "printed on emulsion on a curved piece of glass, with oil highlights applied to the back surface. Beneath it is a second piece of curved glass painted in oil."[18] Curved glass, caressed with paint, all taboo: this "paintograph" is worthy of serious fetishization.[19] Evelyn's body glows in a flesh-colored light that gives way to a surrealistically painted marsh of golden moss-greens. Evelyn, stuck in an everlasting sunset, which is strangely muted by the peculiar pink-yellows that shine below the rather ominous dark violet light, is a modern little Venus of Oxford.

Evelyn is also part animal. Her eyes, mildly vampirish, shine like a fox's at night. A closer look reveals tiny highlights that have been painted on the picto-glass, as if her eyes were marbles. Her face, painted darker than the rest of her pure girl-body, indeed gives the sense that Evelyn, like Alice's

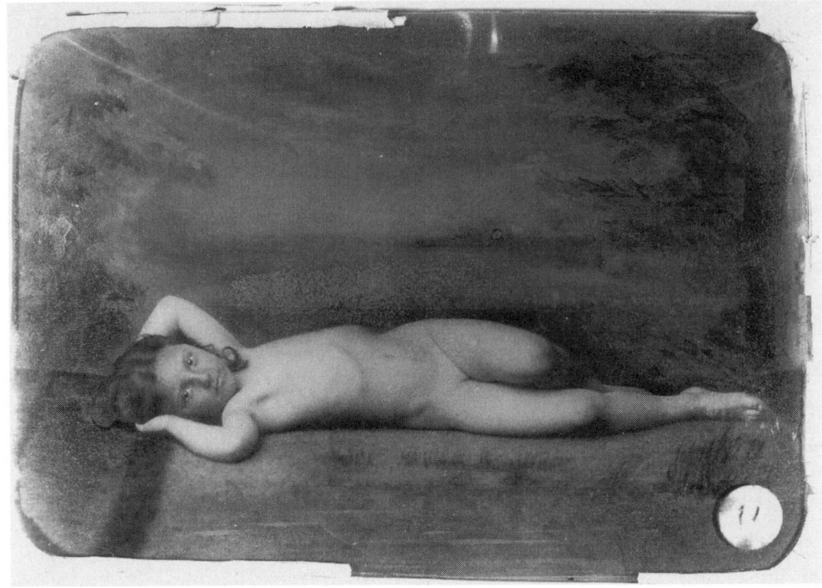

Figure 3. Lewis Carroll, *Portrait of Evelyn Hatch*, c. 1878.
(The Rosenbach Museum and Library, Philadelphia and
The Executors of the C. L. Dodgson Estate)

pig-baby, is part animal and part child. Nina Auerbach has also equated
Evelyn with animality, specifically a kind of animal sexuality. In the current Carroll scholarship, Auerbach's is the only discussion that confronts
this image:

> Some embarrassed viewers have tried to see no sexuality in these
> photographs, but it seems to me needlessly apologetic to deny the
> eroticism of this beautiful little odalisque. Since her sexuality is not
> imaged forth in foils, emblems, or metaphors, Carroll's Evelyn
> Hatch seems to me a far more healthily realized figure than Beards-
> ley's Salomé, who needs the Baptist's purity to define her lust, or
> even than Nabokov's sadomasochistic dream of Lolita, for Evelyn
> Hatch is allowed to be at one with her own implied powers. Thus,
> the achievement of this photograph lies in its pure acceptance of
> what Carroll's contemporaries perceived as demonic and danger-
> ous. Unlike Alice, Evelyn Hatch needs no creatures to inform us
> that she is both animal and dreamer, pig and pure little girl. Carroll
> as camera eye does perfect justice to the self-transforming mobility

of this model. The eroticism, along with the passionate and seditious powers this had come to imply, belongs to the child; the artist
merely understands it.[20]

Auerbach's analysis, like many of her writings, including the groundbreaking *Woman and the Demon,* is exciting for the ways in which it unleashes images (both literary and visual) of supposedly oppressed Victorian stereotypes into spaces of subversive power.[21] She relishes the
images of hungry, aggressive, erotic, violent Victorian women, even if
they often "wear the prim pinafore of that supposed Victorian sugarplum,
the polite little girl."[22] Yet in many ways her analysis feels too celebratory
and too clear. Though I am sympathetic to her criticism of "sophisticated
feminists who purge women of violence and desire with self-imprisoning
alacrity," like Carroll I prefer to "oscillate" between celebration and horror.[23] By granting children sexuality, and by suggesting an inventive and
girl-empowering reciprocity between artist and model (an idea I will
return to later), Auerbach's vision of Victorian subversion transgresses the
prudishness of the "innocent" school of readings. At the same time,
however, her analysis also covers up other contradictions that might be
productive in unraveling the conflicting anxieties of difference in Victorian culture—anxieties that Carroll's photographs of girls make evident.

For example, is Evelyn really a "beautiful little odalisque," as Auerbach
terms her? And if so, what are the standards governing this beauty? She is
a beautiful child, in the ways in which our culture and Carroll's is / was
sympathetic to the beauty of almost all children, especially little girls. But
so much of Evelyn's "beauty" here rests on traditional concepts of beauty
as found in the history of art. The female nude has reigned as ideal beauty
for centuries. Feminist art historians (notably Pollock, Rozsika Parker,
and Linda Nochlin) have been exploring and exposing the objectification
of the female nude in art for more than twenty years. As they have pointed
out, the passivity of the female nude is accentuated by the process of her
production. In looking at this little nude (this photograph of Evelyn
Hatch), I am reminded of the role of women's artistic roles or lack
thereof: that women artists were not permitted to study from the nude
model; that women artists were largely absent from the academies and
the schools; and that since the late eighteenth century, the female nude
was favored over the male nude.[24] In Carroll's image of Evelyn Hatch, like
so many other traditional nudes of the nineteenth century, we find that

"woman is present as an image but with the specific connotations of body and nature, that is passive, available, possessable, powerless."[25] Unlike Auerbach, I would argue that Evelyn is Carroll's "foil," his other. Stretched across a bed of grass, with trees as her headboard and footboard, Evelyn becomes one with nature; (in opposition to Auerbach's reading) she is "metaphor" and "emblem." In capturing Evelyn as odalisque, Carroll is participating in a visual tradition that includes Delacroix and Ingres, "orientalizing" Evelyn, as he often did his other girl-models. Besides using the "primitive dress" of *sans habillement,* Carroll also "orientalized" little girls such as Xie Kitchin by costuming them as Turk or Chinaman (1873, plate 1).[26] The slippage between the spaces of child, primitive, and other becomes a Carolinian dance in a looking-glass mirror: the subjects of his photographs collapse together as othered others.

And what does it mean to be "pure little girl," in Auerbach's phrase? Hélène Cixous has argued that the child is nothing but "an imaginary species, invented by a certain type of psychological literature," and that the little girl is "a complex fantasm" of Carroll's own.[27] Why must we always insist that the child is somehow more pure, or even "healthy," as Auerbach suggests? Does this formulation not extend the same perspective that animated the Victorian "cult of the little girl"?

For, like many of the 500,000 people who bought copies of the *Graphic* Christmas Annual in 1880 for the color centerfold of John Everett Millais's *Cherry Ripe* (1880, fig. 4), Carroll was attracted to the image of the little girl caught before the contamination of adolescence. But, in contrast to an artist like Millais, Carroll was a photographer who undercut the typical representation of the pure little girl. He exposed her, not as a mobcapped girl of pre-industrialized England, but as neological: sexual, sexualized, innocent, childlike, and womanly. A glance at Carroll's rendition of Xie Kitchin mimicking the Joshua Reynolds painting *Penelope Boothby* (on which *Cherry Ripe* was based), reveals a "strangely vampish image very different in spirit from the original"—anything but pure (1879, plate 2).[28] Though clothed, her confrontational gaze and her long, lacy black gloves, pierced by her pure white fingers, image her, like the nude Evelyn Hatch, as differently sexual.

At the time of this photograph (about 1878, given that Evelyn was born in 1871 and here looks to be around six or seven), nudes by such Victorian artists as Edward Burne-Jones, Frederick Leighton, and Lawrence Alma-Tadema were widely recognized, if rather atypical in relation to the popu-

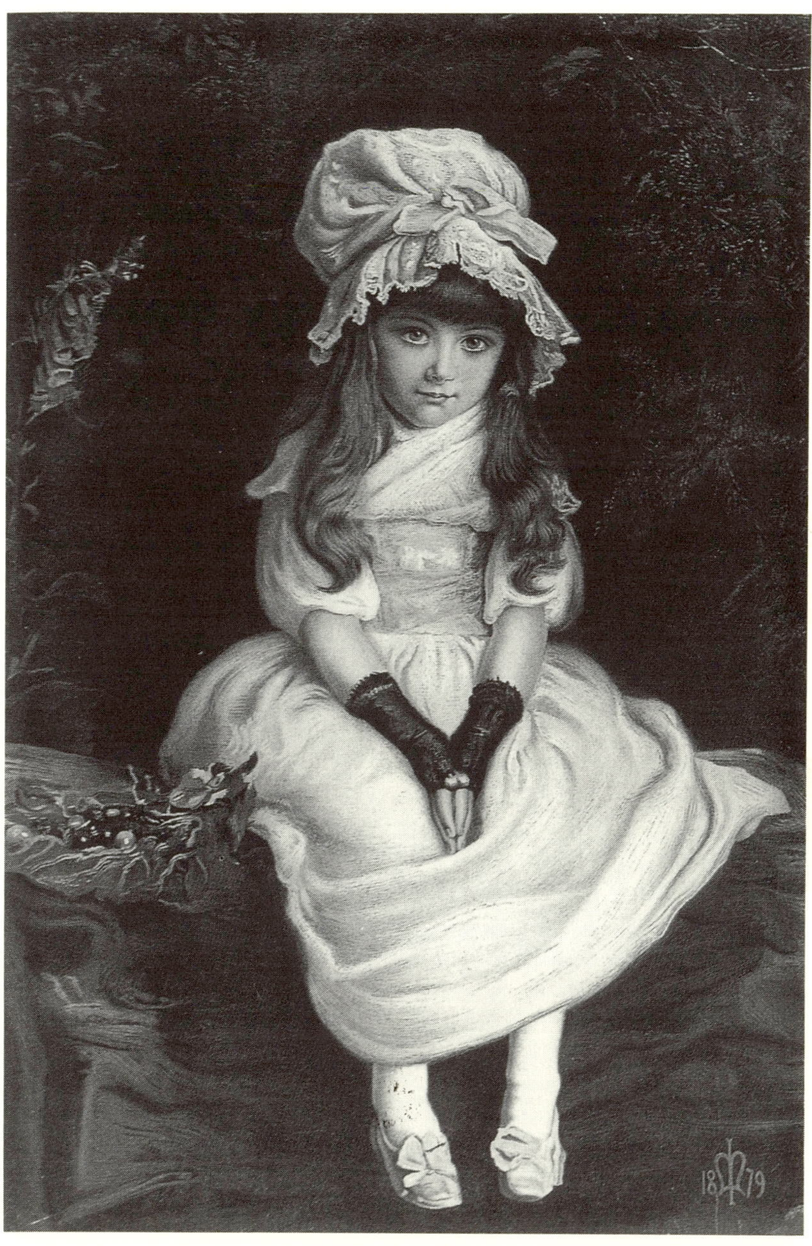

Figure 4. John Everett Millais, *Cherry Ripe*,
1880, in the *Graphic* Christmas Annual

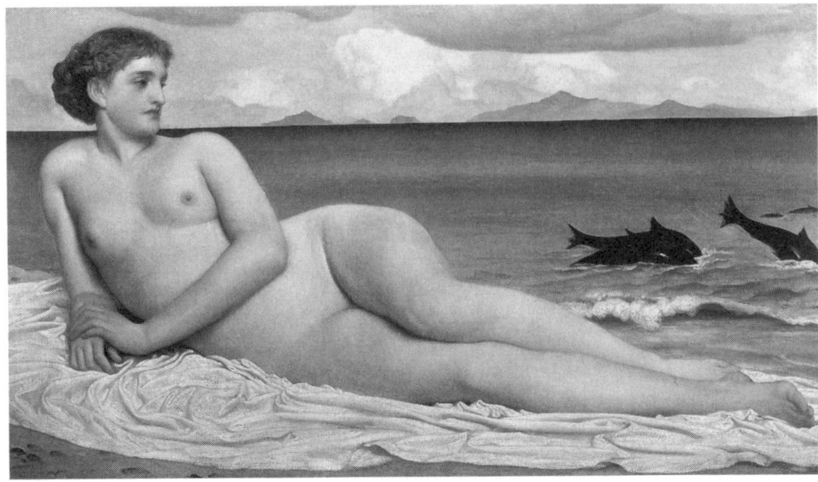

Figure 5. Frederick Leighton, *Actaea, Nymph of the Shore*, 1868.
(National Gallery of Canada, Ottawa)

lar (earlier) work of Dante Gabriel Rossetti's blousy women with bee-stung lips that referenced medieval themes and Romantic poetry. These painters of the female nude imaged their naked women like children, without the telltale marks of development: full breasts and (especially) pubic hair.[29] Leighton's *Actaea, Nymph of the Shore* (1868) is particularly similar to Carroll's photograph, sharing the absence of pubic hair, the unreal background, the reclined pose, and the attachment to the past (1868, fig. 5). The referencing of the past, either through the history of art or literature, was apparently an important manner of veiling what would otherwise be unacceptable. A case in point is *The Sculptor's Model* by Alma-Tadema (1877, fig. 6), roughly contemporary with Carroll's photograph. Alma-Tadema's nude was shocking because it was presented as just that, a nude. It was not a Venus, nor a Galatea, not a classical masquerade. Worse yet, as the Bishop of Carlisle observed, it was "almost photographic."[30]

Evelyn is significantly related to these painted "pure" (yet sexual) women-girls of the period; posed as a grown courtesan, she is their mirror image, not woman-girl but girl-woman. Despite the fact that their bodies have been washed of the markings of "sex," they are not unfeminine. Familiar signs of femininity are offered as emblems of reassurance for the male viewer: pose, transparent draperies, flowers, and so forth all connote the womanhood that is not there. As a result, their sexual difference operates like a fetish and is represented as being both

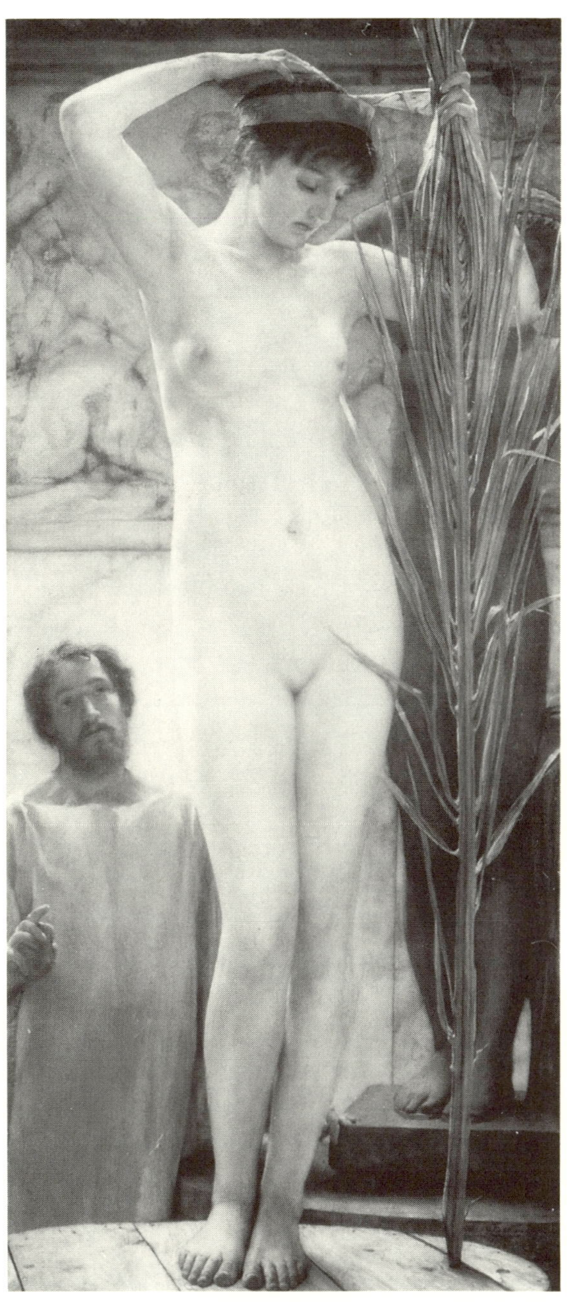

Figure 6. Lawrence Alma-Tadema,
The Sculptor's Model, 1877.
(Christie's Images)

there and not there, simultaneously absent and present. As Abigail Solomon-Godeau argues of the Western female nude, "patriarchy produces a
representation of its desire; sexual difference, like the structure of fetishism, is both there and not there. Nothing to see and nothing to hide."[31]

Unlike Alice, who is constantly eating and changing size, Carroll's
Evelyn will never grow; she is temporally arrested on curved glass, which
prevents her from ever growing curves of her own, let alone pubic hair.
At the same time, unlike the models of Manet and Titian, Evelyn can be as
rude as Alice and has no need to cover her pubic area politely. There is
apparently nothing there, but pure little girl, "a complex fantasm" of
Carroll's own.

Likewise, what Auerbach describes as the animal hidden in Evelyn
Hatch not only gives the image power but plays into the Victorian fear of
the animal in woman. Animality ran riot in the bodies of the hysteric and
the prostitute; it was the source of inspiration in Rossetti's snaky fantasy
portraits of the femme fatale; it was the culprit in the stories surrounding
John Ruskin's failed marriage to Effie Gray.[32] But it also hibernated in the
womb of the secular female angel. This effort to catch hold of the un-
graspable sexuality of good and bad woman alike was the impetus for an
astonishingly wide (and sometimes bizarre) range of suggestions about
the feminine, from the belief that women should not eat meat while
menstruating for fear that their flow would increase, to the induction of
sleep during birth as a form of combat against the gravid uterus. The
manifestations of such anxiety are endless, and have been well documented by historians such as Thomas Laqueur, Mary Poovey, Londa
Schiebinger, and Elaine Showalter, among others.[33]

The conventions of the female nude in the history of art, the animality
of women in medicine and popular beliefs, are all part of a complex web
of social history that Auerbach's powerful celebration spins over, and it is
predicated by her constant slippage between the (fictional) Alice and the
(real) Evelyn Hatch. While such slipping and sliding between imaginary
and real girls may have been the rule of Carroll's world, one must step
outside of Wonderland when coming face to face with a real little girl: she
lived in an actual cultural moment. For example, one might consider the
possible relationship between the picture of Evelyn Hatch and the per-
petuation of the infamously well known fable (that probably very few
Victorians actually believed but nevertheless passed on) that venereal
disease could be cured through intercourse with a virgin. What dis-eases

did the voyeuristic tendencies of this picture cure for Carroll? (Several books provocatively assert that Carroll lost his stutter in the presence of little girls; what happened in the presence of their pictures?[34] Or is this hystericization of Carroll/Mr. Do-Do-Dodgson just another fable that we other Victorians tell in order to feed our own hunger for girl-children?)[35] And, switching to a more grounded level, the jurisprudential, to what extent can the photograph serve as a commentary on the legal system that governed all of the little girls of the period?

The Victorian girl-body was being contested as Evelyn was sitting (reclining) for her portrait. Carroll's photographic years (1856–80) roughly correspond with the years of some of the greatest debates over the female body: the Contagious Diseases Acts of 1864, 1866, and 1869; the Offenses Against the Person Act of 1861; and the Criminal Law Amendment Act of 1885.[36] In her important article "The 'Maiden Tribute of Modern Babylon' Re-Examined: Child Prostitution and the Idea of Childhood in Late-Victorian England," Deborah Gorham has unveiled the ideological contradictions hidden underneath William Stead's famous exposé (in the *Pall Mall Gazette* of 6–10 July 1885) of "white slavery" and the traffic in virgins.[37] The debates leading up to the Criminal Law Amendment Act or the so-called Stead Act (which raised the age of consent from thirteen to sixteen) suggest the difficulty the Victorians faced in determining the parameters of "girlhood."[38]

Part of the problem was that the Victorians did not possess the category of adolescence, which did not begin to come into existence until the end of the nineteenth century. (This partly explains why Carroll was once horrified to discover that he had kissed a young woman of fourteen, thinking that she was merely a child.) Likewise the problem of who and just what a child was animated the legal discourse of the period. And because, as Monique Wittig has argued, only females are "sexed," the laws were only for those beings that were problematically sliding between the categories of girl and woman; male children were outside of "sex," a division set up both to mark women from girls and to mark females from the rest of society.[39] As a result—like Carroll's letters—the various age-of-consent amendments were only addressed to girls. They were about "sex," not about childhood. As Gorham points out, the legislation was significant because it regarded women as less than full citizens, while inscribing them as so different that special laws were required to protect them (the rhetoric of "protection," of course, was merely a thin veil for control). Like a female nude by a great master, the law painted decency over itself, through a highly developed and contradictory rhetoric.[40]

The discourse of the law, which supposedly sought to prevent harm to young girls but actually sought to control female sexuality, is aptly illustrated in the Offenses Against the Person Act. This piece of legislation not only defined as a felony a man's sexual intercourse with a girl under ten and as a misdemeanor his intercourse with a girl between ten and twelve, but also contained special provisions that controlled her economic position and ensured that she would be governed by her guardians, far past "childhood." For example, Gorham notes,

> If a girl under sixteen entered into a relationship with a man, her parents could charge her "abductor" with depriving them of the services of their daughter. If a young woman had property, her parents or guardian could even prevent her marriage up to the age of twenty-one, if they could prove that the suitor had used "false allurements."[41]

Then as now, "sex is a category which women [and girls] cannot be outside of."[42]

Given the law of the period, then, it is hard to conceive that Evelyn Hatch would ever be successful (as Auerbach suggests) in producing an erotic energy of her own, let alone any seditious powers. How could she overcome the odds against it? Her pose suggests that she has "fallen" away from the Victorian guardianship of middle-class girlhood. There were laws against such traveling. Possibly it is not the viewers who are embarrassed, but Evelyn herself. Her darkly painted face may be the result of covering up a blush.

Neutre

As both sexual and not sexual, the body of the little girl marked her as simultaneously different from the male viewer and (according to cultural conventions) lacking the marks of true womanhood. As "pure little girl," she was supposedly not sexual. Yet, given the work of Freud and Foucault, the "cult of the little girl," the artistic treatment of her image, the uneasy law of the period, and so forth, we cannot read her as anything but sexual. She was thus both woman and not woman; she played safely *and* dan-

gerously. In this regard she figures what Roland Barthes and the French
philosopher Louis Marin have described as the *neutre;* both Barthes and
Marin understand the *neutre* as a neverending play of textual and opposi-
tional spaces. In Barthes's words, the *neutre* is "not an average of active
and passive; rather it is a back-and-forth, an amoral oscillation, in short,
one might say, the converse of antinomy."[43] Marin's similar use of the
term, *neutre,* readily and most interestingly references both *neutral* and
neuter, prompting him to play out a series of neither-nor ambiguities
which include the sexual. (For example, *neutre* signifies neither male nor
female—neither subject nor object—neither base nor acid—neither one
side nor the other—etc.) Though Marin's project (a decontructionist
analysis of class ideology through what he terms "utopic spaces") is different from my own, his play with the word *neutre* enriches my understanding of the neither-nor sexuality of the Victorian girl.

In the following passage, Marin writes of *neutre* as both sexual and
grammatical ambiguity. To better understand the significance and the
value of not translating *neutre,* it is worth quoting this selection from
Marin's text in French and English.

Donnons-nous, comme point de départ, une définition abstraite du
neutre: étymologiquement *ne-uter,* ni l'un ni l'autre, la grammaire
le spécifie comme ce qui n'est ni masculin ni féminin, donc hors
genre, comme ce qui n'est ni actif ni passif, donc hors voix. Ainsi on
appellera, en botanique et en zoologie, une fleur ou un insecte
«neutres», une plante ou un animal privés des organes de la généra-
tion, qui ne peuvent ni s'accoupler ni se reproduire. Ainsi en grammaire, on appellera verbes «neutres», les verbes intransitifs qui expriment une action en elle-même, sans aucun régime, auxquels il est
impossible de donner un complément d'objet, comme «marcher»
ou «mourir». Ces verbes expriment une action qui s'applique au
sujet, qui, produite par lui, fait retour à son foyer de production
pour le déterminer.

[As a point of departure we need an abstract definition of the
neutral. Eytmologically *ne-uter,* neither one nor the other, grammar
defines it as neither masculine nor feminine. It is, rather, outside
gender; neither active nor passive, but outside voice. In botany or
zoology a flower or insect is "neuter" if it lacks organs for reproduc-

tion, unable to mate or reproduce itself. In grammar "neuter" verbs are intransitive verbs expressing an action by themselves, without object and without the possibility of an objective case—i.e., "to walk" or "to die." These verbs express an action applicable to the subject that produces it.][44]

Obviously, the sexual ambiguity of *neutre* is of great interest to me here. I am drawn to Marin's representation of the *neutre* as a (neutral) tabula rasa, blank and smooth—it feels like the body of the girl. Yet *neutre* also rustles. It gives voice to the whispering contradictions that transparently veiled the tender body of the Victorian girl, layer after layer, without being readily seen, or heard. These magical veils dressed her in many guises so that she could be understood as determinedly sexed (there were laws to ensure this) as well as without sex (without the organs for reproduction, neither male nor female, as innocent), yet (because of endless discursive grazing) as also full-fed of sexuality.

Turning to another well-known Victorian photographer, Julia Margaret Cameron, who also took fascinating photographs of sexual(ized) children, we can see how this concept of *neutre* unstabilizes any purely "innocent" pleasure that has been taken in and from her girl-pictures. Unlike Carroll's pictures of boyish girls like Evelyn Hatch, Cameron's pictures do not suggest androgyny, they present it overtly. For example, in at least one instance, when Jesus' genitals are exposed, they are clearly female (*Spring,* 1865, fig. 7). Similarly, John the Baptist was regularly modeled by a young girl, Florence Fisher (*Florence / Study of St. John the Baptist,* 1872, fig. 8).

But like Carroll's pictures, one only has to open one's eyes to see sex and sexuality in her androgynous pictures. Looking at *Spring,* one is struck by the charming and seductive looks on the faces of the children— flirtatious really. And how about their beautiful skin, their unkempt precious hair (to be cut and saved later) and their tiny exposed shoulders, soft and round? It is an "erotics of tininess."[45] (If you are wondering about the young Virgin in the picture, hold on, she is the subject of chapter 2.) Returning to *Florence / Study of St. John the Baptist,* one is confronted by the child's all-over voluptuousness: sultry eyes; dark, long, young hair; small lips; porcelain shoulder; her graspable hands. Notice how her left hand is caught gently holding up (or gently removing) the fringed shawl that barely covers her; look at her right hand as it spreads two fingers ever so

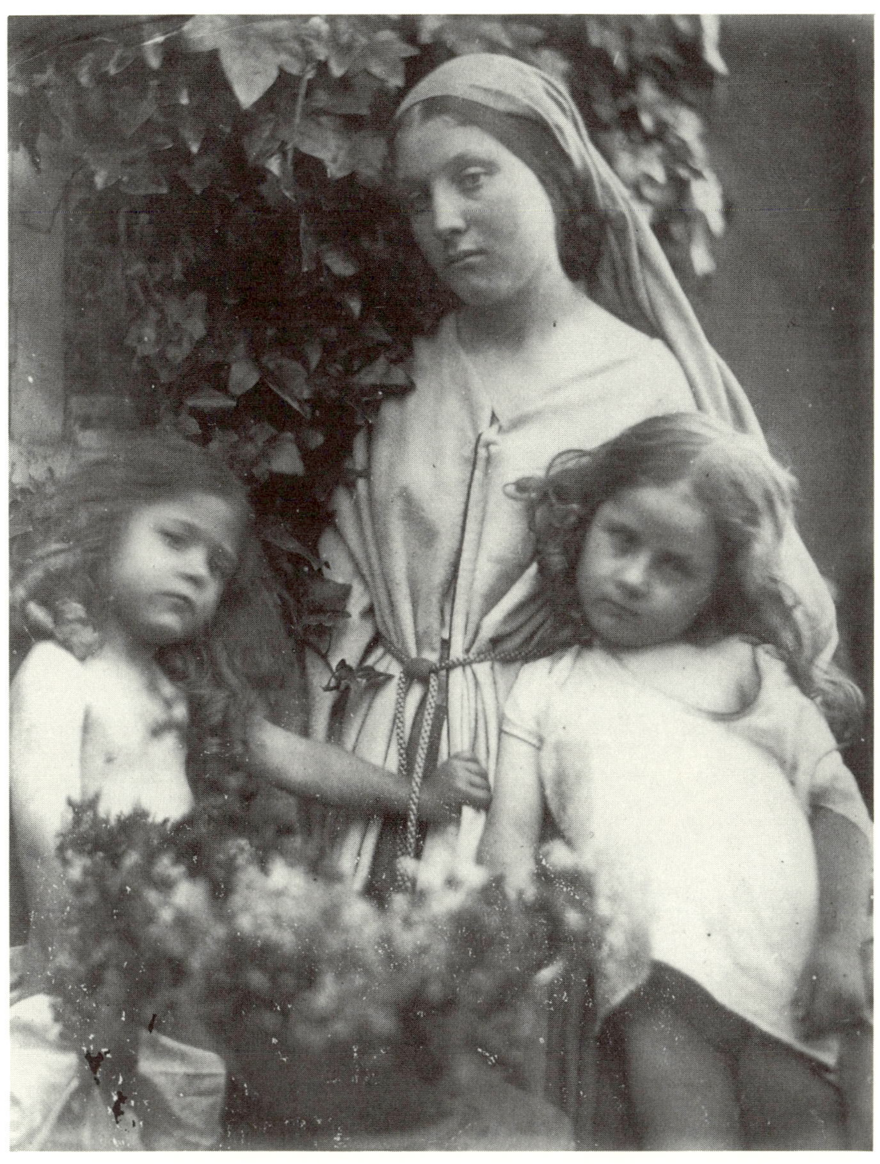

Figure 7. Julia Margaret Cameron, *Spring*, 1865
(Collection of the J. Paul Getty Museum, Malibu, California)

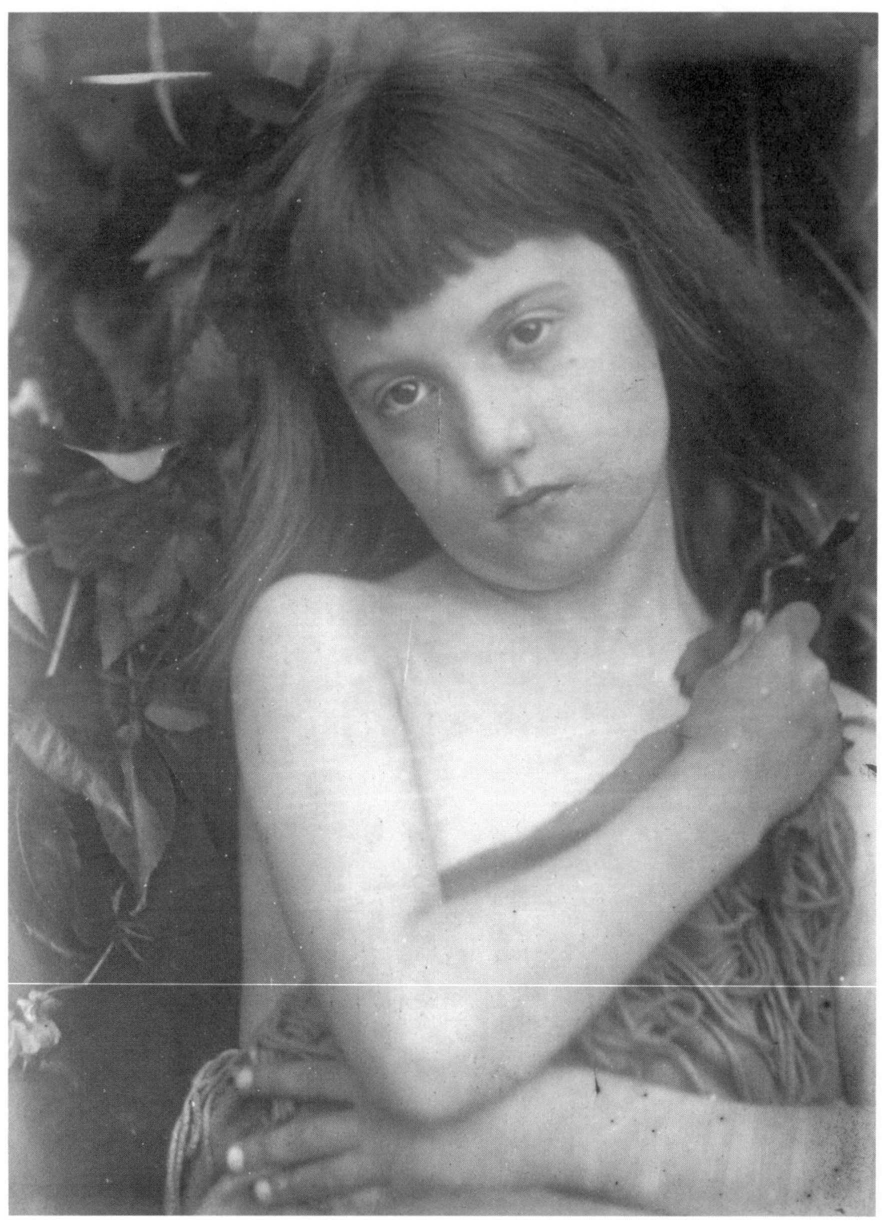

Figure 8. Julia Margaret Cameron, *Florence / Study of St. John the Baptist*, 1872. (Collection of the J. Paul Getty Museum, Malibu, California)

gently in a gesture that is awkwardly childlike (in the way in which children are often unaware of what their hands are doing) and erotic for what it opens up.

And the pictures are also printed with eroticism, as if they have been touched all over. It is as if the messiness of their hair, the touch of their fingers caught unaware, the sensual feel and look of their child-bodies has been magically caught in the emulsion. It is as if the entity of childhood, a strange jelly, has been smeared into these pictures, which were developed without regard for the rules, producing photographs that were (and still are) distinctly fleshly, dreamy, blurry, delightfully sloppy, otherworldly— like the skin of children.[46]

Yet Cameron's work has managed to escape the label of "perversion" that has encumbered Carroll's photographs. Clearly, as the texts on Cameron attest to, she has been saved by her maternal life-style, which included a house full of children. She has been safely inscribed as heterosexual and productive, which is in opposition to the rather common reading of Carroll as a "repressed homosexual." No dangerous penises have appeared in her work to pervert the space.[47] And no one has ever imagined any homoeroticism between Cameron and her maid / model (Mary Hillier), or between the young women who frequently and lovingly embrace each other in many of her images, despite the work of Carroll Smith-Rosenberg.[48] Like good Victorians, historians have preferred to bathe in the apparent "neutrality" (as conventionally defined) and "purity" of her pictures. But I can see the *neutre* in her little girls, and in his too.

Utopographs, or The Myth of Everlasting Flowers

Part of the appeal of understanding little girls as without sex is that it is avoidance of death. For sex is always connected with death. Little girls eventually leave their childhood beds (just like Wendy), only to fly to their wedding bed, which brings them to their birthing bed, which brings them that much closer to their deathbed. (As Carroll wrote in the prefatory poem to *Through the Looking-Glass:* "We are but older children, dear, / Who fret to find our bedtime near.") In order to stop this flight, Carroll ensured that his little girls would always be beautiful and everlasting by capturing them on the photographic plate (an everlasting flower bed), before their eventual bloom of womanly breasts and hips, and their unstoppable wilt. Carroll's little girls, pasted into his albums, were flattened flower buds—some from last spring, others from many springtimes ago—all pressed, pasted, preserved, and arranged into Victorian albums. All about the same age, despite different birthdates. Carroll wanted his child-friends to be forever little, to remain as Persephone was *before* she plucked the tender, sweet-smelling narcissus that metaphorically stood for her own breakage, loss, and marked change. Carroll wanted to avoid the disappointment and anxiety that Alice experiences when she futilely attempts to hold onto her plucked "dream-rushes" in *Through the Looking-Glass.* The "darling scented rushes" are symbols of Carroll's girl-child friends:

> And then the little sleeves were carefully rolled up, and the little arms were plunged elbow-deep, to get hold of the rushes a good long way down before breaking them off . . . with bright eager eyes she caught one bunch after another of the darling scented rushes.
>
> "I only hope the boat won't tipple over!" she said to herself. "Oh, *what* a lovely one! Only I couldn't quite reach it!" And it certainly *did* seem a little provoking ("almost as if it happened on purpose," she thought) that, though she managed to pick plenty of beautiful rushes as the boat glided by, there was always a more lovely one that she couldn't reach.
>
> "The prettiest are always further!" she said at last, with a sigh at the obstinacy of the rushes in growing so far off, as with flushed cheeks and dripping hair and hands, she scrambled back into her place and began to arrange her new-found treasures.
>
> What mattered it to her just then that the rushes had begun to fade, and to lose all their scent and beauty, from the very moment that she picked them? Even real scented rushes, you know, last only a very little while—and these, being dream-rushes, melted away almost like snow, as they lay in heaps at her feet.[49]

The photograph became, for Carroll, the contradictory medium to hold the little girl forever young in the looking glass. We can see the photograph as temporal in the sense that it records a specific moment, a split second in the young sitter's life, yet also as "eternal" in that it is everlasting and not subject to change (neither a moment, nor eternity). The little girls are strange Marinesque flowers, sexual but without the sexual organs to generate themselves; their only reproduction is photographic reproduction, infinitely repeated as sameness. The infinitely duplicative quality of the photograph is hauntingly demonstrated in the bottom right-hand corner of the picture of Evelyn as odalisque. We are confronted with an incongruous number "11," penned in on a tiny white orb that casts a tiny dark shadow on the glass behind. This number 11 is what has always troubled me the most about this photograph. It seems to suggest that not only are such images reproducible, but they are also disposable, like Carroll's own girl-child friends. Their moments with him were fleeting, despite the everlasting nature of their images.[50]

But the split between temporality and eternity is not the only contradiction within the photograph. There is also a play between "real" and "unreal"—much as the little girl is "sexual" and "not sexual" or "woman" and "not woman." Barthes addresses the paradox of the photographic medium in "The Photographic Message," where he argues that the photograph is paradoxical due to the coexistence of two messages,

> the one without a code (the photographic analogue), the other with a code (the "art" or the treatment, or the "writing," or the rhetoric, of the photograph); structurally, the paradox is clearly not the collusion of a denoted message and a connoted message (which is the—probably inevitable—status of all the forms of mass communication), it is that here the connoted (or coded) message develops on the basis of a message *without a code*.[51]

In the case of Carroll's photography, we can see that the photograph is a portmanteau of the art object and reality. Like the large leather suitcase that opens up into two compartments, two bags in one (or even like the invented portmanteau double-words of Carroll's *Looking-Glass* world), the photograph is the baggage that encases the two: the photographic "analogue" / the denoted message and the connoted message / the treatment of the photograph—its "art." That the photograph presents itself as both real and not real allows Carroll to believe in the myth of everlasting flowers, the myth that girls like Alice Liddell will remain "forever little."

The Photographic Condition of the Girl

Despite my earlier criticisms of Auerbach's gloss of the Evelyn Hatch photograph, my intention has not been to obscure the level of performance that her discourse unleashes. Carroll's contradictory photographs certainly document something of the "girl's own." Part of his art was to tap into the child that played within all of the Alices, Evelyns, and Xies. One senses this talent within his sensitive and lovely letters, within the *Alice* books (which turn readers of any age into children), within the unencumbered delightful memories that a number of his girl-child friends recorded as adults. But how much of this has to do with the medium itself? For one also suspects that *all* photographs harbor the sitter's own presence; that is what makes them photographs.

Photographs literally transport light from days gone by to the modern viewer, "like the delayed rays of a star"; this time travel ensures a certain resonance between the sitter and the viewer.[52] The light that touched Evelyn or Alice now touches us. Photography is a visual caress between the viewer and the subject(s) of the picture: a silent performance. Consider how the sitter resonates when Barthes is brushed by sprays of light suspended in collodion since 1852:

> One day, quite some time ago, I happened on a photograph of Napoleon's youngest brother, Jerome, taken in 1852. And I realized then, with an amazement I have not been able to lessen since: "I am looking at eyes that looked at the Emperor" . . . . I was overcome by an "ontological" desire: I wanted to learn at all costs what Photography was "in itself," by what essential features it was to be distinguished from the community of images.[53]

For Barthes, photography is born not of painting, but of the theater. Tracing the origins of the theater back to the cult of the dead, in which the "first actors separated themselves from the community by playing the role of the Dead" by making themselves up as "a body simultaneously living and dead," Barthes finds the theater in the photograph: "Photography is a kind of primitive theater, a kind of *Tableau Vivant,* a figuration of the motionless and made-up face beneath which we see the dead."[54] On a less-poetic level, Ben Maddow remarks, "It's the special naiveté of the twentieth century to think that the artist alone determines the subject; in examining a succession of photographic portraits one is struck instantly by the will and the force of the sitter."[55]

Mirroring the discursive play of Marin, I want to suggest that the girl-models figured on Carroll's photographic plates often oscillate in a performative space: they are "not artist," yet they are "not, not artist." (They are intransitive; they are *neutre.*) The spatial play represented here is uniquely active, and different from the nonplay that is suggested in other Victorian child photographs of the period. The stilted nature of the children imaged by the professional photographers O. G. Rejlander and H. P. Robinson (whom Gernsheim calls "The High Priests of Photographic Art") speaks primarily to the pair's interest in the science of photography—making "composite" pictures—and in the task of illustrating a story.[56] Unlike Carroll, they did not share the desire to capture some essence of childhood. And unlike him again, they had neither the desire nor the talent to entertain children. Carroll's gift in this line, in contrast, enabled him to capture the performances of *his* child-subjects.

Agnes Grace Weld, in *Little Red Riding Hood,* treats us to such a performance (fig. 9, 1857). Her gaze, not unlike Evelyn Hatch's, confronts us and draws us in with a seductive charm reminiscent of Greta Garbo's sultry, wounding eyes. Red Riding Hood / Agnes grows from the strangling ivy bower, caught in some magical, mystical trance, as if she were in the process of overcoming the hold of the vegetation behind her. Hers are the eyes of the wolf that has presumably just eaten her grandmother; we wonder whether she has eaten the wolf, and whether she is about ready to eat us up. The open basket, which displays one delicious bun, is sexually suggestive, and undoubtedly Carroll's doing, but the eyes are Agnes's own.[57] In a four-part series in 1858, Robinson, too, portrayed Little Red Riding Hood (fig. 10). His version, however, is essentially caught up in the narrative, and goes so far as to display a wolf in bed (thanks to the work of a taxidermist). Strangled by the conventions of the story, it is only when Robinson's Little Red Riding Hood stands at her grandmother's door that the model can exhibit herself as "child." In contrast, one could argue that Carroll's / Agnes's play of reciprocity interrupts the narrative of the story by conflating the characters, making it impossible to say just what might happen next.

The performative nature of these prints is intensified when one views them in the actual albums as Carroll arranged them. A large collection of these albums is found in the Gernsheim Collection, housed at the University of Texas in Austin. It includes one of the most notable, *Photographs Vol. III,* the title written in gilt on the front cover. Inside are 115 photographs, all by Lewis Carroll, remarkable for the fact that nearly all are autographed by their subjects. The signatures, all different and often highly individual, are reminiscent of an artist's own signature at the bottom of a

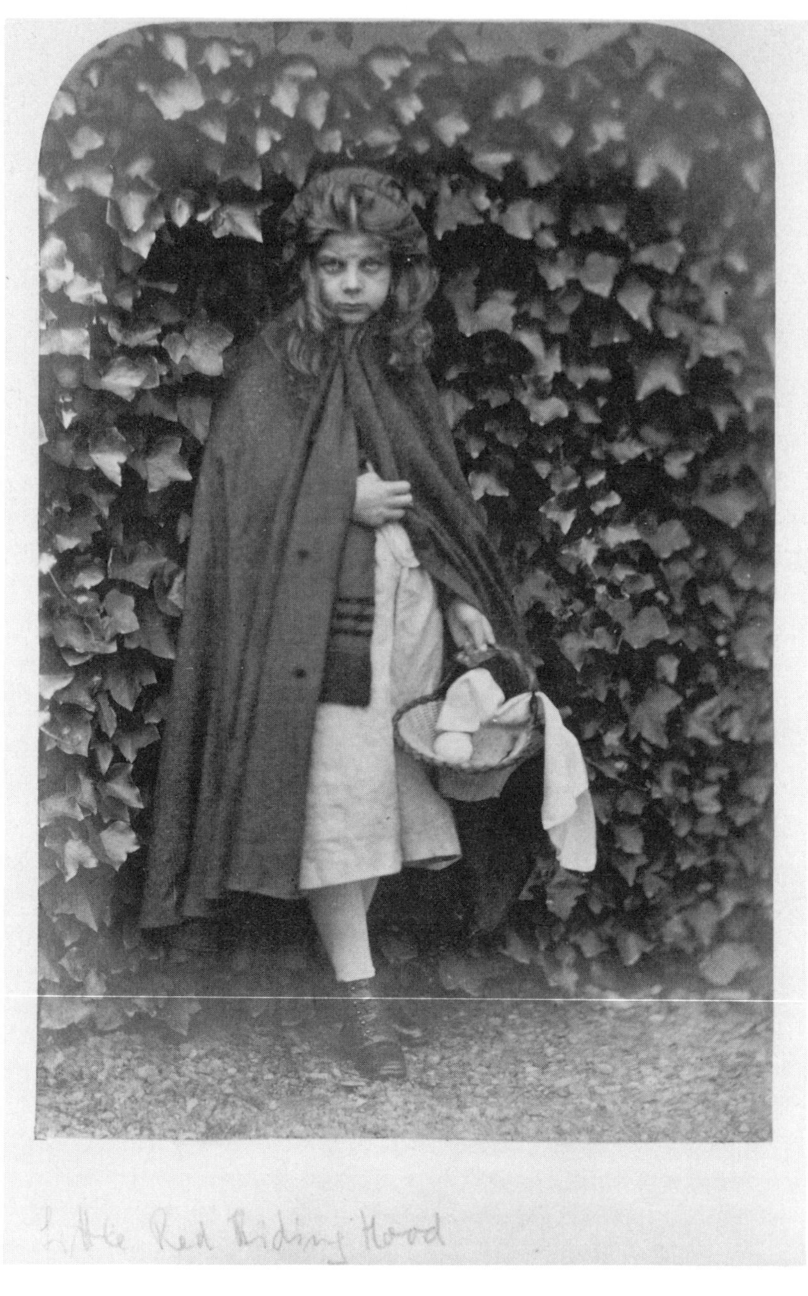

Figure 9. Lewis Carroll, *Agnes Grace Weld as Little Red Riding Hood*, 1857.
(Gernsheim Collection, Harry Ransom Humanities Research Center,
The University of Texas at Austin)

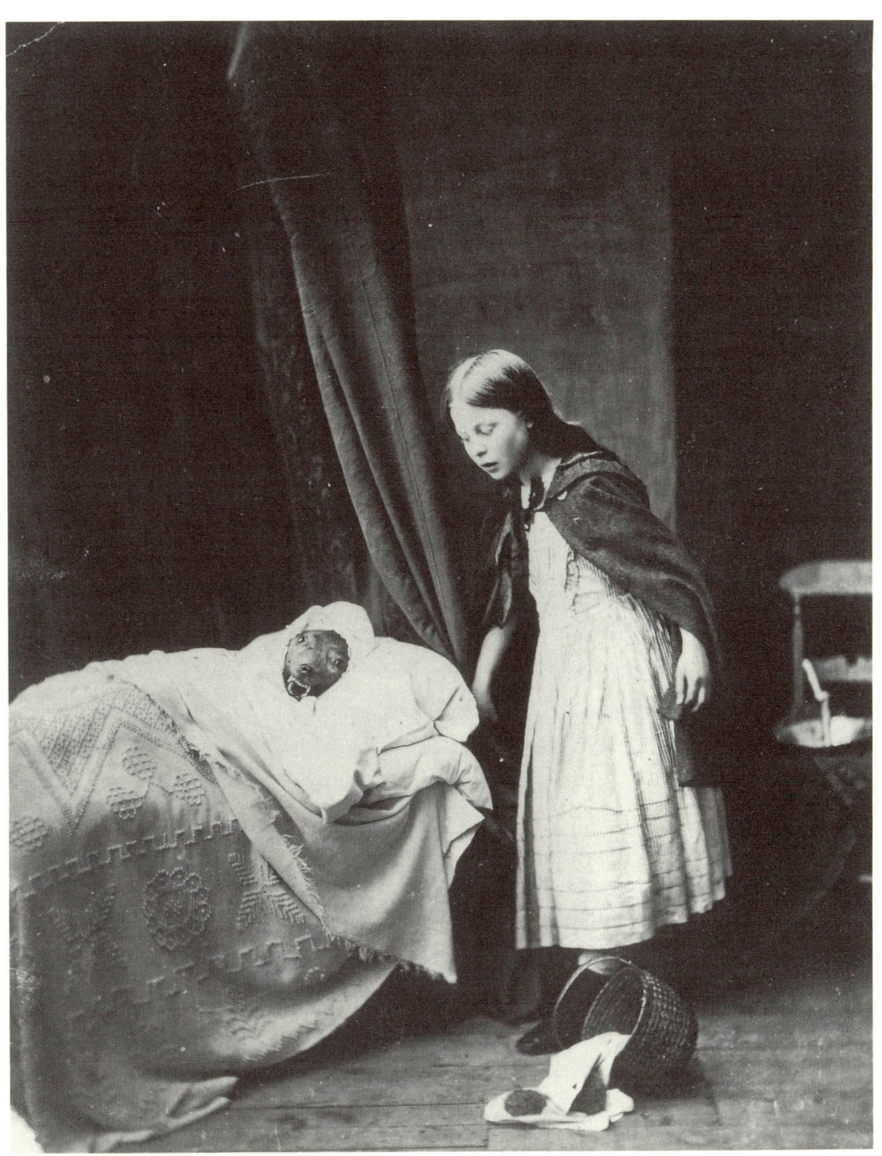

Figure 10. Henry Peach Robinson, from the *Little Red Riding Hood* series, 1858. (The Royal Photographic Society, Bath)

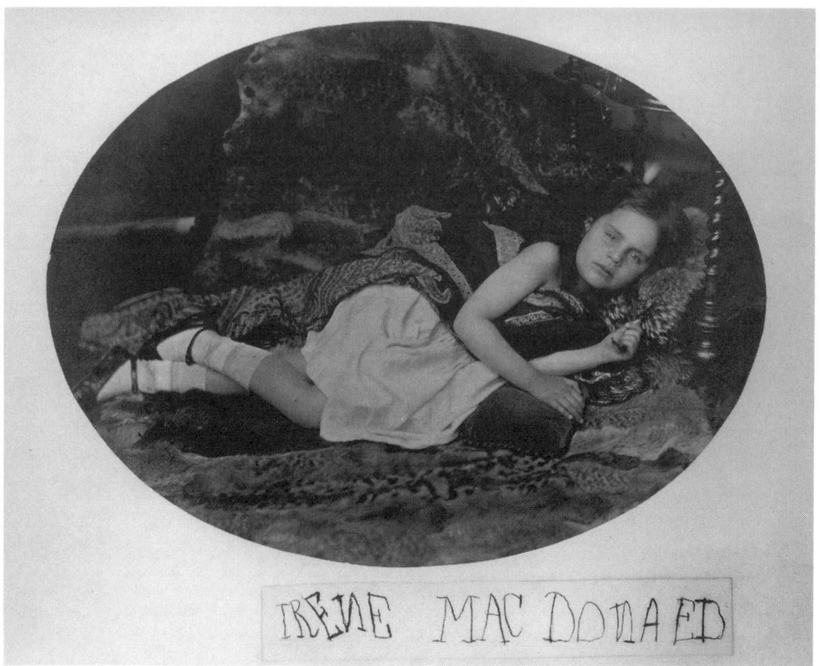

Figure 11. Lewis Carroll, *Irene MacDonald*, 1863.
(Gernsheim Collection, Harry Ransom Humanities Research Center,
The University of Texas at Austin)

painting. Like fingerprints in warm wax, both picture and autograph record the subject's touch: the picture records the body's touch of light, and the ink records the hand's touch of the page.

I am particularly drawn to one of the pages featuring Irene MacDonald splayed before us as a portmanteau of odalisque and Victorian girl (1863, fig. 11). Eyes dreamy (one eye more closed than the other), shoulders bare, an Oriental cloth or carpet heavily veiling her absent bodice, Irene lies on pelts, one visibly that of a tiger, as if she were a bacchante. Her charming and voluminous white cotton skirt, however, and the clean white short socks and black "Baby Janes" that trim her schoolgirl legs, confront all of the picture's Orientalism, marking her image as taboo and thereby heightening its eroticism. There is nothing particularly fresh in this particular play of contradictions. They have long been subsumed by Western culture and rendered frozen. But this image extends beyond the picture's edge and onto the album page, where we find a small piece of paper glued below the scene, collage-fashion. The paper carries Irene's signature, which is cast in a fanciful parade of letters. The originality of her child-scrawl is undeniable. Irene's almost-realized attempt to perfectly spell out her name unfreezes the image by introducing her voice. Two backward *N*s, an *E* that should be an *L,* all compete against the singularity of Carroll's authorship. He may be a man of letters, but hers are the ones that I take in.

Little / Liddell Fetishes

Due to its smallness and its ability to provide a long, lingering look, the photograph is wonderfully suited as a fetish object.[58] The liveliness and individuality of Carroll's photographs of his child-friends turn them into pocket versions of the real thing, just like Alice after she drinks from a little bottle *not* marked Poison. Carroll had always been obsessed with the idea of life in miniature. As a boy, he made his own marionettes and theater. On another occasion he fashioned for his sister a very tiny set of tools, complete with case; at only one inch long, they were probably too small even for Lilliput.[59] The catalog for Carroll's estate sale, after his death in 1898, lists a stationery set consisting of very small notepaper and matching envelopes, all collected in a larger envelope marked "Lilliputian Stationery," in Carroll's own hand.[60] Constructing miniature worlds, writes Susan Stewart, is a way of making "an 'other' time, a type of transcendent time which negates change and the flux of lived reality."[61] Carroll ensured such an other time by cementing a tiny photograph of Alice Liddell inside the end of his telescope; one gaze and the world would stop still, every star would be Alicious. The "Pleasance" of this heavenly image lied in its fetishization; it served to protect Carroll from the brutality of time, as if he, too, were an everlasting star . . . or flower.

Like the Victorian girl, the fetish is always doubled-edged. In psychoanalytic terms as in its everyday usage, it means "both loss (symbolic castration) and protection against loss."[62] Whether it works as in Freud's story of stopping the look of what has already been seen (the mother without a penis) "retrospectively," by fixating on an object that was near before the horrifying primal glance (a tube of lipstick would do), or whether it means carrying a rabbit's foot as protection against failing a logic test—both systems utopically hold contradictory functions. They both avert danger while acknowledging the reality of that danger. The lipstick and the rabbit's foot (Cixous's description of Carroll's White

Rabbit as a "penis on paws" comes to mind) are signs of an everlasting anxiety (fear of loss) that sleeps in all of us, like Alice's own dreams.[63] In this context Carroll's photograph of the little girl—especially Evelyn Hatch as the nude odalisque—become the perfect fetish objects: "her sexual difference is both there and not there." This little nude rests as a small souvenir of days gone by. She is a keepsake of sexual indifference. She wards off sexual fears. She is a pocket phallus (Alice phallus). At the same time, however, she embodies sexual difference, a possibly dangerous difference that he involuntarily acknowledges and fears. He must therefore simultaneously ward off this acknowledgement by fetishizing her as not different at all.

This difference / indifference or absence / presence in Carroll's photographs is not unlike the "Podsnappery" in Charles Dickens's *Our Mutual Friend*. In the famous satire, which speaks to the period's obsessive devotion to the innocence of the young girl, "the cheek of a young person" is shown as a fetishized testing site for (impossible) sexual contradictions. And because Georgiana Podsnap (the owner of the cheek in question) is in the habit of blushing whether it is appropriate or not, all tests are passed— no one flunks, everyone gets to be innocent. Then who is guilty? It seems that there was no way of demarcating her innocence (Georgiana's or any girl's) from her guilt. Like Carroll, "Podsnap's idea of his young person is that of a creature who cannot in fact exist."[64] (Perhaps Carroll best summed up the logic of it all [desiring the impossible] when the White Queen explains to Alice that she could not even have jam today, even if she wanted it: "The rule is, jam to-morrow and jam yesterday—but never jam *to-day*.")[65]

The photograph also works with and against Carroll's preoccupation with time, aging, and developing. As has been touched upon already, the photograph is indexical, due to its "actual contiguity or connection to the world." It is a print of a *real* object, as "lightning is the index of the storm."[66] The indexical aspect of the photograph, the basis for its "message without a code," serves to grant a "reality" to the connoted message (which is based on the "art" of framing, composition, printing techniques, scale, lighting, coloring with oils). This paradox allowed Carroll to believe that little girls remain forever little. But the reality of Carroll's photographic Neverland was double-edged. For on the other side of the photographic plate is the fact that because "photography . . . remains closer to the pure index [we find that it is always] stubbornly pointing to the print of what *was,* but no longer *is.*"[67] In the photograph, a "tiny piece of time brutally and forever escapes its ordinary fate," as Christian Metz puts it, while at the same time it must indicate that all time is forever lost.[68] This is why photography—and not merely our photographs of dead loved ones—is associated with death: every photograph indicates the death of a moment, the passage of time, the fact that we are that much closer to our own deaths. For Carroll, the photograph of the little girl served as a fetish simultaneously to ward off death and to express Carroll's anxiety about the nearness of his own "bedtime." Possibly this is why he himself had such a horror of being photographed.

No Boys, No Women, No Time,
and No Street Urchins

In this last section, I would like to turn back to an early photograph of Alice Liddell posed as a beggar. Captured around 1858, a special version of it was discovered in the possession of Alice's granddaughter. Tinted, like the photograph of Evelyn Hatch, Alice is presented in an oval of gold, centered in a black, lacquered traveling photograph mount (fig. 12). Once again we see bare shoulders, this time exposed by a torn shirt signifying the "beggar's" non-existent poverty. Her crimson rag skirt, tinted with visible brushstrokes, takes on the air of caressed velvet. The reds and greens, the pinkness of her cheeks, the gold and the black of the frame add to the preciousness of the image. The wall behind her suggests a garden wall, as if she had somehow crept into the yard of the Liddell family. Alice as Cinderella. Only the rich could believe such a story. But even beyond photography's usual attachment to death, this image is attached to despair. *Alice Liddell as a Beggar-Child* operates as further evidence of Carroll's uneasy relationship with children outside of the utopian circles of Oxford and the Pre-Raphaelites. Carroll's camera operated like the "cult of the child" industry as a whole; both were directed at the children of the upper classes. Nevertheless, in Carroll's case, there was an exception, a little girl named Coates—though I doubt that she ever received a special letter from him containing an acrostic of her name.

Daughter of one of the Croft employees, Coates was the subject in one of Carroll's rare pictures of working-class children (1857, fig. 13). Unlike Alice, she is not simulating another class: she *is* another class. Heavy work boots peek out from her plain, plaid dress. In stark contrast to Alice's

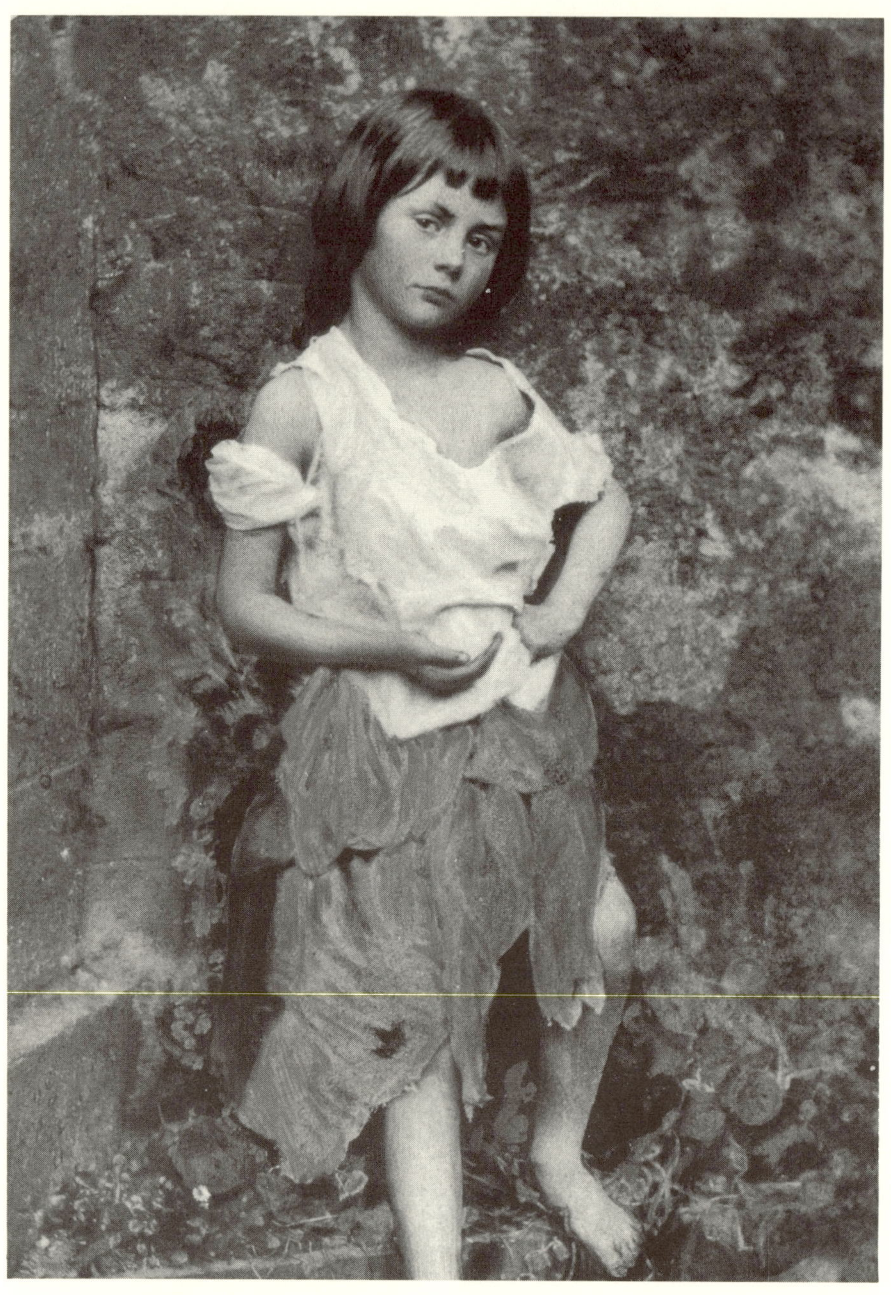

Figure 12. Lewis Carroll, *Alice Liddell as a Beggar-Child*, c. 1858. (Mrs. M. J. St. Clair, Courtesy of The Governing Body of Christ Church, Oxford)

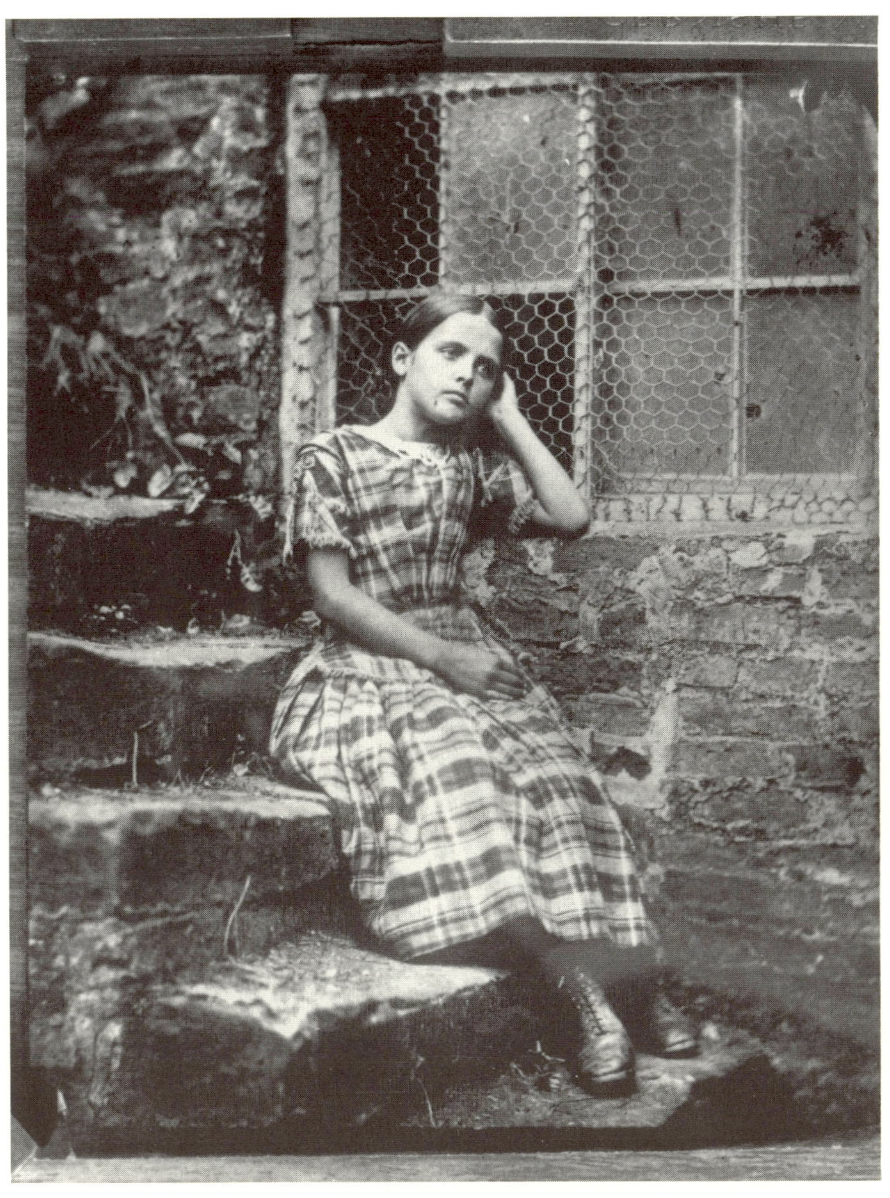

Figure 13. Lewis Carroll, *Coates*, 1857.
(Gernsheim Collection, Harry Ransom Humanities Research
Center, The University of Texas at Austin)

whimsical bob, her hair is pulled severely back from her face. Coates is not lovingly plastered against a garden wall; instead, she is seated on some steps going down to the ground. Wire-covered basement windows, with all of their metaphorical baggage, serve as her backdrop. Gernsheim has celebrated this picture for its intentional naturalness, its lack of pompous setting. Yet what comes through is the difference of Coates's class—a subject of difference not usually apparent in Carroll's work.

Working-class children, with their short-lived childhoods, must have been particularly unnerving for Carroll. In a letter to a grown Beatrice Hatch, he reveals that his utopia was not only cleansed of boys and time but also drew a line at a certain level of class:

> I should like to know, for curiosity, who that sweet-looking girl was, aged 12, with a red nightcap. I think she had a younger sister, also with a red nightcap. She was speaking to you when I came up to wish you goodnight. I fear I must be content with her *name* only: the social gulf between us is probably too wide for it to be wise to make *friends*. Some of my little *actress*-friends are of a *rather* lower status than myself. But, below a certain line, it is hardly wise to let a girl have a "gentleman" friend—even one of 62![69]

This letter raises the contradictions of "class" that afflicted the age-of-consent legislation. For, not only was immoral sexuality always connected with the lower classes, but also economic struggles ensured that by age twelve many lower-class children left home and entered the workplace. The poor child was dangerously outside of the protective surveillance provided by the bourgeois parent. "Below a certain line," the risk that the child might really be an "adult" must have become an unbridgeable difference for Carroll.

On July 18, 1893, Carroll wrote the following letter to his artist friend Gertrude Thompson (requesting her to photograph a nude child for him). The letter reveals Carroll's desire for the body of the *upper-class* girl:

> The "Frena" Hand-Camera . . . is a name new to me. *All* "dry-plate" photography is inferior, in artistic effect, to the now-abandoned "wet-plate": but, as a means of making *memoranda* of attitudes, etc., it is invaluable. Every figure-artist ought to practice it. If *I* had a dry-plate camera, and time to work it, and could secure a

child of a really *good* figure, either a professional model, or (much better) a child of the upper classes, I would put her into every pretty attitude I could think of, and could get, in a single morning, 50 or 100 such memoranda.[70]

Alice *posed* as a little beggar allowed Carroll to play in a space of difference, a simulated difference of class, that was not really different at all, in much the same way that he played with Alice and Xie as Chinamen, Turks, and Danes.[71] The oil painting over the photograph of beggar Alice signifies culture and fantasy and ensures that this is art and not life. But how different the effect might have been if Alice were of the working class. One suspects that he would never have dressed Coates in seductively ripped clothes.

The effect was indeed very different when the famous Dr. Barnardo used "artistic fiction" to image the children brought to his home for destitute children. The pictures were used to advertise the homes, with the hope of raising sympathy and revenue. The bodies of the poor children turned over to Barnardo's care, desperate and without rights of their own, became suitable blank slates for his cause. Consider the case of Florence and Eliza Holder. The two sisters were brought in by their mother around 1876, "poorly but decently clad," possibly in clothes borrowed for the occasion in order that they might be properly dressed for this important moment of their lives (fig. 14).[72] Much to Mrs. Holder's alarm, she was later confronted with a photograph of Florence without the shoes that she came in with, her hair disheveled, and wearing a very tattered dress. To top matters off, Florence was posed as if she were selling newspapers on the street, something she had never done in her life (fig. 15). Barefoot, with her petticoat skirt mysteriously hiked up on one side, she is reminiscent of Carroll's beggar Alice. But her unbelievably disheveled hair, and her sad, angry face, hold no seduction for the viewer. There are no fairy tales for Florence. A portrait of her sister Eliza was also taken; the picture was placed on a collecting box with the legend: "A little waif six years old, taken from the streets." The text, which suggested that she had been living on the street without her mother, was a lie, but the story was made believable through the reality-effect of the photograph (its message without a code). The story came out in an arbitration case in 1877.

Maybe it is because I know the story of Florence that I cannot see anything of the girl's own in her portrait ordered by Dr. Barnardo. How-

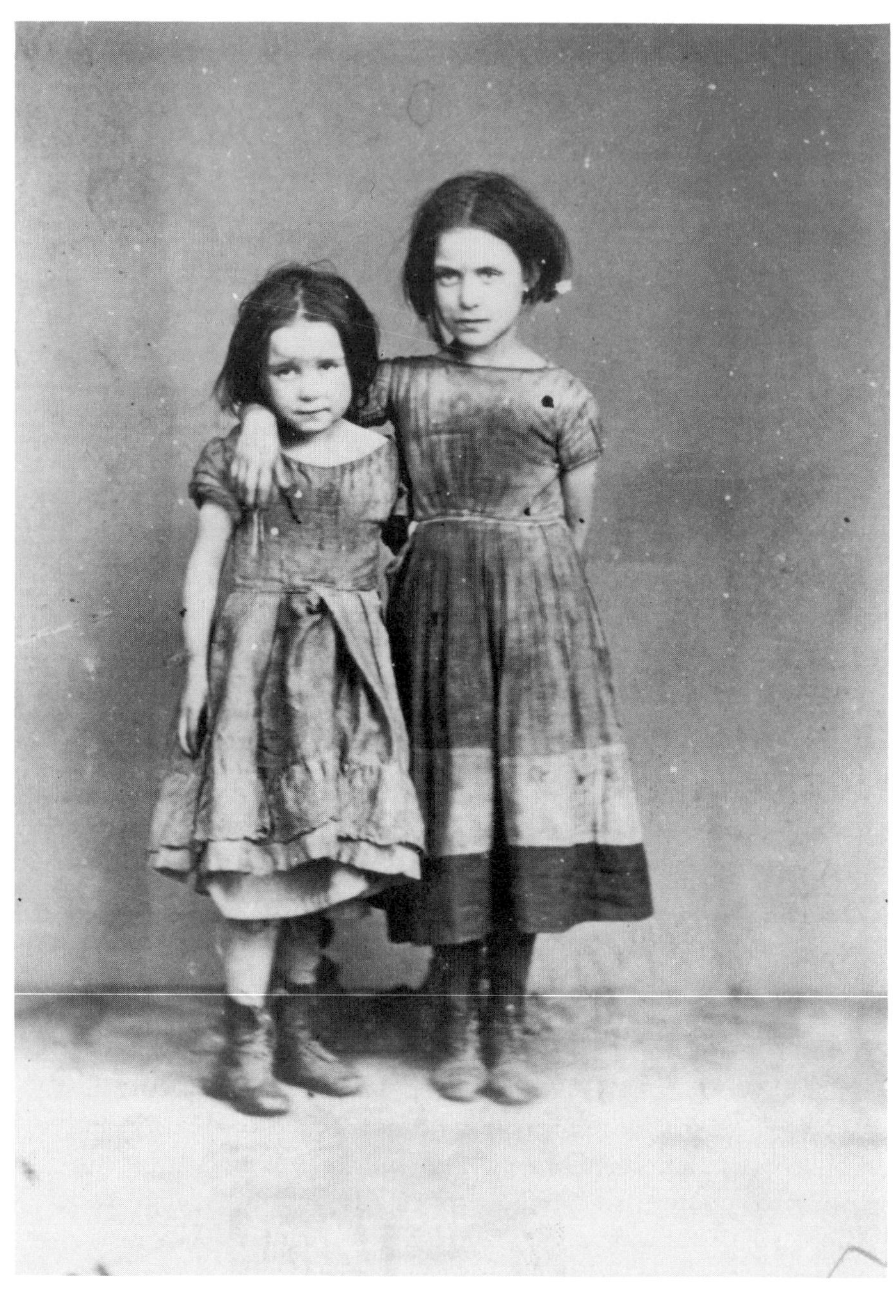

Figure 14. *Florence and Eliza Holder*, c. 1876.
(Barnardo Photographic Archive, Ilford)

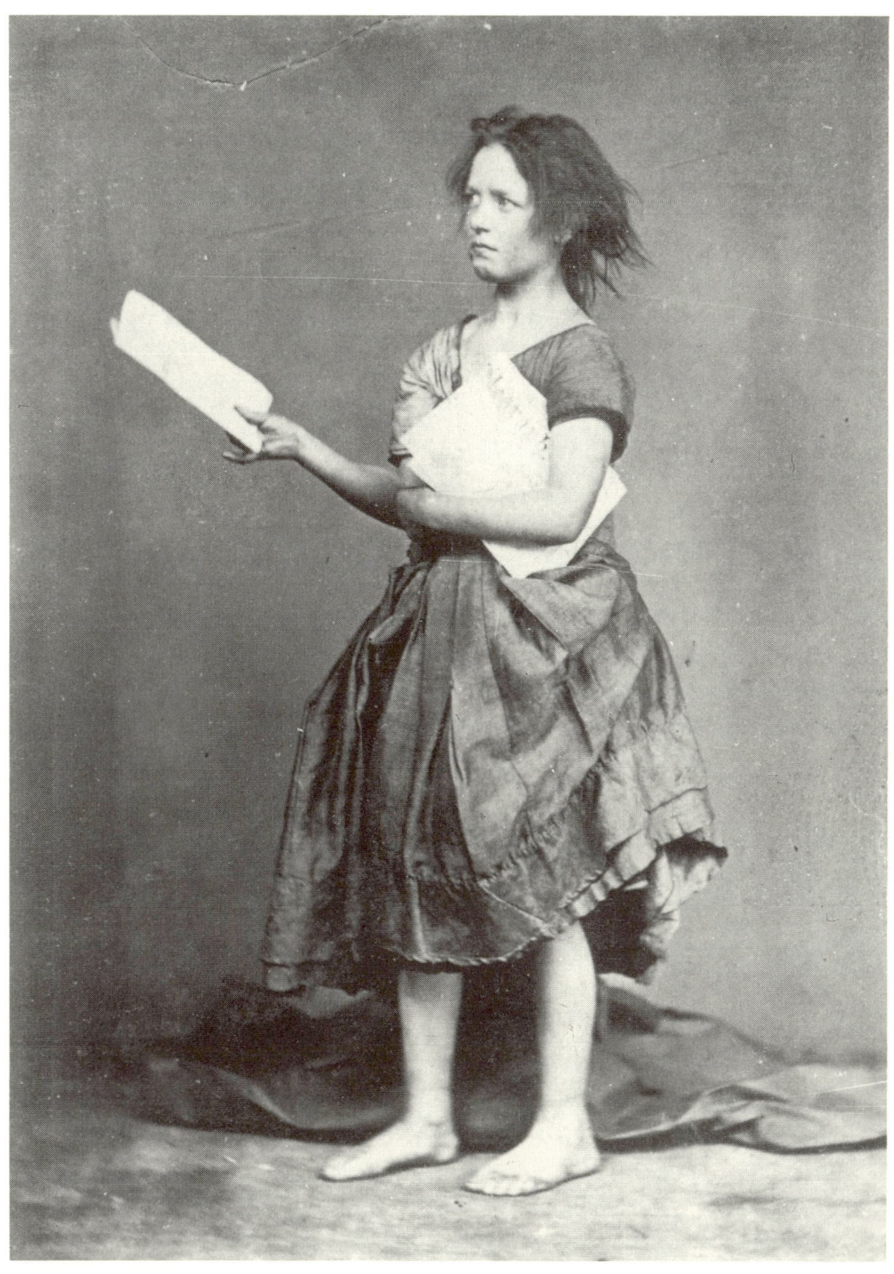

Figure 15. *Florence Holder*, c. 1876.
(Barnardo Photographic Archive, Ilford)

ever, I hear the screams of her mother in court. And I see the manipulation of her and her body for the causes of an upper-middle-class man.[73]

The impetus under the surface of Carroll's fading Victorian prints *can* be traced to a general "cult of the little girl" that was invoked in a range of cultural spaces: from the artists who portrayed her as typically "pure" (sexualized but not actively sexual), as in Millais's *Cherry Ripe* or Arthur Hughes's *Girl With Lilacs* (1863), the painting that Carroll chose to hang over the fireplace in his own study; to the world of children's illustrated books and greeting cards typified by Kate Greenaway's little "dollies"; to the law of the period that sought to determine the parameters of girlhood.[74] But Carroll's actual images remain atypical. They expose a representation of the little girl that feels undecided, as if he too were caught, with the Victorian girl, in an act of blushing and nonblushing at the same time.

This undecidability is poignantly demonstrated in a scene, which is neither fictitious nor true, from Gavin Millar's film, *Dreamchild* (1985). The scene features Alice, her mother, one of Alice's sisters, "Mr. Dodgson," and Mr. Duckworth seated in a row boat that is floating down a beautiful river lined with wild flowers and (perhaps) "real scented rushes." Alice stories have been told. It has been a perfect summer day . . . until now. Mr. Dodgson has begun to stare at Alice. His eyes are filled with an overwhelming, uncomfortable sort of love. His gaze, painful for all involved, does not go unnoticed by Alice. It is clear that she has *experienced* it before and that her sister has seen it before (but neither girl blushes). Without warning, Alice puts a stop to the look by giving Mr. Dodgson a big cold splash of river water right in the eyes. Humiliation washes over his face. The water streams down his cheeks, as if he were crying the incredulous tears of the Mock Turtle—as if he were shedding not drops but gallons of tears (as Alice once did in Wonderland). If Mr. Dodgson were not entirely speechless, he would be stuttering. Mrs. Liddell sternly insists that Alice apologize to him. Then, with unnerving "knowledge" and defiance, Alice not only apologizes but also uses her white lace handkerchief to soak up the water from Mr. Dodgson's pathetic face—sensually drawing the moment out as if the water were tears, tears shared between lovers, until we and Alice's mother cannot take it anymore. His gaze, a white lace handkerchief, a performative little girl, a sexuality without parameters: these are the contradictions at play, in those photographs of Carroll's that feature a "complex fantasm" we call "the girl."

CHAPTER II

To
Make Mary:
Julia Margaret
Cameron's
Photographs
of Altered
Madonnas

Another little maid of my own from early girlhood has been one of the most beautiful and constant of my models, and in every manner of form has her face been reproduced, yet never has it been felt that the grace of the fashion of it has perished. This last autumn her head illustrating the exquisite Maud

> *There has fallen a splendid tear*
> *From the passion flower at the gate*

is as pure and perfect in outline as were my Madonna studies ten years ago . . . The very unusual attributes of her character and complexion of her mind, if I may so call it, deserve mention in due time, and are the wonder of those whose life is blended with ours as intimate friends of the house.—Julia Margaret Cameron (writing about Mary Hillier), "Annals of My Glass House"

Julia Margaret Cameron (1815–79) took photographs of Madonnas. Most of the pictures feature Cameron's parlor maid, Mary Hillier, posing as another Mary: the Virgin. Lovely Mary Hillier, nicknamed the "Island Madonna" by the local folk who lived near Cameron's house, in Freshwater, on the Isle of Wight, not only modeled but also helped with the printing.[1]

Exposing Cameron's Madonnas

While Cameron has been acknowledged by art historians as a great amateur photographer, and has been granted the same kind of admiration that has been given to artists such as Lewis Carroll, Cameron's Madonna pictures (almost all of which were made between 1864 and 1865 and figure amongst her first and earliest pictures) have been among the least appreciated in an oeuvre that features about three thousand photographs in all.[2] Not surprisingly, Cameron is better known for her pictures of great bearded men, such as Charles Darwin and Thomas Carlyle, than for her "Renaissanced" Madonnas holding large, tender babies and full-bloomed white lilies. Gernsheim, who can be credited with rediscovering Cameron for our century, finds only the portraits to be worthy of true admiration, and "no more than sixty, deserve the designation 'master-piece.' "[3] Gernsheim uses words like "affected," "ludicrous," and "ama-teurish" to describe the space of those *other* pictures into which many of the Madonnas fall.[4] I love Cameron's fallen Madonnas. They are *altered* images of Mother, scratched with sexuality and printed with flesh.

However, it is not my intention to suggest that Cameron's Madonna pictures have been totally ignored. The photo-historian Mike Weaver has published two major studies of Cameron's work that include significant studies of the Madonna photographs: namely, in a catalog essay that ac-companied the Getty Museum's 1986 exhibition of her work, *Whisper of the Muse: The Overstone Album and Other Photographs by Julia Margaret Cam-eron* and in his survey of her work.[5] Although Weaver is indispensable in regard to his careful analysis of the typographical characters of the figures, his general historical knowledge of the period, and especially his exper-tise in the history of photography itself, his work remains squarely in the space of the history of art and speaks to a very particular audience. I want to open up the Cameron audience to include not only those interested in the visual arts but also, especially, those who are interested in the theoriz-ation of the maternal and the ways in which Cameron *pictured* the mater-nal *differently.*

My voice for this chapter (it's grain) is heterogeneous, a hybridization textured by four different spatial categories: one, a continuation of the cultural practices of the period, already begun in my discussion of Car-roll; two, Julia Kristeva's maternal theory; three, Mark Taylor's theoret-ical conception of alterity; and four, my connections to these pictures in the context of my own experiences as a mother. The latter is offered cautiously—*not* as a qualification but as part of the impetus behind my desire to enter into these pictures.

Despite the subversion of Victorian concepts of motherhood that I see in Cameron's Madonna pictures, I would like to emphasize further that Cameron herself was, in many ways, the traditional bourgeois Victorian woman. She was religious. She was charitable. She was dutiful in her correspondence, writing an average of three hundred letters a month.[6] And she more than fulfilled her feminine function of motherhood: she gave birth to six children, adopted another three, and took in two family orphans and one "beggar girl."[7]

Although one is in awe of the independence and the tenacity that would have been necessary for a Victorian woman such as Cameron to take up photography, it is important to understand that she greatly reduced the risk of compromising her "femininity" by taking it up late in life: after her children were grown, at the age of forty-eight. Yet beginning photography (with great enthusiasm) at this period in her life was typical of the ways in which Cameron also pushed at the boundaries of femininity (while staying within them). With great creativity, Cameron often managed to safely bypass the confines of her gender by enlarging the bourgeois Victorian woman's part in both her art and life.

Cameron was a performer. She was a highly visible eccentric who wore red velvet in the summer and stirred cups of tea while walking to the train station. She smelled not of delicate flowers but of photographic chemicals. A woman of fascinating inconsistencies, "she presented albums of [her photographs] to the Crown Prince of Prussia and her gardener alike."[8] Never one to turn up her nose at drama, she took great pleasure in meddling in everyone's affairs with overblown sympathy and energy: "Every cold became in her mind whooping cough, and endless were the exhortations and prescriptions which she invented for recovery."[9] A great entertainer, Cameron regularly invited famous people to her house, from Alfred Lord Tennyson to Lewis Carroll and Charles Darwin.

Not only was Cameron a performer, she was also a stage director. She insisted that her guests be actors for her camera. She began by dressing them in jeweled crowns and berets, and she flung great white garments over their heads and *subjected* them to hours of character modeling.[10] It seems that no one could escape her artistic clutches. In the following quote, Laura Troubridge (who had modeled for Cameron as a child) recalls Cameron looming over her and the other children. In Troubridge's account, Cameron feels large and ominous, like Queen Victoria herself. What Troubridge recalls is not child's play:

Aunt Julia appeared as a terrifying elderly woman, short and squat with none of the Pattle grace and beauty about her.[11] Dressed in dark clothes, stained with chemicals from her photography (and smelling of them too), with a plump eager face and piercing eyes, and a voice husky and a little harsh, yet in some way compelling and even charming. We were at once pressed into the service of the camera. Our roles were no less than those of two Angels of the Nativity, and to sustain them we were scantily clad and each had a pair of heavy swan wings fastened to her narrow shoulders, while Aunt Julia, with ungentle hand, touzled our hair to get rid of its prim nursery look. No wonder those old photographs of us, leaning over imaginary ramparts of heaven, look anxious and wistful. This was how we felt.[12]

Even the maids and cooks were exposed as Virgin Marys, Ophelias, Beatrices, and mountain nymphs. And, because she also employed the household servants to help with the printing, domestic order was non-existent: chaos was the order of the day. With Mrs. Cameron sitting up till two o'clock in the morning over her soaking photographs and with the servants busy as models and with the printing and with bringing out huge boxes of photographs to share with the guests, details like what to serve at mealtime were overlooked: the solution was to serve bacon and eggs at every meal. The novelist Anne Thackeray describes her unconventional experience as a guest at "the funniest place in the world":

> I cannot tell you how much we enjoy it all; of a morning the sun comes blazing up so cheerfully, and the sea sparkles, and there is a far-away hill all green, and a cottage which takes one's breath it looks so pretty in the morning mists. Then comes eggs and bacon. Then we go to the down top. Then we lunch off eggs and bacon. Then we have tea and look out the window, then we pay little visits, then we dine off eggs and bacon, and of an evening Minny and Emmy, robed in picturesque Indian shawls, sit by the fire, and Miss Stephen and I stroll about in the moonlight.[13]

And, as might be expected, the performances continued far beyond the confines of Cameron's glass house and well into the night:

> After the day's photography was over, the hostess always thought of something for the pleasure of others. There were parties and dances in the big paneled entrance hall . . . Cammy was also a keen orga-nizer of amateur theatricals, in which the Tennysons' and the Cam-

erons' sons and the younger generation of visitors participated with great gusto.[14]

A woman of unexpected contradictions, Cameron subverted the representation of the Victorian bourgeois woman (who was metaphorically confined like a fine bird in an elaborate cage of domestic order), even if she was not consciously critiquing its image. Cameron ruffled her feathers, decorated herself with red plumes, covered her cage with white sheets, and left the tiny wrought-iron door slightly ajar, so that she could fly both in and out, or simply perch herself on the threshold of confinement.

Cameron not only subverted the image of the Victorian woman through her *performed* life but also subverted its representation in her Madonna pictures, again, even if she was not consciously critiquing it. For at first glance, Cameron's photographic images of the Virgin Mary appear to conform with the expectations of a Victorian woman. Using Christian typology, the pictures properly contain woman's sexuality within a space of holy motherhood. Yet upon closer investigation, the pictures manage to bleed through the plastered walls of confinement that encircled the period's "angel in the house."[15] The images, which are often literally blurred, move metaphorically between categories, smearing the lines between sexual and not-sexual, male and female, earthly and heavenly. They move like an apparition, leaving the viewer perplexed about what has been seen.

Because she is photographed, however, this *altered* Mother appears more *real* than mythical. Unlike most apparitions, Cameron's Madonnas are fixed on photographic plates. Because Cameron imaged her Madonna through an everyday "real" woman, Cameron's Mary embodies death and sexuality (something that the biblical Mary is robbed of). Cameron's "Madonna pictures" become undecidable in their representation: they are a tribute to both the Virgin and Mary Hillier. They are just as much indebted to portraiture as to religion. They verge on sacrilege. The viewer is caught between the idealism of the Virgin Mary and the actual "complexion of her [Mary Hillier's] mind."

In photographing her maid as the Madonna, Cameron blurred not only the hierarchical distinctions between women but also the sharp focus many considered essential to photography. Cameron once wrote: "What is focus and who has a right to say what focus is the legitimate focus?"[16]

The blurry effect was caused by Cameron's soft focus as well as by the movement of the models, and all of the dirt, fingerprints, and hair that she allowed to accumulate on her glass plates.[17] "Even if she dropped and cracked the negative she would still make prints from it and boldly send them to exhibitions, when any other photographer would have discarded the picture."[18] Cameron's style went against the conventions of photography at that time, which sought clarity, reality, and truthfulness. Her work was in opposition to the "focused" work of other Victorian photographers, such as Carroll, Lady Clementina Hawarden, and Robinson. As a result, her distinctly foggy style has been read as more closely connected to the later hazy paintings of Pre-Raphaelitism than to the photography of the period.[19]

Cameron's pictures are haptic in the fullest sense of the word. Not only did she physically scrub, scratch, brush, and fingerprint her glass plates, she also focused on the ways in which women touch. Cameron further dramatizes this touching and what it feels like to be touched by featuring appealing folds of drapery in the Madonna pictures. Cameron recorded women touching their babies, with their fingertips and even with their lips. This "maternal touch" can also be found in those pictures that feature the Madonnas (and Madonna types) touching other women. Cameron *altered* her Madonnas to make Mary (and maternality itself) with a difference.

Altering Madonna

Mark Taylor's explorations of alterity are largely dependent on the work of the French philosopher Emmanuel Levinas. According to Levinas, the other is independent and autonomous, with its own qualities and attributes, and is prior to the subject; in other words, the other is the "alterer" of our own subjectivity. Levinas's is a notion of the other that exists outside of the traditional binary conceptions of the split between self and other. My own maternal experiences have fed into my understanding of what it means to be altered by an other who is autonomous yet continually calls on me to respond. "For Levinas what makes the other person other is not a unique attribute or a unique combination of attributes but the 'quality' of alterity itself. The other is other because his [or her] alterity is absolute, indeterminate, and indeterminable."[20] Of interest to my writing (with its particular emphasis on the haptic) is the fact that the indeterminacy of Levinas's *other's* absolute alterity is stimulated through the experience of the caress. Levinas tells us that "in a caress, what is there is sought as though it were not there, as though the skin were a trace of its own withdrawal, a languor still seeking like an absence which, however, could not be more there."[21] Similarly, the photographic skin that Cameron's Madonnas shed onto her glass negatives and albumenized papers can be read as traces of an absence that could not be more there. After all, Mary Hillier is dead and gone; yet she is there before us. Of course, all photographs are traces of such skin. Balzac understood this, which is why he feared losing thin ghosts of himself, like layers of skin, with each photograph "taken."[22] With Cameron, we are also left with the photographer's own skin (her fingerprints) on a plate that gives way to women touching the skin of infants and other women.

In *Blessing and Blessed* (1865, plate 3), as with so many of Cameron's Madonna images, there is an emphasis on touch. Touching upon the velvet light and darks, Mary Hillier emerges as the Madonna. She traces the forehead of a child with her lips. The softness of the photograph can be attributed to the slight movement of her head, which also gives this stilled picture the effect of movement: the two are caught in an eternal kiss. Mary Hillier's nostrils quietly quiver at the salty, warm smell of a brow that gives way to a full head of hair that ends in weightless curls. The child's hair falls back unnaturally, as if it has been stroked and caressed repeatedly in a single direction. The child's chin is smudged with a fingerprint or a touch of dirt that must have landed on the wet plate. The child's shoulder, composed of bony flesh, finds a perfect space between Hillier's breasts. She feels it. The child feels it. (I feel it as I recall my own head against my mother's breast in a memory that may or may not be real.) Hillier's hand, covered by her soft woolen shawls, finds its own way into the ever so slight curve of the child's forearm. Hillier's loosely covered hand, as opposed to a gloved hand, seems to emphasize the "feeling of" caressing the child's body.[23]

In contradiction with the lovely caressing that unfolds in *Blessing and Blessed,* the picture is punctured (as always) by death. Death, as I argued in the previous chapter, is directly connected to the medium of photography itself. Although Cameron's camera has frozen Mary Hillier and a beautiful child as forever young (just as Carroll did, only Cameron lets the mother into the picture), one cannot deny the morbid sense of mortality that is promoted by this picture: here, death is exaggerated by the child who poses as an infant pietà. Again, I call on Metz to compound the photograph and death: "Even when the person photographed is still living, that moment when she or he *was* has forever vanished. Strictly speaking, the person *who has been photographed*—not the total person, who is an effect of time—is dead."[24] Looking at *Blessing and Blessed,* nineteenth-century viewers would understand that Mary Hillier and the child are going to die; twentieth-century viewers already know that they are dead. And of special interest to this chapter, Mary Hillier's absolute specificity, "Lo, she was there," indeterminably alters the Madonna to the ground, altering alterity into a space of alt*a*rity.

"Altarity" is Mark Taylor's term for the semiotic play that the concept of alterity invokes within a space of Derridean undecidability. According to Taylor, "Altarity is a slippery word whose meaning can be neither stated clearly nor fixed firmly. Though never completely decidable, the field of the word 'altarity' can be approached through the network of its associations: altar, alter, alternate, alternative, alternation, altarity."[25] Through various complex wordplays, Taylor associates his concept of altarity with Christian deities, the family altar, the hymenal altar, the altar of pleasure, a slang version of altar which means pudendum, etc. Specific to my concerns is Taylor's celebration of the ways in which altarity contains, but is not withheld by, a semantic range of "altar," which includes high and low, sacred and sexual. For this is precisely the reading I attribute to Cameron's Madonnas: they too are sacred and sexual, as they quote images of "high art" (Renaissance paintings) through a medium considered to be "low art" or "not art" at all. My thesis has now doubled up: Julia Margaret Cameron both altered and *altared* her Madonnas to make Mary (and maternality itself) with a *difference*.

Making Angels

Cameron's work feels particularly subversive when one considers how Victorian women "lacked" their own narratives of difference, biological or otherwise. Here are a few of the more familiar stories: In order to deter other women from overintellectualizing, a Harvard doctor revealed that in performing an autopsy on a Radcliffe woman, he discovered that her uterus had shrunken to the size of a pea.[26] Nineteenth-century scientists used skeleton studies to confirm that women's bodies were underdeveloped, and therefore lower on the evolutionary scale. Due to their smaller stature and larger animal-like pelvises, women were envisioned as an intermediary between primate and man. One of the first female skeletons to be drawn featured her in front of an illustration of the skeleton of an ostrich; this emphasized what the two supposedly held in common—a small head (not fully equipped for intellectual thought) and a very large pelvis (fully equipped for birth).[27] Despite discoveries of actual difference, principally the discovery of spontaneous ovulation in 1840, doggerel verse still maintained that a woman was not different from man, that she was merely man turned outside in and was lacking the sufficient heat to push her male genitals out.[28] Despite the confirmation that hysteria was *not* connected to the uterus, smelling salts were still used to chase her wandering womb, her hysterical sexuality, back into place.[29] All of these stories served as "prefaces" to Freud's "Lecture on Femininity" (1931), which confirmed that "the little girl is a little man," with her insufficient clitoris standing in for the "lost" or "tucked in" penis.[30]

But despite all of the debates over skeletons, or whether or not an untamed uterus came up into the throat and made an hysteric cough, or whether or not women could ovulate and conceive, like a fish "in cold blood," without sexual stimulus, it was the biological process of motherhood that clearly marked woman as different from man. For the image of mother is the "only function of the 'other sex' to which we can definitely attribute existence."[31] This caused particular anxiety during the Victorian period, with its emphasis on the bourgeois family, the sacredness of motherhood, and the desired purity of women. How could masculinist culture celebrate her as mother while erasing her difference and her "sexuality?" It seems that the solution may have been to envision her not as an ordinary, biologically functioning sexual mother but as a pure, decorous, nonthreatening, virginal mother. As Bram Dijkstra writes:

> The practical impossibility of having their household nuns and modern madonnas duplicate the original Mary's immaculate conception must certainly have become rather an embarrassment. However, it was Auguste Comte, who came to the rescue in 1854, suggesting in his *System of Positive Policy* what he certainly had a right to call "a daring hypothesis." Comte in effect suggested the exploration of artificial insemination as a means of keeping women as close to the Madonna ideal as possible, while still allowing them to fulfill their function as mothers.[32]

Comte's outrageous proposal, to keep the Victorian angels of the house as close to the Madonna as possible, was born of anxieties surrounding the debates over sexual difference. But despite Comte's fantasies, the Virgin mother, the Madonna, still stands alone, "alone of all her sex."[33] For, the Blessed Virgin Mother is the only woman to have given birth as a virgin, to have been born of immaculate conception, and to have escaped death through "assumption." As Catherine Clément points out, "She [the Virgin] is a woman because she is a mother and a man because she conceives by herself . . . The Virgin is androgynous . . . She is a man."[34]

In the age of Victorian religious doubt, we find that the bride of the bourgeois Victorian male, the angel in the house, replaces Mary as a source of worship. This new secular yet angelic bride, crowned the bourgeois home and family as the new temple of purity. It was she who maintained sacredness within an age of modernist doubt. But as a result of the heightened fear of sexual difference that had erupted in the Victorian era, she too, like the Virgin Mary, had to maintain her "motherhood" as sexually indifferent. This angel in the house, like so many women of her time, found that her wings were merely decorative—rendering her powerless.[35] (Queen Victoria wrote to her own daughter that being pregnant made one feel so pinned down, as if one's wings were clipped.[36]) Such Victorian household angels were caught within the double-bind of having to be a mother (her ultimate achievement) without acting upon her sexuality so as announce her sexual difference. The contradictory image of the Victorian angel-mother as fecund yet sexually pure brings to mind the semiotics of the Victorian blush that colored my earlier discussion of Carroll's equally impossible girl-child. When faced with sexual innuendo, a blush would indicate the angel-mother's knowledge of sexual practice, and a nonblush might indicate her familiarity, ease, and lack of embarrassment with the very act that produced her children. As a result, she had to maintain herself on a difficult flight that traveled across the threshold of blushing. She must always be in the act of blushing and nonblushing at the same time. She was doomed. Thus, preserving the secular virgin mother became dangerous work, forcing Victorian society to keep her locked up in her heavenly home, a throne removed from the streets of London, far from civilization, so as to make each pregnancy appear immaculate, a work of God. For she really belonged in heaven, as Coventry Patmore, the famous Catholic convert, friend of Cameron's and author of *The Angel in the House* indicates when he speaks and writes of his own wife.[37] Patmore enthroned his angel within a virginal space that belonged not to him, but to God and to the heavens. Is it sheer coincidence that the Immaculate Conception was raised to dogma status in 1854, the year that Patmore wrote *The Angel in the House,* and the year that Comte proposed that all women might partake in artificial insemination?

Not surprisingly, Cameron spoke a language that was similar to the Grand Victorian Angel: the queen herself. The queen's wedding-night advice to her daughter, "Lie still and think of the Empire," is mirrored in Cameron's own advice to young girls before a dance: "If ever you fall into temptation, down on your knees, and think of Aunt Julia."[38]

And, like a good household angel, Cameron never ran the risk of letting her art conflict with her family. Because Cameron did not take up such a time consuming hobby until the children were grown, motherhood was *not* something to fit in with her art. Unlike her French contemporary, the painter Berthe Morisot, Cameron never had to hire a wet nurse to feed a child while she busied herself with her art.[39] If anything, for Cameron, motherhood was poetically and emotionally tied to the camera. For it was Julia, Julia Margaret Cameron's only daughter, a mirror of her own mother in name and face, who gave Cameron her first camera, as a gift, in hopes of amusing her mother when the children had grown up. In the words of Cameron from her "Annals of My Glass House" (1874): "Therefore it is with effort that I restrain the overflow of my heart and simply state that my first [camera and] lens was given to me by my cherished departed daughter . . . with the words 'It may amuse you, Mother, to try to photograph during your solitude.' "[40] Daughter Julia, Cameron's first child, gave birth to Cameron's photographic career, only to die young, at age thirty-four, in childbirth, after having given birth to six children, like her own mother. For Cameron, her photographic images must have always been literally tied to her daughter.

*The Photographs: Tied to the Maternal
and Tied to Death*

Like a photograph, the child is always connected to its referent: its mother. A photograph carries its referent with it, just as a mother carries her child with her body, even after birth. Kristeva speaks of the process of maternity as a graft: "What connection is there between myself, or even more unassumingly between my body and this internal graft and fold, which, once the umbilical cord has been severed, is an inaccessible other?"[41] Similarly, Rosalind Krauss writes of photography as a graft: "Photography can only operate with the directness of a physical graft; photography turns on the direct activity of direct impression as surely as the footprint is left in the sand."[42] And to Krauss's words I would add, as surely as the footprint is made on the birth certificate. Perhaps that is why Barthes speaks of the relationship between the photograph and its referent as being like an umbilical cord. Likewise, our mother's body is that to which we are physically tied and from which we are externally severed. It is birth that guarantees our death. The womb is never far from the tomb. Birth is the greatest catastrophe of our lives.

Barthes's most famous book on photography marks such a place: written after the death of his mother, and hauntingly right before his own unexpected death, *Camera Lucida* is a photo album that marks those pictures that are (personally) poignant to him—that pierce him with *punctum,* that simultaneously trigger birth and death. Barthes's punctum-pictures pull at the beauty and the horror of all that is metaphorically implied by the small scar that cuts into the smoothness of our all our bellies, our navel: the irreducible mark of our birth and our guaranteed death. Our umbilical scar always pulls at the lost mother, just as a photograph pulls at its lost referent. That is why (some) photographs *wound* Barthes: he feels it like a stab in the abdomen.

Cameron's photographs of the Madonna often feature Mary as a figure of maternality tied to death. In *La Madonna Esattata / Fervent in Prayer* (1865, plate 4) and *La Madonna della Pace / Perfect in Peace* (1865, plate 5), Mary Hillier cradles a child who appears dead. In these two pictures, the deathly effect of the child stands in contrast to Hillier's movement. (The pictures were part of a special album, containing 111 photographs, that Cameron presented to her friend Lord Overstone in 1865. When the album was intact, the viewer would have seen *Fervent in Prayer* first, then, with a flip of the page, *Perfect in Peace.*)

In *Fervent in Prayer,* the expression on Hillier's face is of great interest: her humbly raised eyes are undermined by a slight, but certainly remarkable, smirk that she wears on her lips. Is she showing love and devotion to God or to the fascinating woman standing behind the camera? Hillier looks as if she is about ready to break into laughter. Is Cameron provoking her underneath the great black sheet that shields the camera from light and the artist's gaze from her subject?

In contrast, Hillier's face in *Perfect in Peace* is washed with melancholia. Seeing the two pictures together reveals that Hillier's face is as much a part of the masquerade as the white sheets. Visibly, Hillier, like the photographer herself, is a performer too. They must have enjoyed performing together. Cameron credited her first accomplished picture, which she entitled *My First Success* (1864), to her "Sweet, sunny-haired little Annie!" and showered her with gifts.[43] This sense of reciprocity between artist and model continued throughout Cameron's photographic career. Mary Hillier (like Agnes Grace Weld, Irene MacDonald, and Alice Liddell herself) appears to be no exception to the *play*.

But despite Hillier's altered performances, the child is exactly the same in both pictures. His immobility is accentuated by his frozen and furrowed brow, his stiffened lips, and his lost body, wrapped in Hillier's sheets. Propped in a mother's arms, he is reminiscent of the period's funerary pictures, which sometimes depicted the deceased as asleep. The literature and the postmortem photography of the period often linked sleep with death: it was a way of denying death. Sleepy photographs of death (fig. 16) gave the impression of everlasting life, not unlike photography itself. Photographs of dead children appearing to sleep are beautiful fetish objects that allow us to believe in everlasting life (in dream-rushes that will never lose their scent and will never ever melt), while they force us to confront our own mortality. Dan Meinwald explains that "the making of a postmortem photograph is, like embalming, a preservation of the body for the gaze of the observer."[44] Cameron must have known something of this and that is why she invites us to take long looks at her (un)dead.

Shades of death touch upon *Fervent in Prayer* and *Perfect in Peace,* but in *The Shunamite Woman and Her Dead Son* (1865, plate 6) the viewer is exposed to an even stronger tone of death. The beautiful child whom we long to read as asleep haunts us with his closed eyes. We anxiously wait for them to open, knowing full well that the baby is merely a child-friend, or perhaps a relative of Cameron's, yet the photographer keeps them shut forever through her naming of "dead son."[45]

Looking even closer at this picture, the voyeurism of our gaze at this child is doubled by the sensuality of the child: shirt rumpled up, a slightly

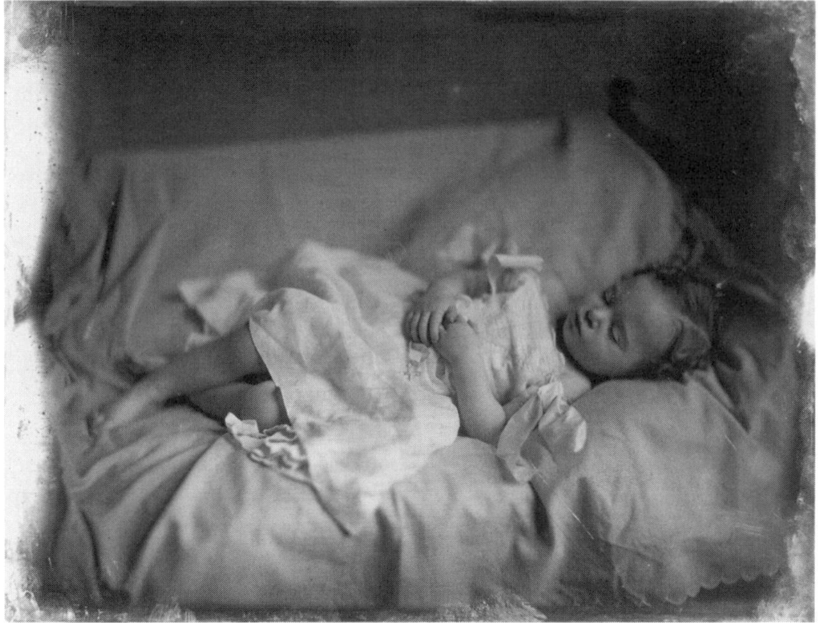

Figure 16. Southwares and Hawes, *Photograph of a Dead Child*
(as indicated by the rosary), 1865. (International Museum of
Photography, at George Eastman House, Rochester)

arched back that gives way to a lovely rounded belly, delightful thighs that
have fallen open in complete disregard. The sensuality of Cameron's picture is especially striking through a contemporary lens. When comparing
it, for example, with Sally Mann's *The Wet Bed* (1987, plate 7), which
features Mann's daughter Virginia asleep, the sexuality of Cameron's child
is suddenly heightened.[46] As both Mann's and Cameron's pictures *display*
children in situations that only the family should see (a wet bed, a death
bed), they are taboo images.[47] Kincaid has written that "the child is the
embodiment of desire and also its negation."[48] How true this feels in these
two pictures, where the child embodies death and negates it (through
sleep and in Cameron's case Christianity), just as the child embodies sexuality and denies it (also through sleep and inexperience / innocence). Like
the Victorian postmortem photographs of children in their most precious
clothes, framed by breathtaking flowers and silky pillows, these are attractive images that are disturbing to look at. Cameron and Mann, as mother-
artists, speak a surprising mother-tongue that enlarges our vision of the
relationship that motherhood, sensuality, sexuality, and death share.

In *The Shunamite Woman and Her Dead Son*, Cameron's representation of maternality is further expanded by the reciprocity of sexuality between her and her child. The woman and the baby share lines of sensual erasure where the mother's arm sinks into the belly and thighs of her child. Wearing only a touch of a garment that is impossible to see, the Shunamite Woman looks as unclothed as her child. Her hair, an overdetermined sign in the Victorian sexual imagination, slips beyond her madonnaesque veil and hints at Magdalene eroticism. This mother, deep in thought, takes up even more space when one realizes that she looks elsewhere, beyond her child.

The Theater of the Mother: On Stage and in the Wings

Cameron's dramas are focused on the theater of "mother," not the stage of the child. Refusing to reiterate only the child's side of the story, which is characteristic of psychoanalytic thought (from primary narcissism, to a glance in the Lacanian mirror, to the oedipal moment and concepts of fetishization), Cameron lets the mother into the picture.

In Cameron's *Goodness* (c. 1864, plate 8), the mother is actively looking. Mary Hillier looked at Cameron's camera eye, and now she looks at us straight in the eye. The child is looking intently at us too. The child's clasped hands are inadequately masquerading those of an infant Christ. Yet the child's drama does not overshadow that of the mother. They both share a strong presence as they perform for the camera, for Cameron, for us. With a closer look, it appears that Christ is really a little girl: the biblical narrative is subverted.[49]

The drama that is performed is that of maternality. Hillier's gaze is so strong that it has a materiality of its own, throwing out an invisible barrier between her and the child and the viewer. The child's eyes seem to be saying, Do not come near. The two girls, one older, the other very young, both with undraped shoulders and chest, are both nakedly there. They are indeterminably close, yet *not* one. For Levinas, being for the other is *goodness*. The paradigm of an ethical relation is that of goodness, precisely the mother's response to the needs and the requirement of the child. Hillier looks as if she is doing just that. In the words of Levinas, "To be for the Other is to be good . . . . The fact that in existing for another I exist otherwise than in existing for me is morality itself."[50] Hillier is able to

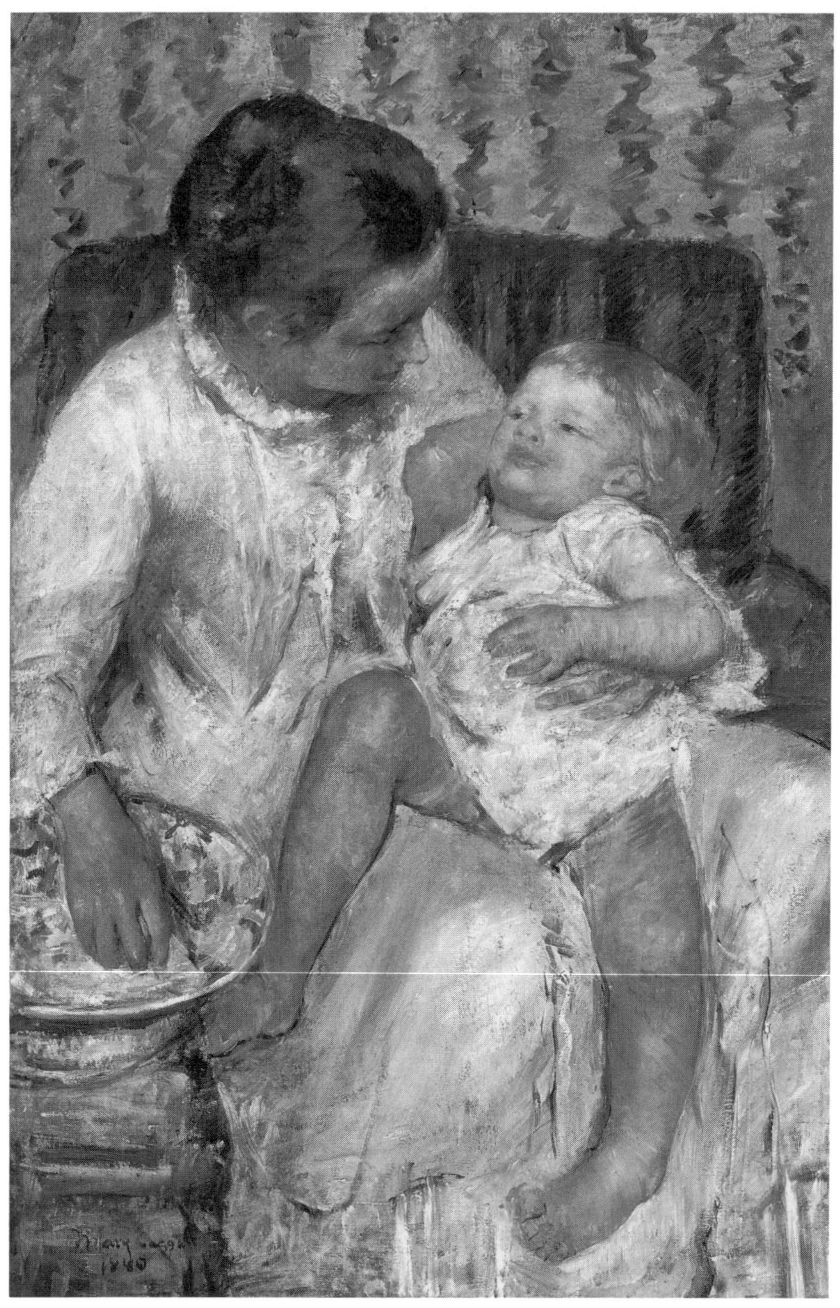

Figure 17. Mary Cassatt, *Mother About to Wash Her Sleepy Child*, 1880. (Los Angeles County Museum of Art, Mrs. Fred Hathaway Bixby Bequest)

perform *Goodness,* precisely because she can do so without losing sight of herself.

Cameron's portrayals of the mother and child, though couched in Christian iconography (a space that undoubtedly promoted her acceptance as a woman "art maker"), let mother into the picture, much more so than Mary Cassatt, the other great nineteenth-century "imager" of mother and child. Looking at *Mother About to Wash Her Sleepy Child* (1880, fig. 17), Cassatt's first *maternité* image, we find that most of the surface is filled with the white and monumental enfolding presence of not the mother's face, but the holy garments that cloak the mother as ethereal Queen. Cassatt has imaged a contemporary nineteenth-century woman as "modern Madonna." This Madonna's subservient maternal role is reinforced by whisking the mother's individuality and human characteristics out of the picture. Her face is turned and obscured, as she presents herself not as mother, but as a religious icon who gives way to her "sleepy child," who is truly the subject of the painting. This "focus" on the child is characteristic of most of Cassatt's images of mother and child.

The difficulty of revealing, finding, and releasing the mother in art is curiously inherent to the metaphors of artistic production itself. As Susan Suleiman writes in "Writing and Motherhood,"

> Just as motherhood is ultimately the child's drama, so is artistic creation. In both cases the mother is the essential but silent Other, the mirror in whom the child searches for his own reflection, the body he seeks to appropriate, the thing he loses or destroys again and again, and seeks to recreate. A writer, says Roland Barthes, is "someone who plays with the body of his mother."[51]

Barthes continues this play with the body of the "mother" in *Camera Lucida,* which lyrically writes itself around the search for the photograph of his mother, which might finally allow him to rediscover her, which might reveal her truth, which might bring back the face that he had loved. Surprisingly he finds her *not* in the photograph in which she is hugging him as a child against the rumpled softness of her crêpe de Chine. She is *not* there in that very same photograph in which he can waken in himself the perfume of her rice powder. She is *not* in any photograph in which Barthes himself is present; instead, he finds her in the Winter Garden Photograph, where his mother is found facing the photographer at the tender age of five:

She was holding one finger in the other hand, as children often do, in an awkward gesture . . .

I studied the little girl and at last rediscovered my mother. The distinctness of her face, the naïve attitude of her hands, the place she had docilely taken without either showing or hiding herself, and finally her expression which distinguished her, like Good from Evil, from the hysterical little girl, from the simpering doll who plays at being grownup.[52]

Acknowledging that the "truth" of his mother was not in the photograph of him with her, not even in a photograph in which she was a mother, allows the concept of mother to expand beyond Mother with a capital *M,* beyond our cultural metaphors of her, beyond her place in stories of psychoanalysis, beyond her place in the Family. Barthes seems to reiterate this concept by never reproducing for us the Winter Garden Photograph. In his book filled with other provocative photographs, which "wound" him, which "pierce" him, which "prick" him, which "sting" him and "cut" him because of their *punctum,* we never see the picture of his mother. Her presence is felt at the center of the text, but her image is outside of his own drama, his own search. Barthes allows his mother to move outside of his own drama as child, into a world of her own, into her own childhood space, where he has not even been conceived. We feel her strong presence, but she is not there, she has other things to do, she is free to move outside the constraints of traditional stories of motherhood.

Cameron plays out the same trick in *The Bereaved Babes / The Mother Moved!* (1864, plate 9). Through its suggestive and humorous title, we imagine that the mother has, if only momentarily, refused her role as Mother, as she chooses to move outside of the frame and the framework of motherhood. She is not there, but she is "not, not there." Her meaning and her presence, like Barthes's own mother, is allowed to flow beyond the edges of the page. Cameron not only lets mother into the photograph: she lets her out.

The Split Tongues of Maternality and Photography

In "Stabat Mater," Julia Kristeva presents not only an account of the traditional representations of the Virgin, but also the birth of her own son. Written near the time of his birth, Kristeva constructed the article in two pieces that are deliberately and typographically fragmented from each other. A column of bold type, which is a moving and free account of her own desire and experience of motherhood (her *jouissance*), is placed next to a column in plain type, which is a historical and psychoanalytic critique of the cult of the Virgin (fig. 18).

The bold text, which indeed I do see as a bold move on Kristeva's part, plays with the notion of attempting to represent a preoedipal and postoedipal space, before and beyond conventional language. The bold text is an enactment of Kristeva's refiguring of the semiotic. Usurping the word "semiotic" from Ferdinand de Saussure, Kristeva unfixes and refixes it to mean this preoedipal, *maternal* space.[53] Kristeva's semiotic is a rupture in the symbolic, and a rupture in her own text. This bold portion of the text de-privileges traditional verbal speech by performing within a constellations of senses that is linked to the bodily contact with the mother. There is ecstasy in touch: "stream of hair made of ebony, of nectar, smooth darkness through her fingers, gleaming honey under the wings of bees, sparkling strands burning bright . . . silk, mercury, ductile copper: frozen light warmed under fingers."[54] There is ecstasy in smell: "Scent of milk, dewed greenery, acid and clear."[55] There is ecstasy in sound: "Taut eardrum, tearing sound out of muted silence. Wind among grasses, a seagull's faraway call, echoes of waves, auto horns, voices, or nothing? Or his own tears, my newborn, spasm of syncopated void."[56]

The *sound* of Kristeva's *bold* text makes sense / *sens* (*jouissance* sounds just like *j'ouïs sens*), and it looks different.[57] Her *full* text is torn between two languages, one expressive, the other critical, which mirrors the experience of the maternal body held on the threshold between nature and culture. It is a place of growing contradictions. Kristeva tells her listeners, "Obviously you may close your eyes, cover up your ears, teach courses, run errands, tidy up the house, think about objects, subjects. But a mother is always branded by pain, she yields to it."[58] Her subjectivity, the mother's and Kristeva's, is violated by pregnancy and subverted by lactation and nurturance. She is altered by her child.

Cameron's pictures embody the look of and feel of Kristeva's split text. Both operate in incongruous spaces. I have already examined several sets of interwoven contradictions that Cameron constructed: sacred (the Madonna) and profane (Mary Hillier); alive and dead; negation of time and its absolute loss; sexual and not sexual; there and not there. These are all double-spaces that facilitated Cameron's *altaring* of her Madonnas.

especially, as early as 1328, to the promulgation of Salic laws, which excluded daughters from the inheritance and thus made the loved one very vulnerable and coloured one's love for her with all the hues of the impossible, the Marian and courtly streams came together. Around Blanche of Castile (who died in 1252) the Virgin explicitly became the focus of courtly love, thus gathering the attributes of the desired woman and of the holy mother in a totality as accomplished as it was inaccessible. Enough to make any woman suffer, any man dream. One finds indeed in a *Miracle de Notre Dame* the story of a young man who abandons his fiancée for the Virgin: the latter came to him in a dream and reproached him for having left her for an 'earthly woman'.

Nevertheless, besides that ideal totality that no individual woman could possibly embody, the Virgin also became the fulcrum of the humanization of the West in general and of love in particular. It is again about the thirteenth century, with Francis of Assisi, that this tendency takes shape with the representation of Mary as poor, modest and humble – madonna of humility at the same time as a devoted, fond mother. The famous nativity of Piero della Francesca in London, in which Simone de Beauvoir too hastily saw a feminine defeat because the mother kneeled before her barely born son, in fact consolidates the new cult of humanistic sensitivity. It replaces the high spirituality that assimilated the Virgin to Christ with an earthly conception of a wholly human mother. As a source for the most popularized pious images, such maternal humility comes closer to 'lived' feminine experience than the earlier representations did. Beyond this, however, it is true that it integrates a

Scent of milk, dewed greenery, acid and clear, recall of wind, air, seaweed (as if a body lived without waste): it slides under the skin, does not remain in the mouth or nose but fondles the veins, detaches skin from bones, inflates me like an ozone balloon, and I hover with feet firmly planted on the ground in order to carry him, sure, stable, ineradicable, while he dances in my neck, flutters with my hair, seeks a smooth shoulder on the right, on the left, slips on the breast, swingles, silver vivid blossom of my belly, and finally flies away on my navel in his dream carried by my hands. My son.

Nights of wakefulness, scattered sleep, sweetness of the child, warm mercury in my

Figure 18. Julia Kristeva, page from the English translation of "Stabat Mater." (*The Kristeva Reader*, ed. Toril Moi [New York: Columbia University Press, 1986])

But, as I have pointed out, Cameron also dramatically altered traditional photographic protocol (through focus, lighting, and general untidiness), in order to inscribe (masculinized) science with (feminized) art. Photography has always played out the contradiction between science and art: Cameron's success was her ability to enlarge art to such an extent that it threatened to encroach upon science.

The split in photography between science and art is analogous with Roland Barthes's contradictory categories of denoted and connoted (as discussed in chapter one). In Cameron's Madonna pictures we find that the denoted (the message without a code) ensures that we believe that Hillier was actually *there*—while also (nearly) believing the Madonna was actually there. On the other hand, the connoted enables Cameron to use her "art" to manipulate this corpo*reality* with her fantastic play of light, her tolerance (and one might even say her love) for smudges and dirt, and her desire to let figures blur and quiver as they literally move through her constructed sexual-ethereal spaces. Cameron's *connoted* message altars Mary (and maternality itself) on the basis of a *denoted* message that pictures a (real) woman.

Though many artists and critics of the period held Cameron's work in high esteem, she received as much criticism as she did praise: the regard for her work was *split*. Cameron was especially snubbed by her fellow photographers. They were irritated by her style, which went against recognized standards. Carroll wrote the following about Cameron's blurry vision of the world:

> In the evening Mrs. Cameron and I had a mutual exhibition of photographs. Hers are all taken purposely out of focus—some are very picturesque—some merely hideous—however, she talks of them as if they were triumphs of art. *She* wished she could have had some of *my* subjects to do *out* of focus—and *I* expressed an analogous wish with regards to some of *her* subjects.[59]

Robinson was even more pointed in his criticism of Cameron:

> The arguments of the admirers of these productions were, that the excellences existed because of the faults, and that if they were in focus, or more casually executed, their merit would be less. This is not true, and, if it were, I should certainly say, Let the merits go; *it is not the mission of photography to produce smudges* . . . . If studies in light

and shade only are required, let them be done in pigment or charcoal, with a mop if necessary, but photography is pre-eminently the art of definition, and when an art departs from its function it is lost.[60]

Like Kristeva, Cameron's voice interrupts the symbolic with a language that resists mastery. They both take pleasure in speaking with at least two tongues: the mother's and the father's.

More Tongues: Touching on Color and Smell

Within the space of her mother tongue, Cameron has other feminine tongues that connote, whisper, click, lick, sniff, and hum into the prescribed languages of motherhood and photography. I have already commented on Cameron's double use of "touch"—the touching of the photographic plate and the touching between women and children. In the remaining pages I will elaborate on Cameron's particular use of touch and color and even olfaction as waxy spaces of resistance within her images that appear, at first glance, to respect traditional style and iconography.

Color. Nearly all of Julia Margaret Cameron's photographs have the impression of having been painted with color. There are several reasons for this: one, the blurriness of Cameron's photographic style suggests painting more than photography; two, her habit of quoting Italian Renaissance paintings, which again brings her work closer to painting; three, Cameron's attraction to actually brushing on, or giving the effect of brushing on, colored tones on the pictures; four, the velvety saturations of plum-sepia, auburn-sepia, gray-sepia, cream-sepia, charcoal-sepia, and pink-sepia that her pictures achieve; and five, the pleasurable fading and oxidation that has taken place since the pictures were first developed, "which can be attributed to insufficient washing and inadequate toning of the prints."[61] Anne Thackeray wrote, "There is a quality about many of them as pictures which I do not remember in any other photographs. They suggest colour so completely that it does not seem that painting could add anything to their beauty."[62]

The Double Star[63] (1864, plate 10) is remarkable for its color. This painting-photograph glows in warm mulberry-brown light. The picture, as if fixed in thick, dark fruit juices, features passion between what looks to be girls. I am reminded of Christina Rossetti's "Goblin Market."[64] Both picture and poem are bruised with the eroticism of childhood. The photograph—though mostly dark, as if smeared with the flesh of an over-ripe plum—has the appearance of also being underpainted with thick cream, ocherous earth, and something crimson: like "Plump unpecked cherries" or "Wild free-born cranberries, Crab-apples, dewberries."[65] One can see snatches and blotches of this eerie sienna rosiness rising up into the children's faces, in the ominous background, and along the picture's edges. Satiated by these baths of filling color, the *two stars,* "plums . . . Fresh on their mother twigs," kiss.[66] "Hug me, kiss me, suck my juices / Squeezed from goblin fruits for you, / Goblin pulp and goblin dew. / Eat me, drink me, love me."[67] Their faces have gently nudged their way into a sleepy coital lock. A hand barely spreads its fingers on a childish breast. "Cheek to cheek and breast to breast / Locked together in one nest."[68] Dark gray watercolor-juices flow down from the middle right. Large milky white dots sit on top of pin-dots of pink, gray, and cream. The dots wander and punctuate wherever they please. A mysterious arc behind them (a heavenly sun eclipsed by the moon?) suggests a mysterious night-light source. For, even in the darkness, the children manage to glow like the pink-gold of a childhood bracelet. Indeed, the colors speak a language of their own.

Julia Kristeva has richly explored the notion of color as an independent and uncodified language in "Giotto's Joy" and "Motherhood According to Giovanni Bellini."[69] The latter is of particular interest to me because of its emphasis on the representation of motherhood. In this text, like "Stabat Mater," Kristeva locates *jouissance* in a preoedipal, preconscious "mute" space before and beyond speech. Meaning is suggested this time, not through a double-text but through Bellini's *breaching* color. According to Kristeva, Bellini has succeeded in representing *jouissance* through "a predominance of luminous, chromatic differences beyond and despite corporeal representation."[70] In other words, the production of color challenges the importance of the figuration itself, creating a *jeux d'espaces* through the working of the signifier *jouissance.* Similarly, Cameron's use of color, which includes her use of pure white light, exceeds figure and outline.

Touch. Cameron also engraved lines onto her photographs, which, like her use of color, exceeded figure and outline: she touched and let things touch the emulsion, the skin of her glass plates.

The Double Star is fractured by such lines. The bottom left of the picture is filled with cracks, which scarifies the child's body with history and pain, like a delicate garden sculpture photographed by Atget. But what moves me are the double lines on the right of the picture; they become my punctum; they pierce me with history and pain. I know that Mary Hillier helped Cameron with the photographic process; whose hair is this?

Olfaction (Scent with a Kiss). While there are no pictures of Cameron really touching an *actual* Mary Hillier, there are many pictures of Hillier touching other women. In *The Kiss of Peace* (1869, plate 11), which Cameron sent "with a kiss" to her friend Mary Frazer Tyler, two young women (one older, the other a girl-child) press and nudge their bodies together.[71] The taller dark-haired figure, a suggested Virgin Mary and the real Mary Hillier, bestows a tender and nearly invisible kiss on the forehead of what might be presumed to be an Elizabeth.[72] Yet because of Hillier's arousing and impressive display of hair, which *clouds* the picture, "Mary" appears to be as much Magdalene as Virgin. This trick of letting Hillier's hair out to weave two discourses together, the pure and the impure, both of which are contained by the signifier "Mary," is a stratagem that Cameron played out in many of her pictures.[73] Such *play* between categories makes for a slippery kiss that smacks of unholy devotion. With typical Cameronian finesse, *The Kiss of Peace* pictures all of the contradictions of altarity by tangling up Mary Hillier, Mary Magdalene, and the Virgin Mary: through long flowing hair (wild, tangled, and beautifully lit) and through faces that appear smudged, caked, and scratched as a result of Cameron's sloppy photographic process. The marks shared between these two women act as a sign of their love, the love between women.[74]

Although this picture can be seen as a re-imaging of Mary Hillier's kiss on the temple of the Christ child in *Blessing and Blessed* (1865, plate 3), the effect, this time around, is much different. In *Blessing and Blessed,* Hillier invisibly touches and barely rubs the marblelike arm of the beautifully carved baby-child with an unseen hand, gloved by the cashmere shawl; in *The Kiss of Peace,* her hands, and even her arms, appear bound and fixed underneath the (same?) shawl, as do those of Elizabeth. This denial of touch makes touch feel all the more urgent. Hillier copes with this urgency by slipping her face into the character of hands: "Mary" caresses the young girl with her lips, her cheek, her nose. The palpability of it all is further enlarged, not only by the print that grew out of a plate that gives evidence of having been touched all over but also by the half-closed eyes and the averted gazes of the girl and the woman.[75] In fact, they have the appearance of not seeing at all, as they seek each other through kisses and blind groping, as if they were in the womb.

I also *see* olfaction. The picture's emphasis is not only on Hillier's wild hair, shot with light, but also on the pleasing line of her nose. The same light can be found dancing on the pale tresses and nose of the other girl. But it is Hillier's nose, featured in elegant profile, that thrills me. It is my *punctum*. I love Hillier's nose. I know it and its subtle curves well. I am able to distinguish the "Island Madonna" from Cameron's other young beautiful models by her lovely nose.[76] Somewhere in between a sniff and a kiss, Hillier audibly breathes in the young girl. I recognize this gesture: I always smell my children before and as I give them kisses. The scent with a kiss is a maternal memory.[77]

But the sentimentality of the picture is punctured by erotic over-tones—not only because of the fact that it is a visual-haptic-olfactic repre-sentation of love between women but also because of the Cameron's embracement of the textual representation of Mary Magdalene. Cam-eron, famous for her photographs of Victorian women with bowers of hair caught in never-ending growth, surely was intrigued by Mary *Mag-dalene's* synecdochic signifier: perfumed hair. As is written in John 12:3, "Mary therefore took a pound of right spikenard [a costly ointment with a musky odor valued as a perfume in ancient times], of great price, and anointed the feet of Jesus, and wiped his feet with her hair; and the house was filled with the odor of the ointment." Feet and hair—objects of fetish-ization noted for their strong smell, in combination with the smell of musk (an odor that has been historically associated with animality and sex)—paint this story and this picture with an erotic "texture of per-fume."[78]

The Most Altering *Madonna*

Cameron may have let hair and other debris fall onto her glass plates, but in *Holy Family* (1864, plate 12) she literally scratched into its emulsion.[79] The effect feels blasphemous; one is not supposed to draw on photographs (it is rather like writing in ink on the pages of a beautiful book). And to top it all off, since the halo is so clearly a construction, the effect is rather ridiculous. When I have shown this image to my students they take delight in trying to figure out how it got there. At first, not understanding that it has been drawn onto the plate, many imagine that Cameron, in her typical theatricality, merely concocted a halo out of wire, stuck it onto Hillier's head with "a piece of kitchen dough" (a makeshift glue that Cameron is famous for using in such *dramatic* situations), and then photographed her. Hillier (the maid) is not transformed into a queenly Madonna; instead, she reads as a mimicked version of the Madonna. Dressed as if she were in a small-town play, the holy crown calls attention to the incongruity of the entire scene and the crown does not *fit*. As a result, this portrait of the purest and most magnificent woman in all of Christianity (that is also a portrait of a magnificent maid) is altered into Taylor's place of altarity: the image is read as both high art and (ridiculously) low art, utopically held together by Cameron's emulsion.

Yet despite its comic overtones, this picture (which I first came across—and touched—at the Royal Photographic Society among batches and batches of Cameron's large colored and discolored pictures), is the one that I always remember, the one that I always think about. The fact that it not only traces Hillier's lovely head but also gives way to Cameron's own haloed tracing of it, touches me. The halo serves as an index of Cameron's own hand, a place that she was. The effect is not unlike coming across the handwriting of someone you greatly admire. And, in fact, her handwriting is there. Look closer at the bottom of the photograph's watery edge. There, written in white ink, thick and chunky, like frozen milk, Cameron has signed the glass: "Taken From Life Julia Margaret Cameron." This writing on the plate is totally unconventional, and only appears (rarely) in her very early prints. I picture Cameron's hand, stained by photographic chemicals, *writing* the halo above Mary Hillier's angelic head. I long to caress this picture, to run my finger in the printed crevice that marks Hillier as Cameron's own holy angel, as her saint, in a private religion between them.

In the *Holy Family* (and in all of Cameron's pictures, which are all more or less haptic), I better understand what I see through the sense of touch, even if I am not actually touching them. The topic of sight's relationship to touch is a perennial philosophical topic (Johann Gottfried von Herder and Denis Diderot come to mind), but most important to my concerns is the fact that Cameron's husband, Charles Hay, wrote a treatise, *An Essay on the Sublime and Beautiful* (1835), that considered this very relationship. Working from the treatise, Weaver tells us that "Mr. Cameron acknowledged the primacy of the eye among the organs of sense; but attributed its pre-eminence to touch."[80] This *point of view* feels very much like Julia Margaret Cameron's own work, which is, of course, visual, but can be characterized as having a predilection for the sense of touch.[81] The following is an excerpt from Charles Hay Cameron's hand that Julia Margaret Cameron might have recalled, some twenty-six years into her marriage, when her blackened hand granted Hillier a halo in one fell swoop:

> It is by the sense of touch only that we at once acquire the notion of externality, and perceive external things. By the eye we perceive nothing but light, with its varieties of colour and intensity. Experience, however, very soon teaches us that many of these varieties represent the varieties belonging to objects of touch, and, as soon as this connexion between the two senses is once firmly established in our minds, we trust to our eyes to give us information in all ordinary cases, concerning the distances and figures of external objects; and the touch, which originally explained to us the meaning of the modifications of light, is neglected, like the Dictionary of language with which it has made us familiar.[82]

I am taken by the words of Charles Hay Cameron, which tell us that we initially understood how to see the world through touch (in a place that I imagine to be not unlike Kristeva's preoedipal space of the "semiotic"). And according to C. H. Cameron, we still understand vision through the haptic; it is only because we have become so firmly entrenched in the connection that we no longer realize it. Touch is the "Dictionary" for sight. Julia Margaret Cameron reopens the Dictionary that has long been closed and invites us to touch its forgotten pages. I am altared. I feel Mary.

CHAPTER III

Touching Netherplaces: Invisibility in the Photographs of Hannah Cullwick

"He took me for his housemaid," she said to herself as she ran. "How surprised he'll be when he finds out who I am!"—Alice, talking about the White Rabbit, ALICE'S ADVENTURES IN WONDERLAND

On May 11, 1988, I had my first appointment to see the Munby Box (fig. 19) at the Wren Library of Trinity College, Cambridge. I was led through the center of the magnificently beautiful space (a small wondrous castle lined with ancient books and crowned by promising windows) to an old lovely library table. I took a seat. A soft crimson cloth was laid before me. Two men then heaved the heavy box onto the velvety cloth. The box, an odd construction from the 1970s (manufactured of wood veneer and plexiglass), had an overall awkward effect. Even one of the brass handles at the box's side had been attached upside down. It was ugly. But it was also enigmatic. It gave the sense that something beautiful was inside. It invited inspection. I was captivated. They gave me a pair of white gloves.

A Story in a Box

The Munby Box is a creation of the Wren Library to hold the photographs of working-class women that were obsessively collected by Arthur Munby (1828–1910): a Cambridge-educated man who was a second-rate poet, an acquaintance of the Pre-Raphaelites, and a man about London with plenty of family money and an insignificant career with the Ecclesiastical Commission that did not interest him. What did interest him were

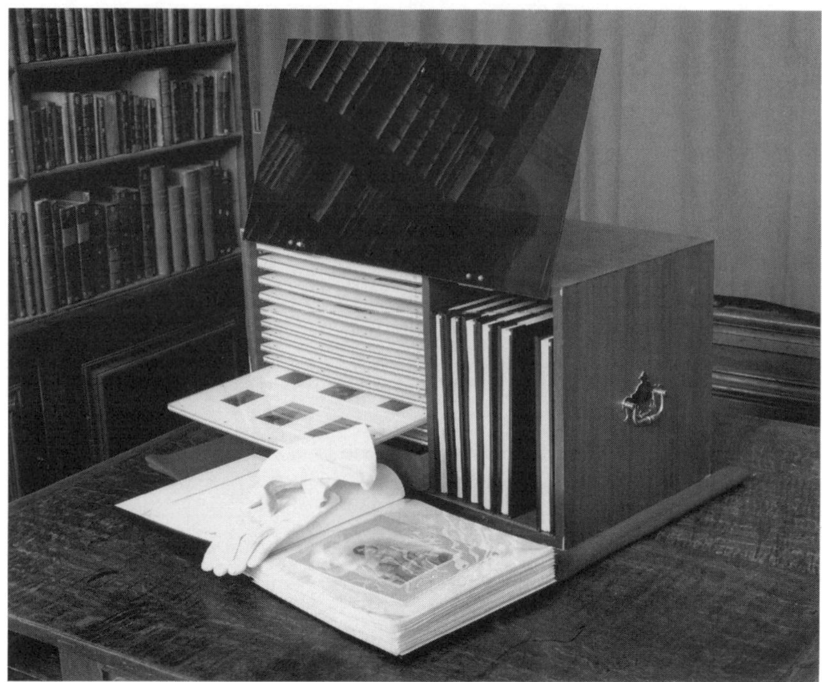

Figure 19. The Munby Box, c. 1970.
A creation of the Wren librarians to hold
Munby's collection of photographs of working-class women.
(Master and Fellows of Trinity College, Cambridge)

working-class women, especially those involved in manual labor (despite the fact that he "had never worked with anything heavier than a pen in his life"), and especially those who upset conventions of gender.[1] For example, there were the mining women who wore pants, lifted heavy rocks, and nearly approached Munby in size. There were harnessed milkwomen with big red hands and broad shoulders. Besides the many manual workers, there were also performers, like the girl acrobats (small and skinny without flesh and without curves) who looked like boys in their skintight tights. He also wrote about these women in his diaries and made sketches of them. The Wren Library also holds these, but they are not in the Munby Box.

Hannah Cullwick (1833–1909), a lower servant for all of her life (beginning at age eight), met Munby in 1854. The two developed a strange, secret courtship that lasted for more than thirty-six years. Their relationship circulated around Munby's voyeuristic interest in her work and her pride in being obsessively hardworking. She began writing her own volumes of diaries, at his request; he found her accounts of her endless drudgery tantalizing. He also was very interested in having photographs of her taken "in her dirt" and often made arrangements for this. And he was very interested in Hannah Cullwick's special ability to masquerade as a lady (fig. 20), and there are photographs of this as well. There are also some very unusual photographs of her as other, rather shocking, characters: a chimney sweep, who looks more like a slave (fig. 21); a bare-chested Magdalene (fig. 22); a man with short hair (fig. 23). Interestingly enough, the character of Magdalene was decided upon cooperatively, between Hannah Cullwick and a photographer by the name of Mr. Stodart. It was Cullwick who first suggested that Munby cut her hair. It was Cullwick who once suggested that she go about with Munby, dressed as a man, so that no one would know her identity. The two were married in 1873. (Almost all of the photographs of Hannah are of her as an unmarried woman.) Yet all through their long courtship and all through their marriage, Hannah Cullwick preferred to remain a lower servant, working mostly as a maid of all work.[2] Hannah Cullwick's diaries end soon after the marriage. After the two were married, she refused the name "Hannah Munby," preferring to be called simply "Hannah." Hannah preferred to remain, in her own words, "his slave," which she saw as being a more honored position than a "wife nor equal to any vulgar man."[3] Of course, even before her marriage (because of her class and her station), Hannah was rarely referred to by her surname. I want to keep this difference intact: for the remainder of this chapter I will honor Hannah as simply Hannah.

Despite the volumes of diaries that they both kept, and despite the forty-odd photographs of her in the Munby Box, it is hard to get ahold of Hannah.[4] One wonders if her invisibility within this space of excess representation is not tied to her own desire to defy visibility. She made invisibility into an art. She wore her thirteen-and-one-half-inch biceps as proudly as she wore her dirt. Her dirt, her masculine stride, her lack of womanly manners enabled her to go through the streets of the city freely, without the usual constraints placed upon the Victorian lady. As Liz Stanley has pointed out, Hannah "goes out alone to public houses late at night, walks through crowds of drunken men without fear, wanders at night

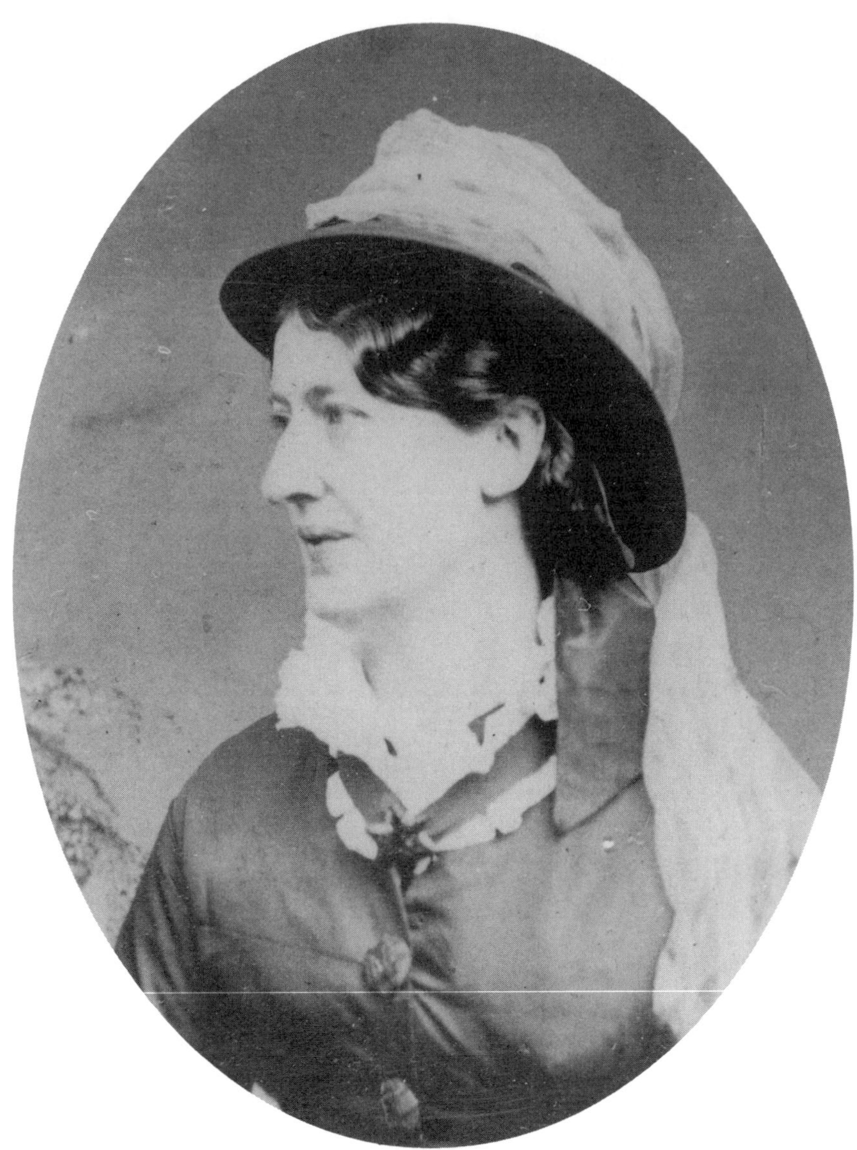

Figure 20. Howl, Hannah as a lady, 1874.
(Master and Fellows of Trinity College, Cambridge)

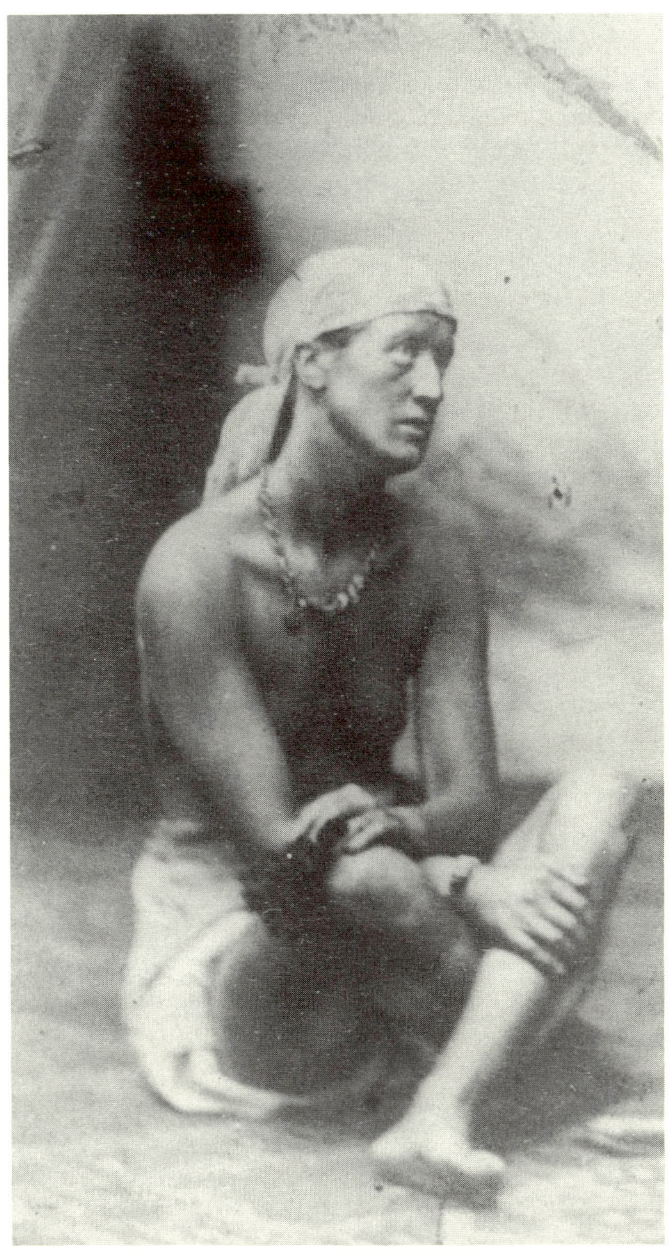

Figure 21. Hannah as a chimney sweep, 1862.
(Master and Fellows of Trinity College, Cambridge)

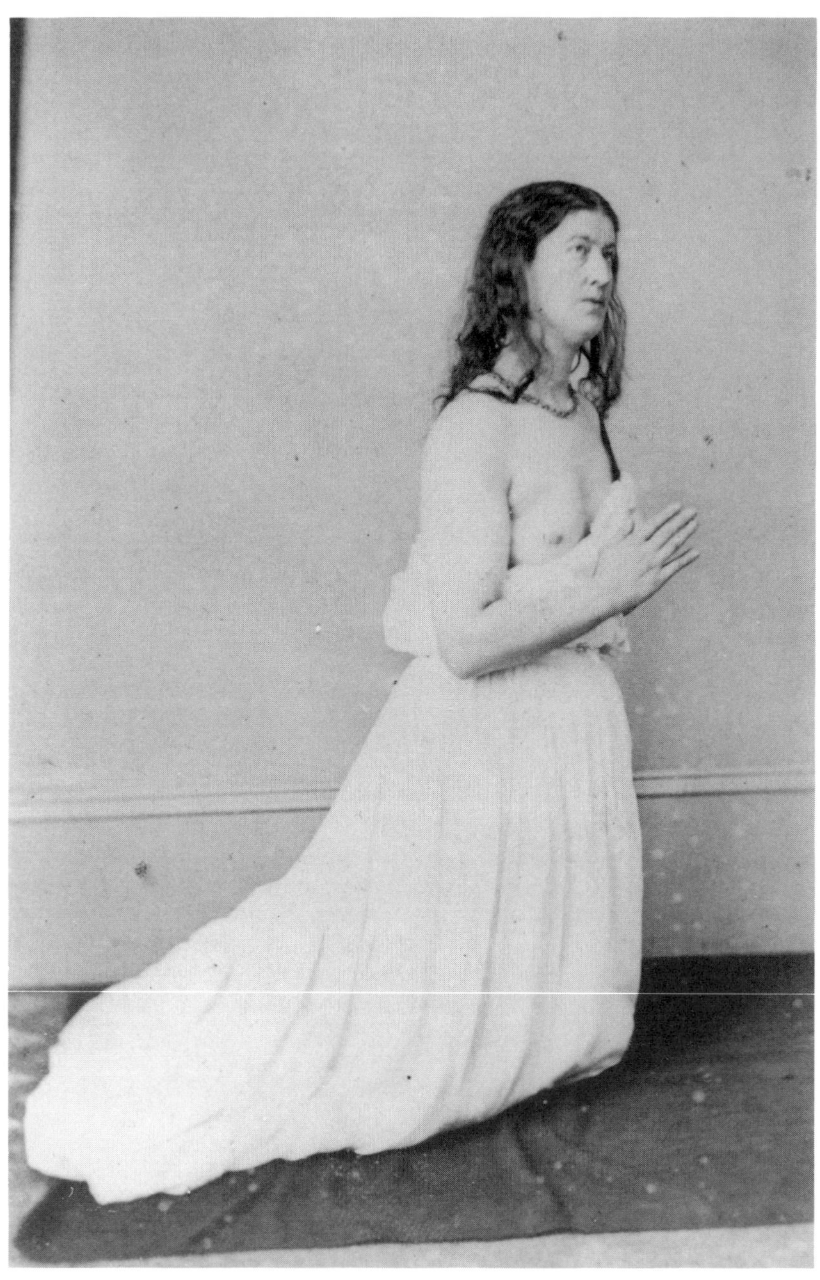

Figure 22. James Stodart, Hannah as Magdalene, 1864.
(Master and Fellows of Trinity College, Cambridge)

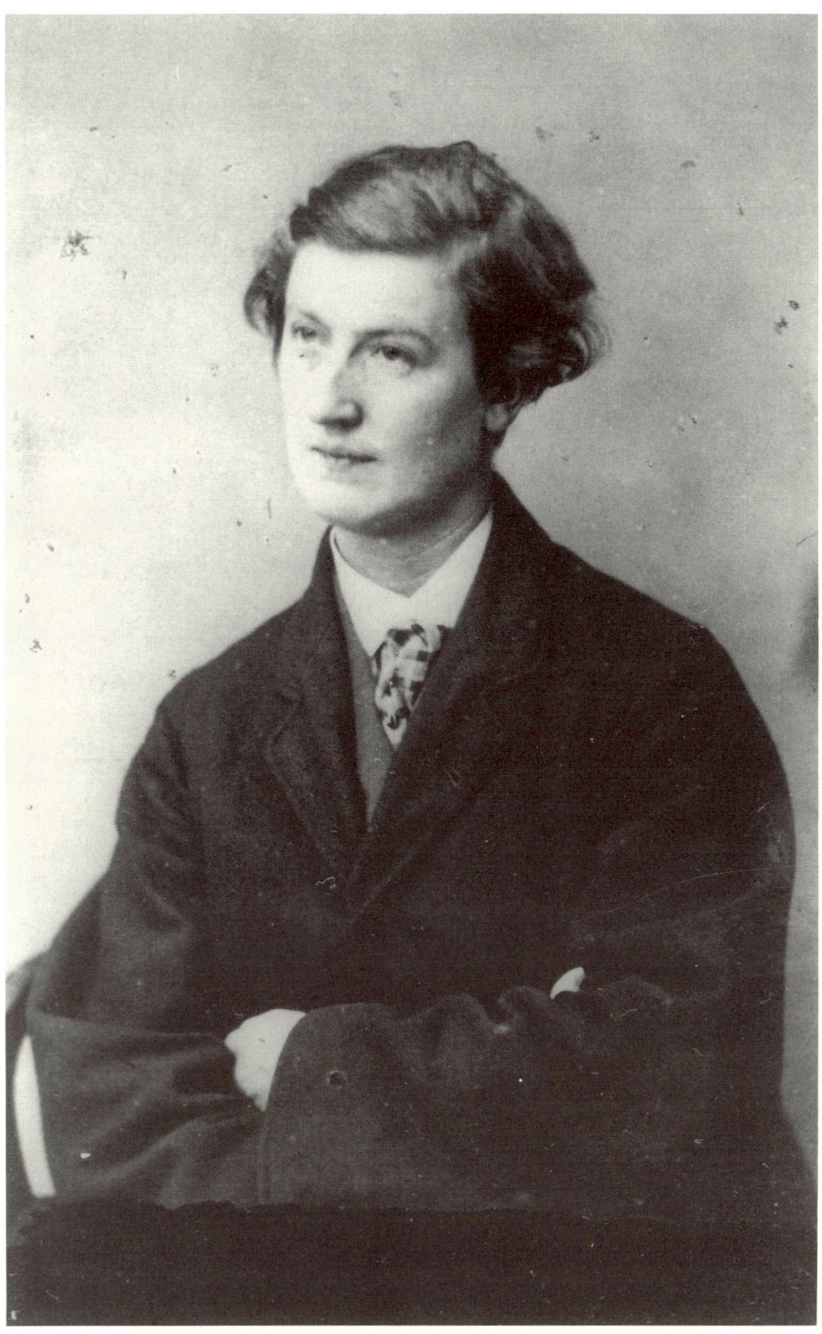

Figure 23. Fink, Hannah wearing men's clothes, 1860.
(Master and Fellows of Trinity College, Cambridge)

across fields and waste ground, and all without molestation or harass-
ment."[5] Hannah writes in her diaries: "That's the best o'being drest
rough, & looking 'nobody'—you can go anywhere and not be wonder'd
at."[6]

Hannah's job also required that she not be visible to her employers and
their guests. The work must look as if it was done invisibly. Hannah's
diaries are filled with passages about her struggles not to be seen and the
outrage that her employers bestowed upon her when she was, especially if
she was seen dirty, covered with signs of her occupation. But for the most
part, Hannah was as good at covering up her traces as she was at removing
household dirt and grime. This skill, of making one's presence invisible,
turned out to be quite useful when she desired to spend the night with
Munby. Munby explains it well in a passage from his diary:

> She [Hannah] had leave to stay out a few nights during her mistress's
> absence: and she wished to spend them with me. In her innocence
> and confiding love she wished it: ought I to refuse? Her coming
> would compromise neither herself nor me, because it would not be
> known to any one: *she who washes dishes and makes beds can remove all
> traces of her own presence.*[7]

In one curious place, deep inside the mysterious Munby Box, Hannah
has been washed away entirely; she is *unpictured*. Pulling out Tray 12, of
the box, one confronts a small copper frame with a note describing a
photograph that is not there (fig. 24). The note, which doesn't really say
much, moves me more than any of the actual pictures. Its words are
simply:

> <u>Hannah</u>, going to the Public house for the Kitchenbeer as she does
> daily.
> Taken in the street about noon on Friday, the 2nd of February 1872.
>
> B. The house in Pochester Square against which she stands, is that of
> an acquaintance of mine.

All that remains is a trace of her remembered presence, written in
Munby's hand.[8] I am drawn to this missing picture: it represents Hannah's
invisible flesh. I want to touch it. I caress the place of her absence with
gloved fingers. I am reminded of my continual longing to caress Mary
Hillier in *Holy Family*—my insatiable desire to run my finger along the

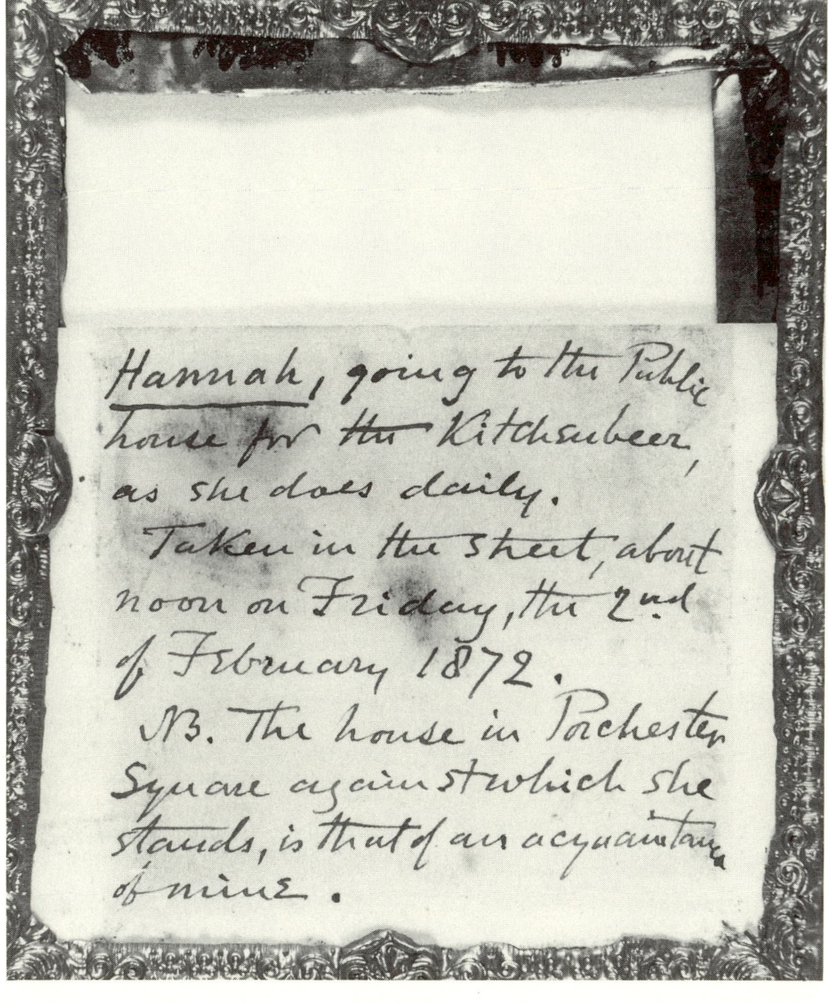

Figure 24. Copper frame with note describing a photograph of Hannah that is missing from the Munby Box, n.d. The note, written in Munby's hand, reads as follows: "*Hannah*, going to the Public house for the Kitchenbeer as she does daily. Taken in the street about noon on Friday, the 2nd of February 1872. B. The house in Pochester square against which she stands, is that of an acquaintance of mine." (Master and Fellows of Trinity College, Cambridge)

printed crevice of the halo inscribed by Cameron's hand. Again, I recall and recite Levinas's lovely words: "In a caress what is there is sought as though it were not there, as though the skin were a trace of its own withdrawal, a languor still seeking, like an absence which, however, could not be more there."[9]

Invisible Gloves

May 11, 1988
Very strange to be writing with white gloves on as I search the photographs for meaning behind "dirty" working-class women.—My first diary entry on the Munby Box

In two early articles on the photographs of Hannah, photo credit is given on the one hand to Hannah (by Heather Dawkins) and on the other to Arthur Munby (by Leonore Davidoff).[10] Although the photographs were, in fact, taken by several photographers (none of whom were either Munby or Hannah), these two articles express the conflict over who is empowered by these images. I am led to ask, alternately—as though turning a glove inside out again and again—whether the photographs are expressions of Munby's own fantasies about a working-class woman, not unlike a painting of Jane Burden by Dante Gabriel Rossetti? Or are they Hannah's own self-portraits that unexpectedly prefigure the work of current feminist photographers and performance artists like Cindy Sherman and Eleanor Antin? As complex representations over an equally complex space of negotiation (the space of Hannah's body), they are neither and both. Which side of the glove is the right side—the inside or the outside? The leather or the fur? Like Alice's White Rabbit, this chapter has dropped its gloves.[11]

However, in my searching I will not be seeking a singular conclusion about the relationship of power between Munby and Hannah. I choose not to imagine them as simply the subject and object and vice versa—like a loom, stuck in "permanent weaving," moving backward and forward, until the discourse becomes so tight that the other is strangled by its sealed-up world. I will not pattern Hannah.[12] Instead, my writing registers her as invisible, which far from making her disappear, renders her flesh a palpable-palpating specter. Though you may not see her, she will touch you.

My grasping at the "invisible" has been induced by Maurice Merleau-Ponty's unfinished book, *The Visible and the Invisible*.[13] I am drawn to his

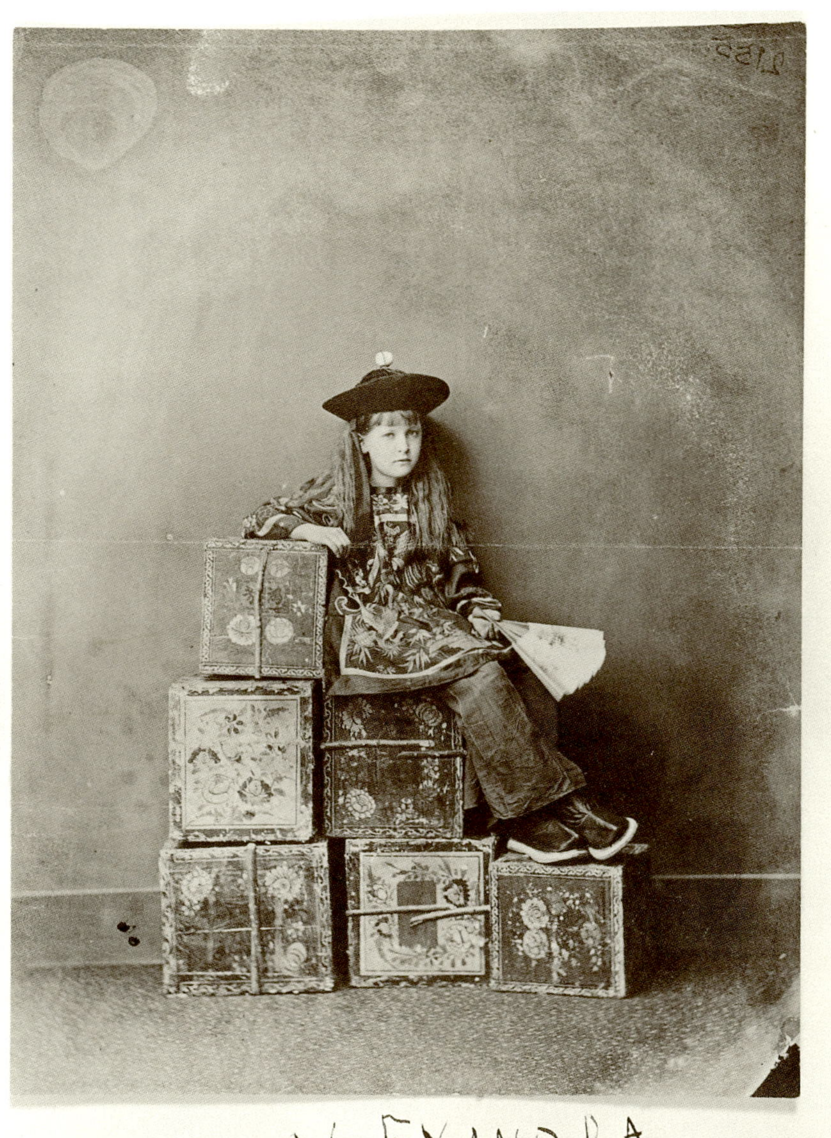

Plate 1. Lewis Carroll, *Xie Kitchin as a Chinaman*, 1873.
(Gernsheim Collection, Harry Ransom Humanities Research Center,
The University of Texas at Austin)

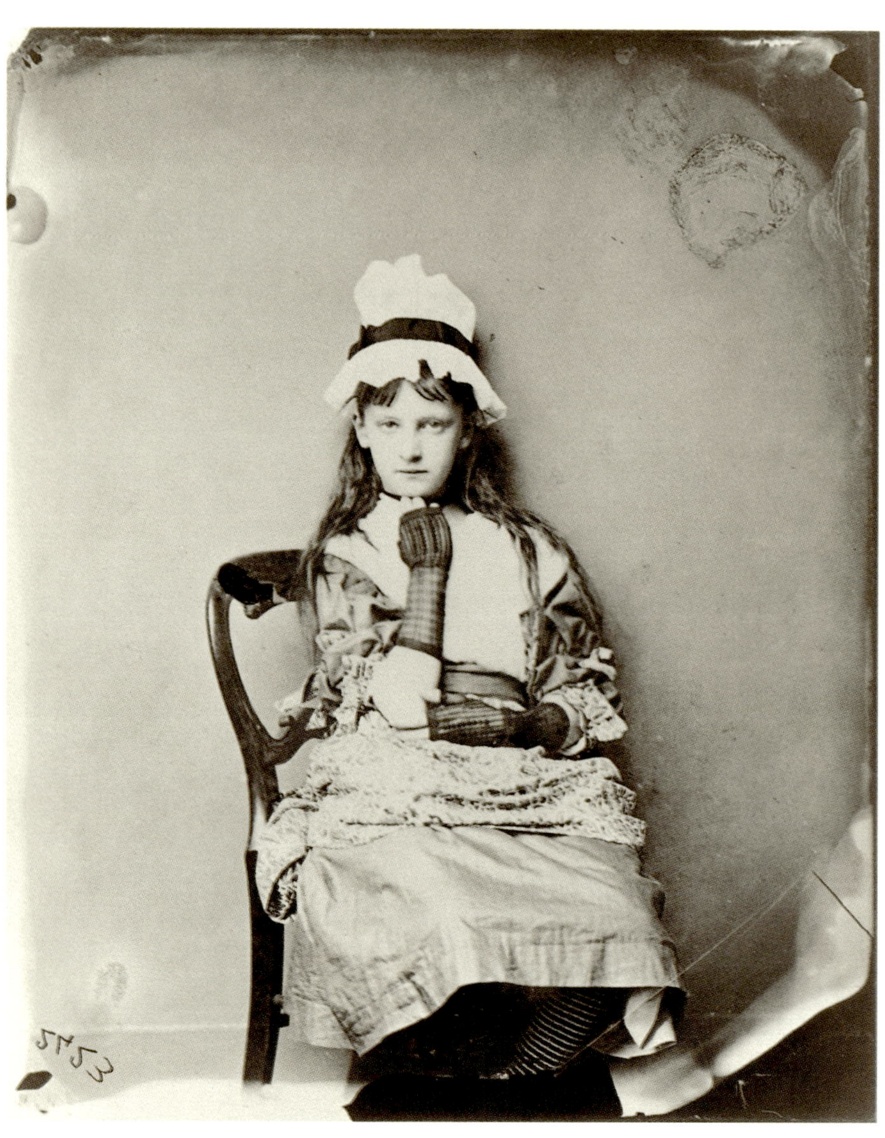

Plate 2. Lewis Carroll, *Xie Kitchin as Penelope Boothby*, 1879.
(Gernsheim Collection, Harry Ransom Humanities Research Center,
The University of Texas at Austin)

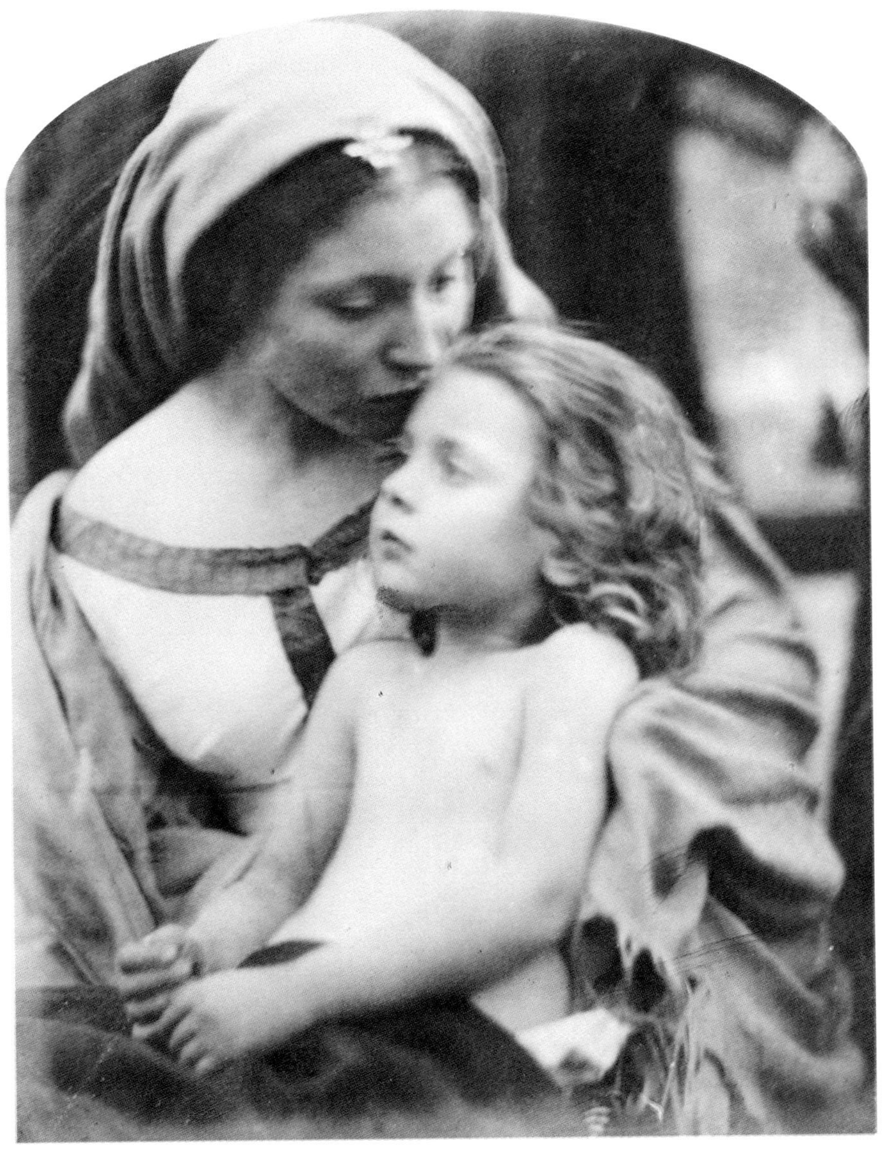

Plate 3. Julia Margaret Cameron, *Blessing and Blessed*, 1865. (Collection of the J. Paul Getty Museum, Malibu, California)

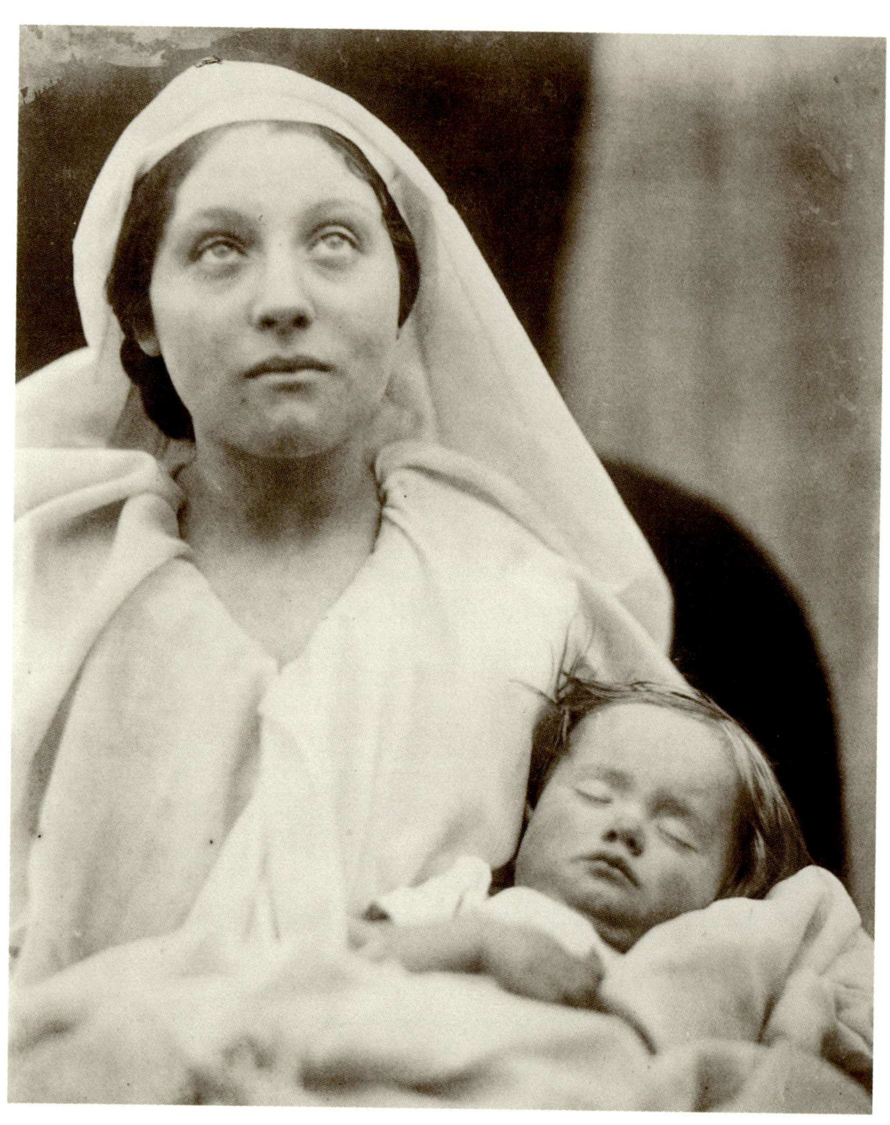

Plate 4. Julia Margaret Cameron,
La Madonna Esattata/Fervent in Prayer, 1865.
(Collection of the J. Paul Getty Museum, Malibu, California)

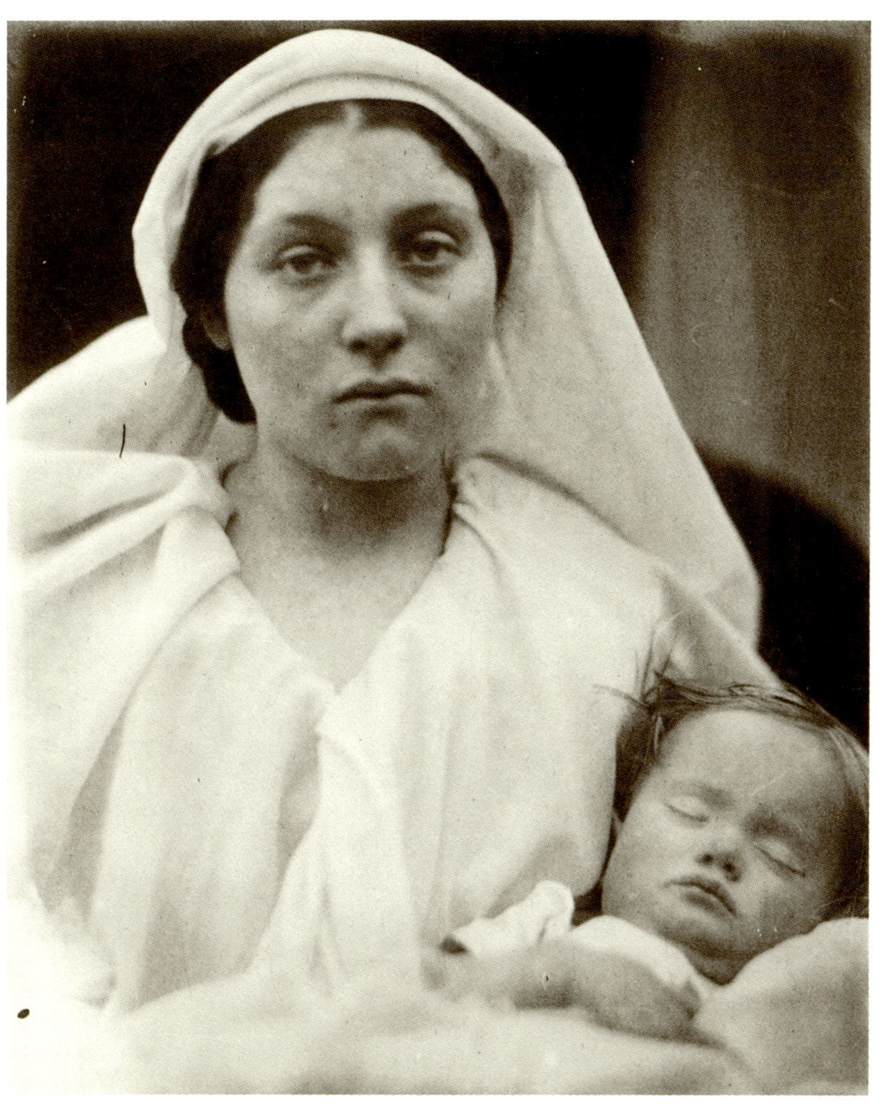

Plate 5. Julia Margaret Cameron,
La Madonna della Pace/Perfect in Peace, 1865.
(Collection of the J. Paul Getty Museum, Malibu, California)

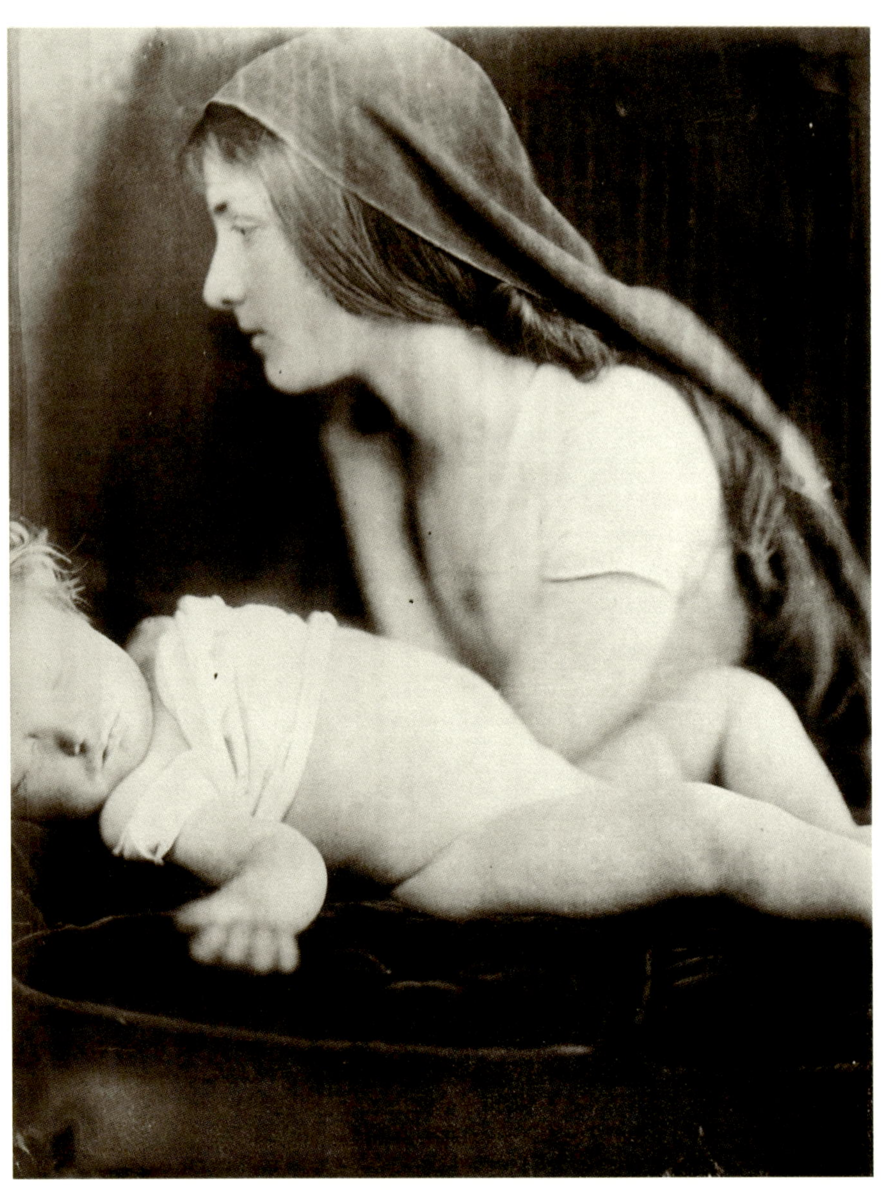

Plate 6. Juliet Margaret Cameron,
The Shunamite Woman and Her Dead Son, 1865. (Collection of the
J. Paul Getty Museum, Malibu, California)

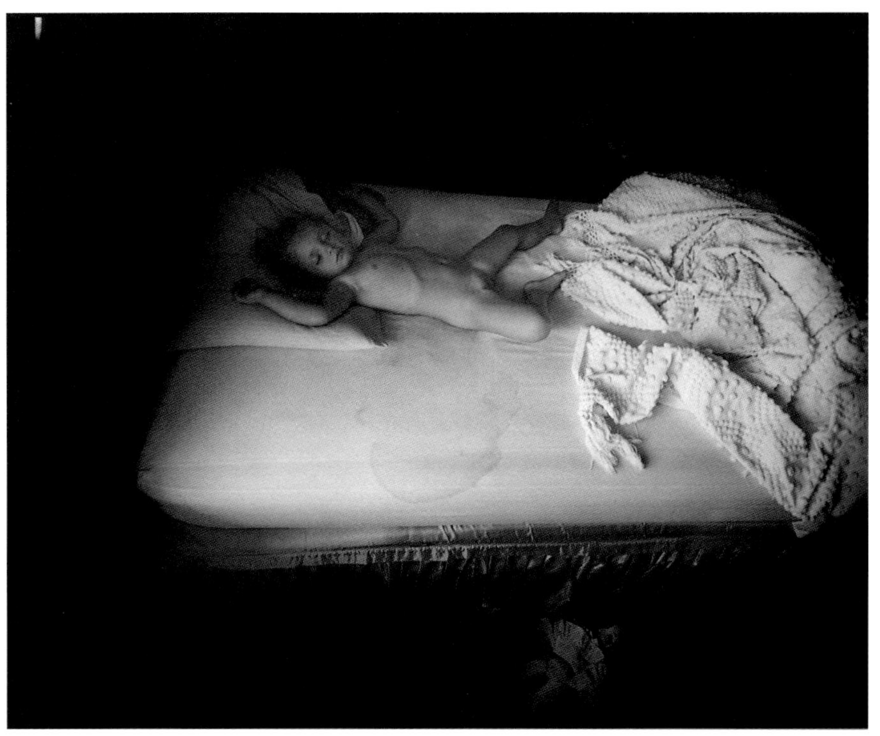

Plate 7. Sally Mann, *The Wet Bed*, 1987.
(© Sally Mann, Courtesy of Houk Friedman, New York)

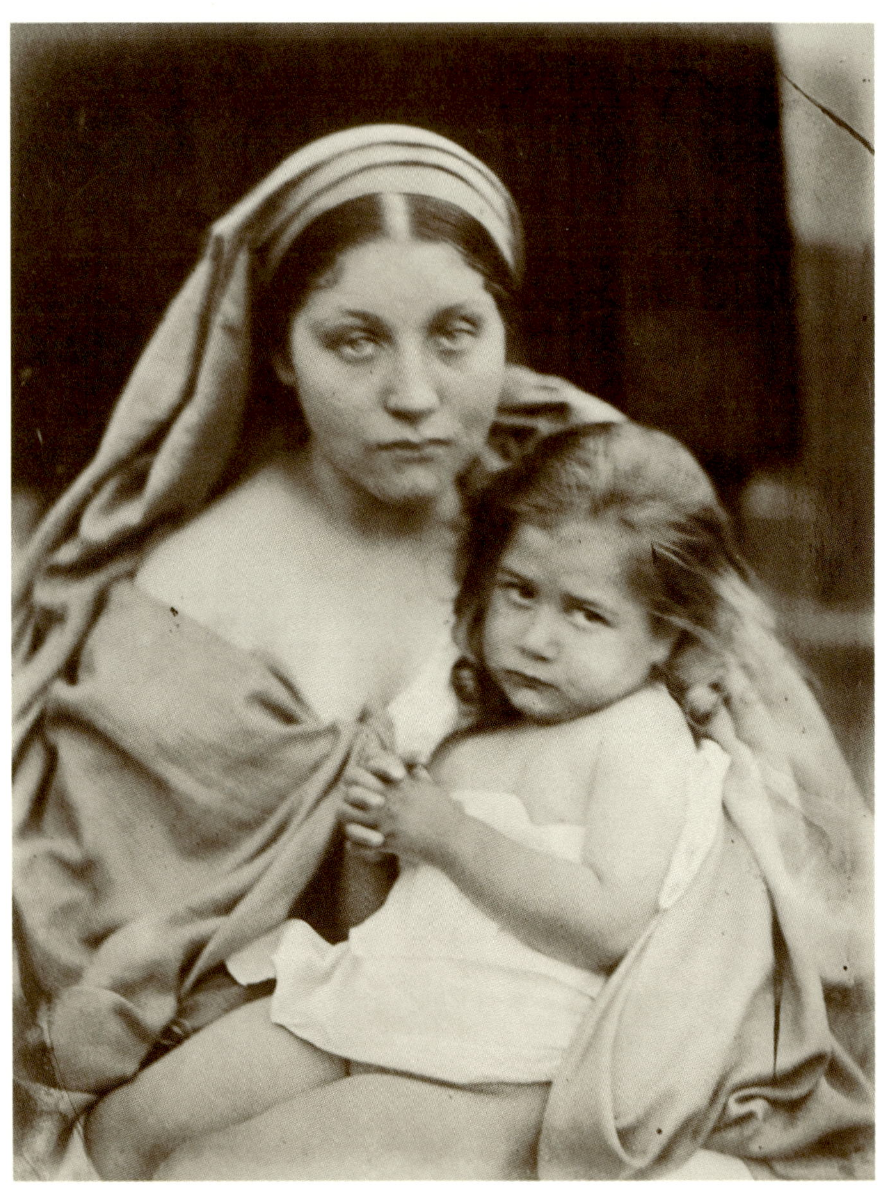

Plate 8. Julia Margaret Cameron, *Goodness*, c. 1864.
(Collection of the J. Paul Getty Museum, Malibu, California)

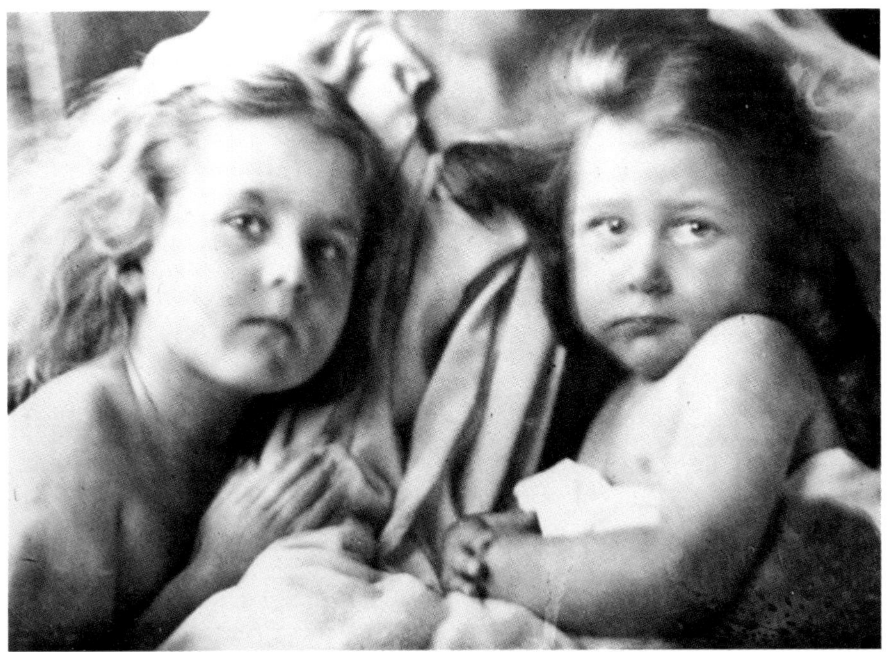

Plate 9. Julia Margaret Cameron,
The Bereaved Babes/The Mother Moved!, 1864. (Collection of
the J. Paul Getty Museum, Malibu, California)

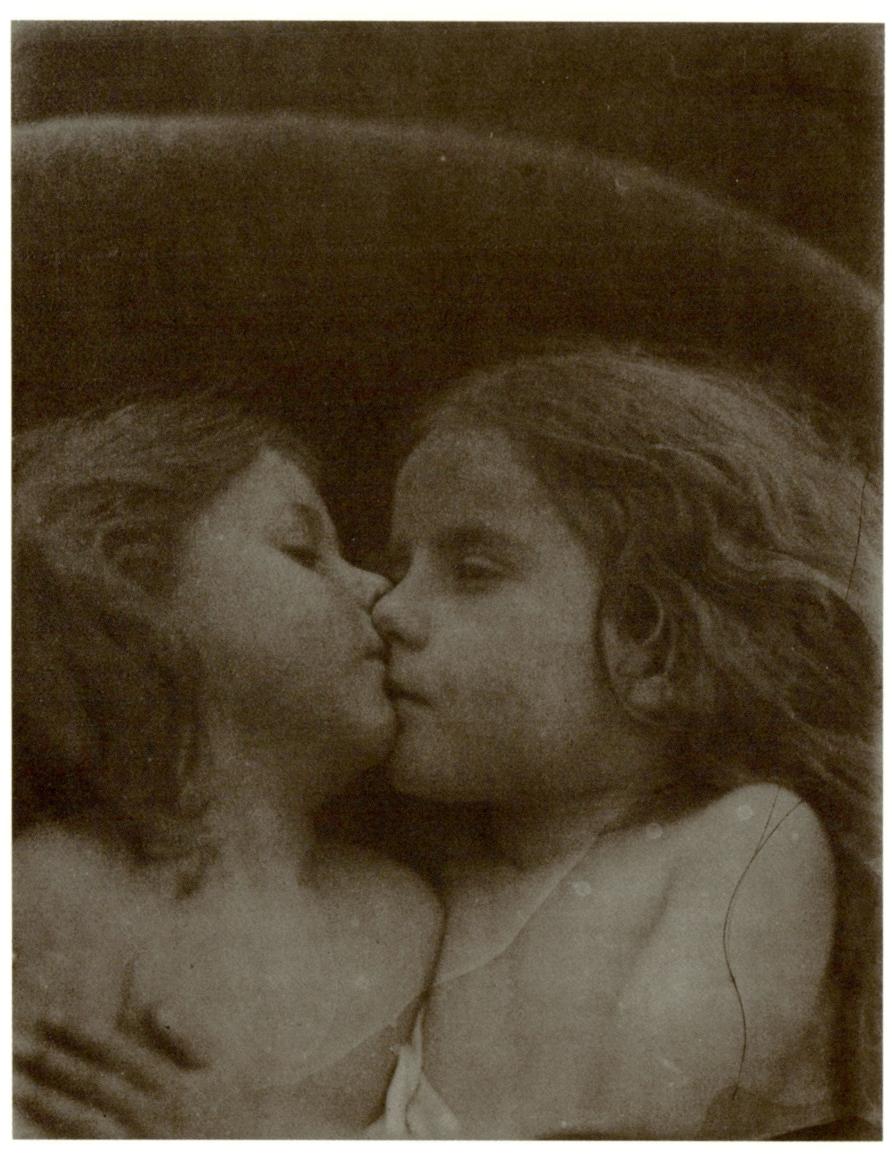

Plate 10. Julia Margaret Cameron, *The Double Star,* 1864.
(Collection of the J. Paul Getty Museum, Malibu, California)

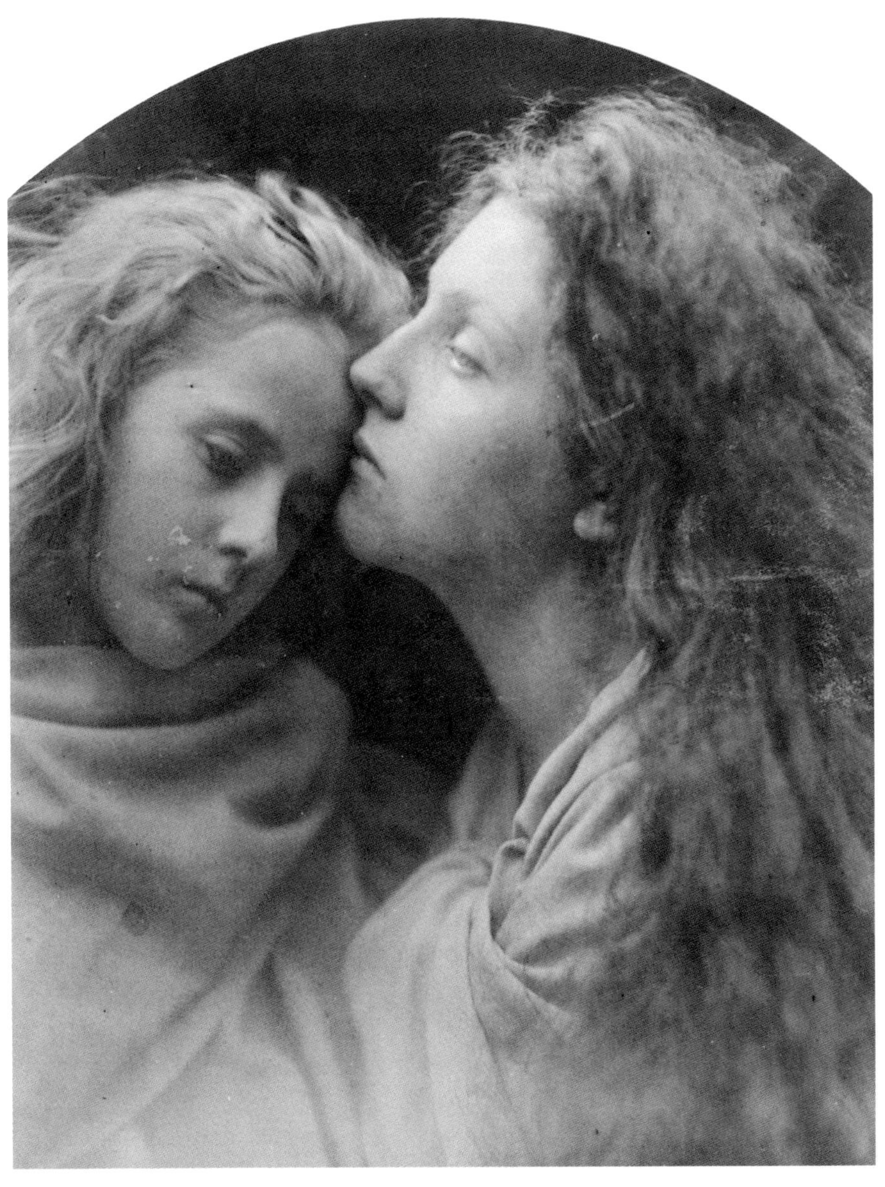

Plate 11. Julia Margaret Cameron, *The Kiss of Peace*, 1869.
Inscription: "My best photograph sent with a kiss to the beautiful
artist and dear friend Marie." (International Museum of Photography,
at George Eastman House, Rochester)

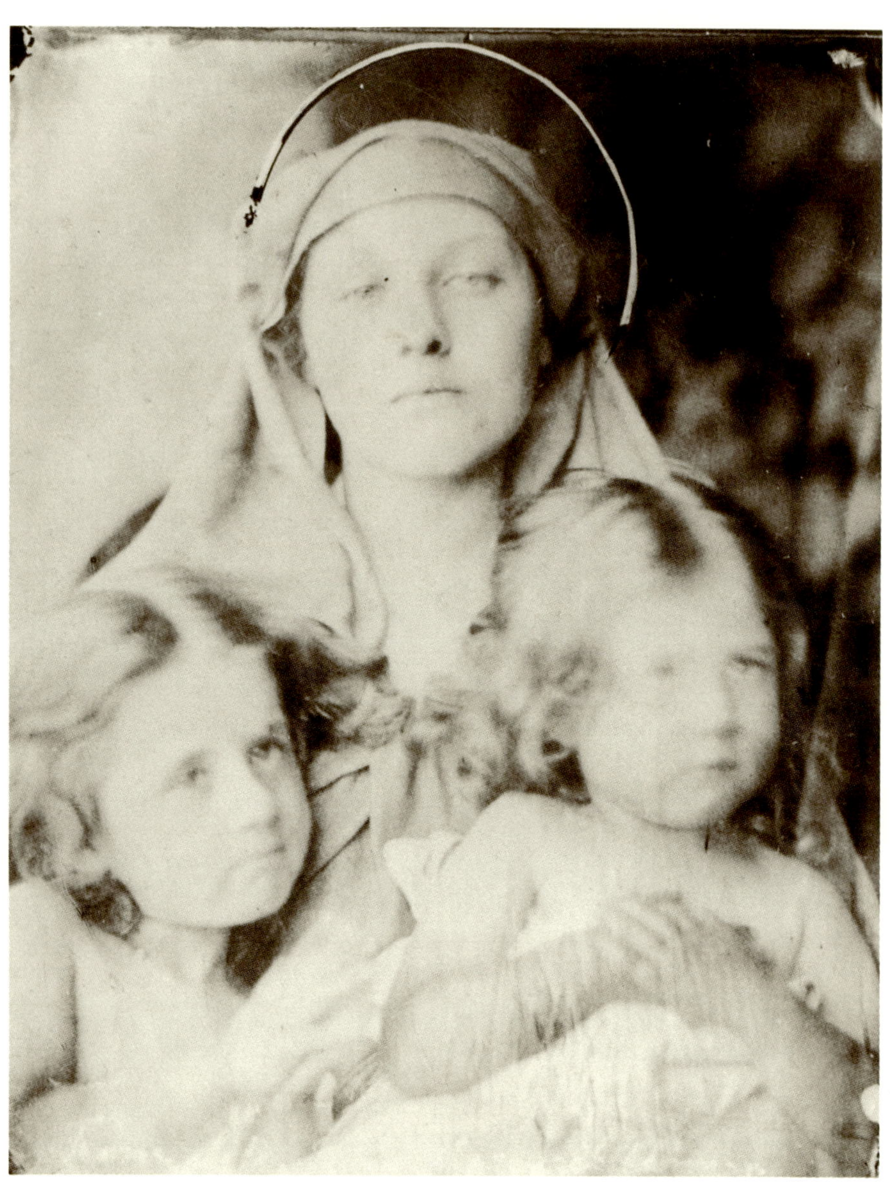

Plate 12. Julia Margaret Cameron, *Holy Family*, 1864.
(The Royal Photographic Society, Bath)

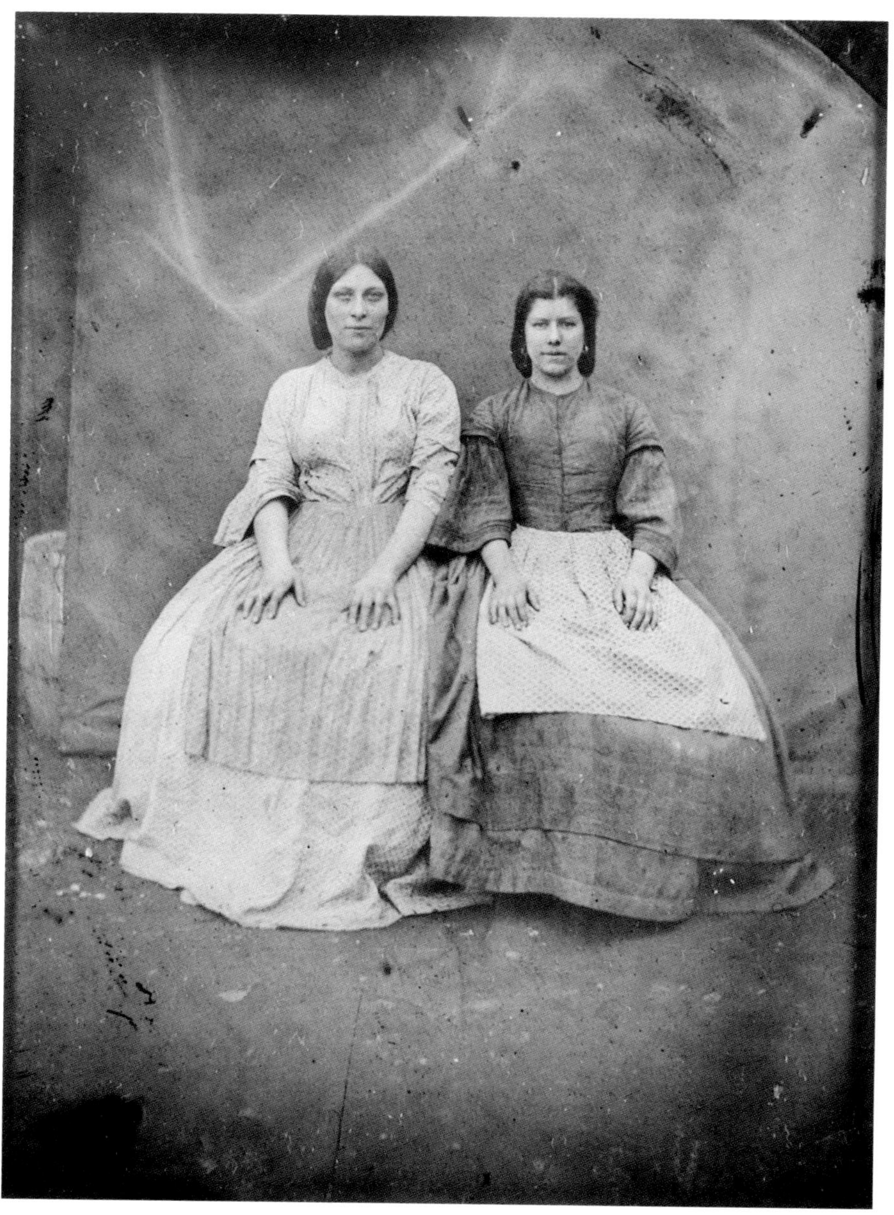

Plate 13. Paper mill girls, Dartford, 1863.
(Master and Fellows of Trinity College, Cambridge)

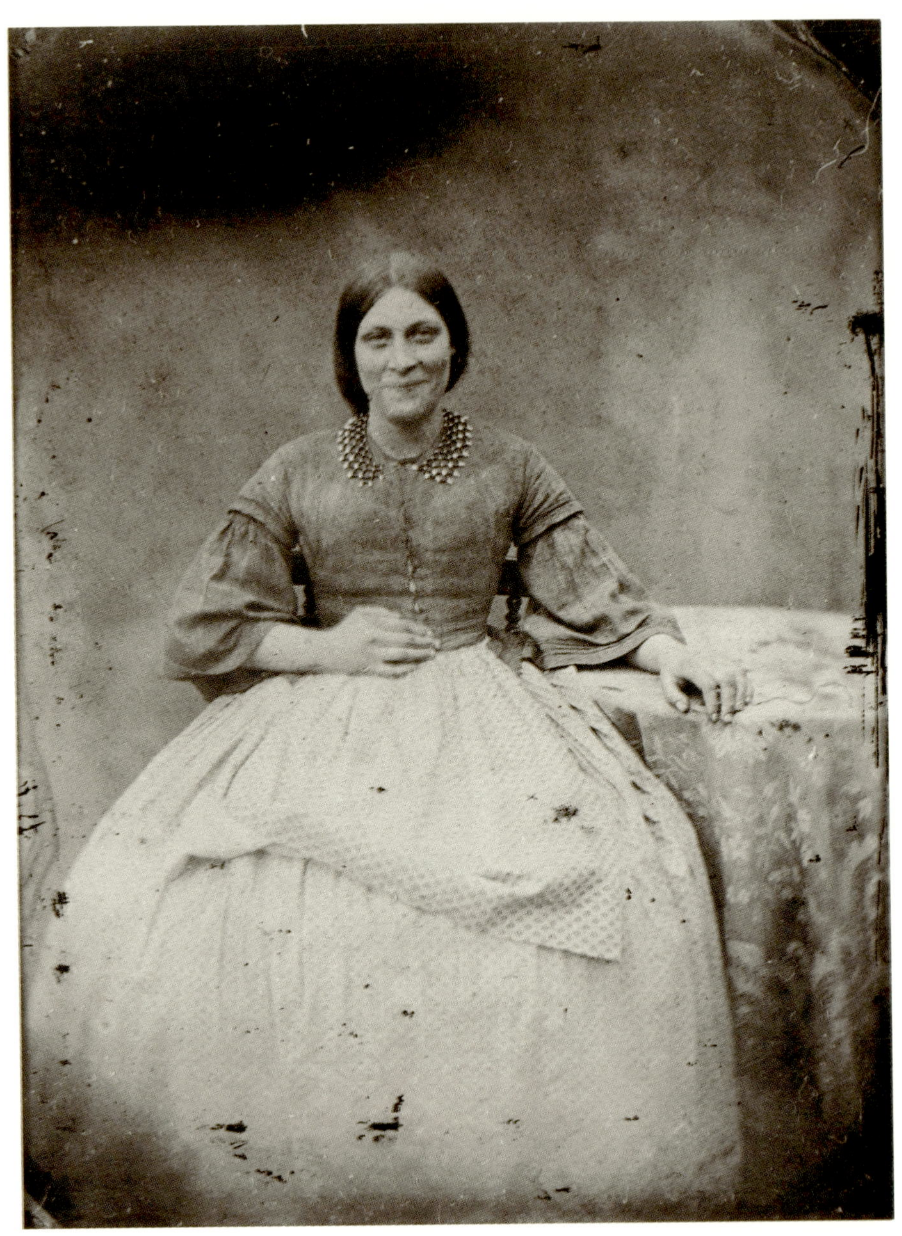

Plate 14. Paper mill hand, Dartford, 1863.
(Master and Fellows of Trinity College, Cambridge)

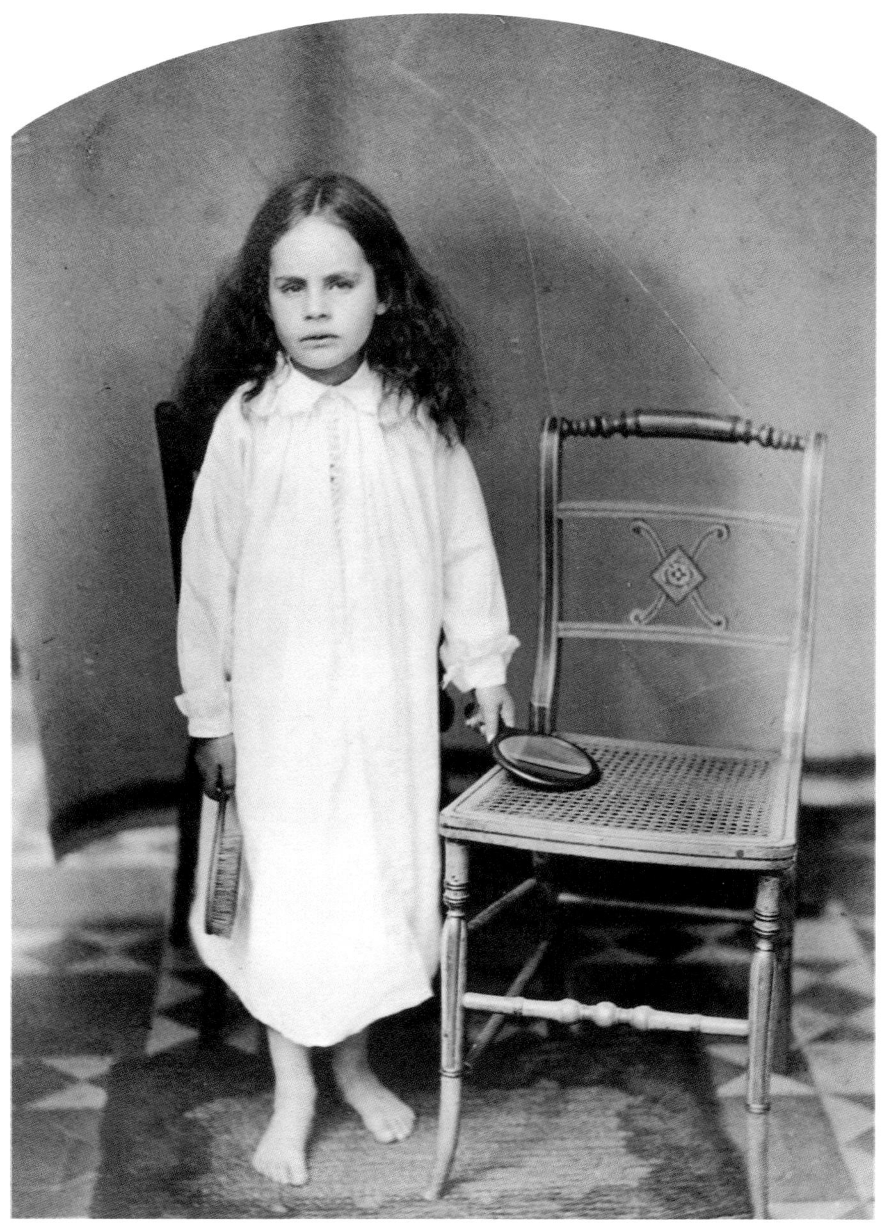

Plate 15. Lewis Carroll, *"It Won't Come Smooth"*
(Irene MacDonald), 1863. (Gernsheim Collection, Harry Ransom
Humanities Research Center, The University of Texas at Austin)

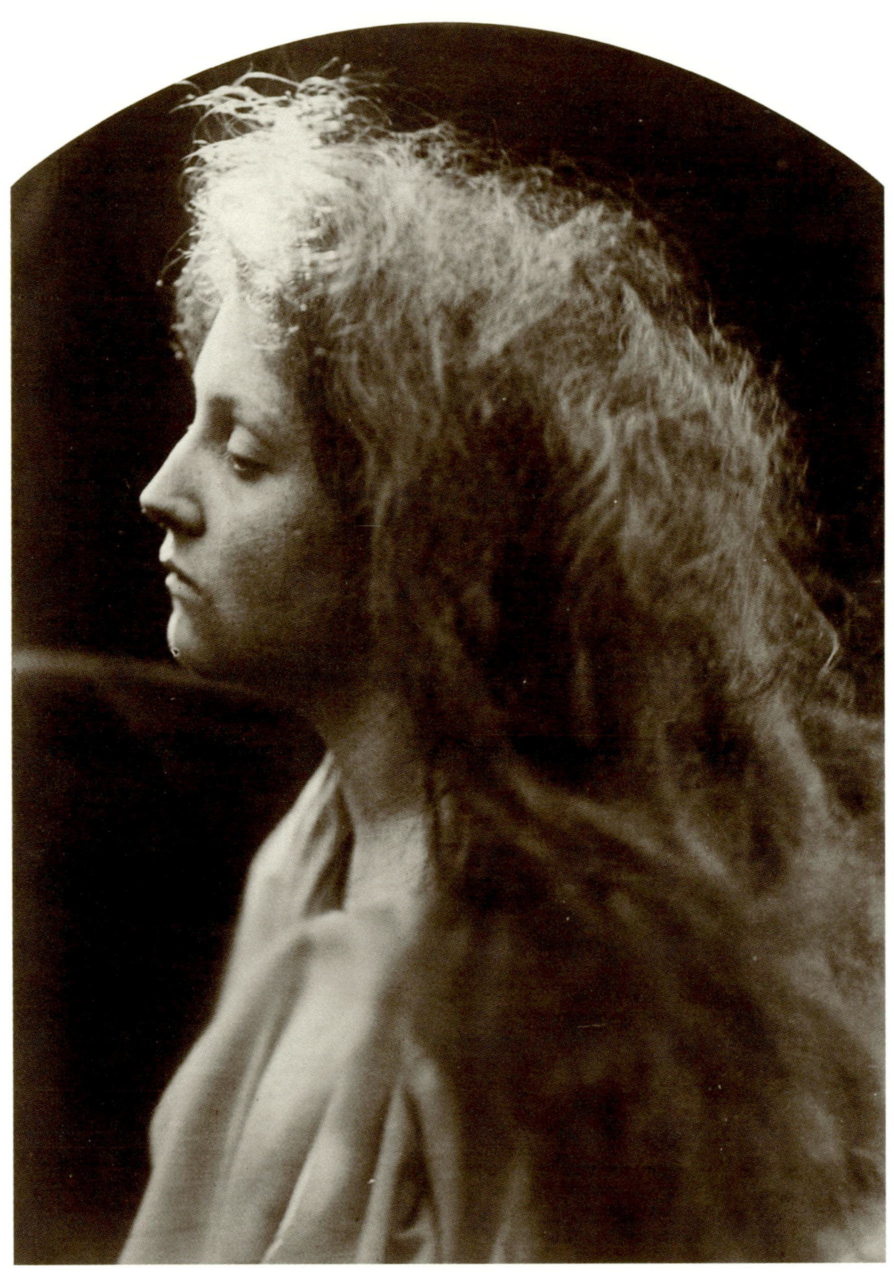

Plate 16. Julia Margaret Cameron, *The Angel at the Tomb*, 1869.
(Collection of the J. Paul Getty Museum, Malibu, California)

efforts to imagine the other (as well as the subject) without sacrificing or closing off the possibilities of his or her identity. Merleau-Ponty uses the inside-out, outside-in structure of the glove (its reversibility) as a model of this double-open space in which subjects perform. In clarifying the metaphor, he points out that we understand the reversibility of a glove (what he would call its chiasm) without the need for a spectator on each side:

> It suffices that from one side I see the wrong side of the glove that is applied to the right side, that I touch the one *through* the other (double "representation" of a point or plane of the field) the chiasm is that reversibility—
>
> It is through it alone that there is passage from the "For itself" to the For the Other—In reality there is neither me nor the other as positive, positive subjectivities. There are two caverns, two opennesses, two stages where something will take place—and which both belong to the same world, to the stage of Being.[14]

In this passage, not only are both parties invisible (erasing subject / object asymmetry)—like "two caverns, two opennesses, two stages where something will take place"—they are understood through sight's relationship to touch and touch's relationship to sight. Like the visual understanding of a layered collage, one knows just what is on top, what is buttressed, what is nearly touching but not: by either actually touching the collage or by imagining what it would feel like to touch it. As Merleau-Ponty puts it, "The invisible is what is not actually visible, but could be . . . what exists only as tactile or kinesthetically, etc."[15] In other words, the invisible can include the visible (as it does in the word "invisible" itself); yet the invisible goes beyond the visible and is not limited to the visible. However in a culture that privileges the seen over the unseen, invisible caresses, invisible sounds, and invisible smells are often elided (overlooked).

Jacques Lacan uses *The Visible and the Invisible* (in *The Four Fundamental Concepts of Psycho-analysis*) to provide his audience with an unfamiliar and expanded notion of the gaze that will be of further use to this chapter.[16] Lacan develops Merleau-Ponty's theory with a stronger emphasis on how we see—more precisely, how we don't see. For Lacan, all that is not visible is part and parcel of the gaze as well. Lacan maintains that the gaze is everywhere and all-encompassing—that when we look at someone we are also being looked at by someone else who is also being seen by another, and so on and so on. (Sometimes, we get unseen glimpses of this: for example, when we hear a sound that suggests another's presence, or when we smell someone that we cannot see.) The gaze, for Lacan, is not what we see (that is vision), but the fact that we are always being *gazed* at on all sides from all directions. According to Lacan's gaze, one is in a space of "radiated reticulation."[17]

By analyzing Merleau-Ponty, Lacan suggests the possibility of what I will call a *gaze of the invisible:* a sensate gaze from inside the body. This interiorization forces us to confront our own subjectivity. After all, we can feel ourselves touching ourselves, but we can never see ourselves seeing ourselves. "There is no coinciding of the seer with the visible," except in a mirror, which itself is only representation, a copy of ourselves on a cool icy surface: Lacan's "Mirror Stage" par excellence.[18] Thus the seeing of ourselves seeing is purely constructed, suggesting the falsehood of our visual perception of self (the mendacity of our subjectivity), which is part and parcel of our mythical visions of the other. Traditional seeing-ness, as Lacan explains, is focused on the exteriorization of looking. In his words, "The phenomenologists have succeeded in articulating with precision, and in the most disconcerting way, that it is quite clear that I see *outside,* that perception is not in me, that it is on the objects that it apprehends."[19]

Lacan then continues to tell us that we (also) try to imagine that we can see ourselves seeing (that we can see *inside*), in order to defeat the fact that vision is always outside of us and that we could never know how the other perceives us. This unproblematized (and mythical) approach to looking is sustained in order to carry the all-seeingness of the vision we desire—so that we can see what we want to see:

> And, yet I apprehend the world in a perception that seems to me to concern the immanence of the *I see myself seeing myself.* The privilege of the subject seems to be established here from the bipolar reflexive relation by which, as soon as I perceive, my representations belong to me.[20]

In such a scheme we entertain vision *falsely* as outside and inside at the same time, in order to hold onto representations of the other that are subject to our own constructions—in order to ensure that representation belongs to us—in order to colonize seeing. Differently, my emphasis on the *gaze of the invisible* seeks truly to entertain a sensate gaze from both inside and outside of a reticulated body, which must come at the cost of shattering the *visualized* construction of the subject-object dichotomy.

However, my enthusiasm for Merleau-Ponty's invisible is continually gloved and lined by Luce Irigaray's critique and reconceptualization of the invisible in her essay "The Invisible of the Flesh: A Reading of Merleau-Ponty, *The Visible and the Invisible*, 'The Intertwining—The Chiasm.' " Although Irigaray understands Merleau-Ponty's invisible as a fecund place for representing the other, she also sees his conceptualization of it as problematic. But rather than abandoning Merleau-Ponty's text completely, Irigaray reconceptualizes the invisible in (feminist) terms that are also particularly useful here.

According to Irigaray, Merleau-Ponty is unable to acknowledge the other's difference from his own subjectivity and thereby he actually (despite his stated intention) does *not* make a space for the other. Thus, Merleau-Ponty's invisible remains otherless: barren. Fueling this problem is the basic fact that Merleau-Ponty refuses to let go of his overall privileging of the visual; Irigaray describes it as his "love for painting":

> His [Merleau-Ponty's] analysis of vision becomes even more detailed, more beautiful, as it accords him the privilege over the other senses, as it takes back a great deal of the phenomenology of the tactile, but by giving it the privilege of closing up the aesthesiological body . . . His phenomenology of vision almost mistakes itself for a phenomenology of painting or of the art of painting . . . he speaks of it with the lyricism of one who loves art rather than with the rigor of a philosopher, as if one must give oneself over to its weight and measures.[21]

This, in turn, sets off a theoretical bartering that simply exchanges "seer and visible, touching and tangible, 'subject' and 'things' in an alternation, a fluctuation that would take place in a milieu that makes possible their passage from one or the other 'side.' "[22] This easy slipping and sliding from one side to the other is a nonstick exchange system that works (mythically), with *apparently* nothing left over, because the categories are, in fact, (perplexedly) undifferentiated by Merleau-Ponty.

Nevertheless, Irigaray, moved by Merleau-Ponty's conceptualization of the invisible, recasts his theory so as to emphasize that reversibility always leaves something "remaining." According to her, all of the other cannot be caught: "it is impossible to have relations of reversibility without remainder."[23] The remainder, which cannot be seen, is, for Irigaray, the invisible: a body full of holes that moves spatially without clear form, an aesthesiological body, a flesh that has been sublimated, a specter, a body that moves beyond visualization. Irigaray's focus on the rich possibilities of "remainder" are in keeping with Michel de Certeau's notion of alterity, in which the other, even while under the fingertips of citation in the ethnographic text, "keeps nothing of its own, it remains capable, as in a dream, of bringing forth something uncanny: the surreptitious and altering power of the repressed."[24] De Certeau's dream body flows into Irigaray's *invisible* aesthesiological body, which together suggest Hannah's body, which is "not there," yet it is "not, not there."

My approach here, then, draws specifically from a braid of invisibility, one that twists through and around the work of these three very different but related authors: Merleau-Ponty, Lacan, Irigaray. In addition to this braid (this *gaze of the invisible*), I will also draw upon my encounter with the miraculous box in Cambridge.

Sexuating Hannah

Swept the passage & took the things out of the hole under the stairs—Mary uses it for her dustpans and brushes. It is a dark hole & about 2 yards long & very low. I crawl'd in on my hands & knees & lay curl'd up in the dirt for a minute or so & then I got the handbrush & swept the walls down. The cobwebs & dust fell all over me & I had to poke my nose out o' the door to get breath, like a dog's out of a kennel. —DIARIES OF HANNAH CULLWICK

Valentine's day was while I was there & I slipp'd out in my dirt to get one for Massa. It took me a few minutes to select one. I found one—a dog with a chain round his neck & thought it fit for me. —DIARIES OF HANNAH CULLWICK

There have been a number of studies of Hannah, but not one has granted her sexuality, flesh, desire.[25] I find this surprising because the photographs (and the diaries), for me, are overflowing with sexuality, flesh, desire. Those texts that have broached the subject of sexuality find it only in Munby's world—at least that has been their focus (Derek Hudson; Peter Stallybrass and Allon White). Those authors who have centered on Hannah have dealt with other issues of her representation: Davidoff has represented Hannah's very real oppression as a female servant; Stanley has celebrated her tenacity and virtue; Dawkins has read her deconstructively as a textual effect. Their texts, then, register Hannah in four ways: simply invisible (Hudson; Stallybrass and White—and I am using this description *not* in Merleau-Ponty's sense of the term); as victim (Davidoff); as heroine (Stanley); as text (Dawkins). Although all of these works have contributed to my understanding of Hannah, they are unsatisfactory because she is *all* of these things plus more; and one of the most important aspects of this space of "more" is that Hannah too, like Munby, was a person who acted on and acted out desire.[26]

So, although Hannah left "thousands of closely written quarto-size pages," "penned at a breathless pace," and although there are many photographs of her in the Munby Box, her own sexuality has, curiously, been written out of the stories of her life.[27] Represented as if without her own sexuality, without her own desire, and certainly without her own perversion, she has been imagined as extremely desirable, but not desiring. Falling again into Foucault's repressive hypothesis, we other Victorians have continued to dream Hannah as Fair Woman in much the same way that Carroll's girl-children have been read as innocent without sexuality.

Not surprisingly, Munby (in contrast to Hannah) has been granted various spaces of sexuality, albeit limited in how he has been imagined: the repressed homosexual (Hudson); the sexual exploiter of cross-class relationships with manly women and blackened women (Davidoff); the actor of an unnamed, but nevertheless present and very erotic form of sexuality (Dawkins); or the neurotic, analogous to Freud's "Rat Man" or Freud's "Wolf Man" or even Freud himself, because he shares their confused (and highly sexualized) fantasies of an elision between "pure" mothers and "dirty" nurse maids (Stallybrass and White).[28]

Liz Stanley's introduction to *The Diaries of Hannah Cullwick: Victorian Maidservant* remarks on the absence of Hannah's point of view in Hudson's *Munby: Man of Two Worlds*:

> The publication of Derek Hudson's biography of Munby in 1972 has led to a resurgence of interest in Munby himself as a "man of two worlds," as the biography is sub-titled. Much of this interest seems to derive from Munby's life-long obsession with lower-class women—and women who were truly *working* women, whether in the coal pits of Wigan or digging the roads of London. A further and related interest comes from theorizing about Munby's possible sexual proclivities. Whether he was sexually interested in and aroused by lower-class women only, whether he was impotent, or

whether, in displaying little interest in women of his own class sexually or otherwise, he could be considered a repressed homosexual, are the kinds of questions explored. However, little of this interest has focused on Hannah, even though a large proportion of Munby's writings are about her and indeed a significant amount of the Munby collection at Trinity College, Cambridge, is by *her.* And so, although Hudson writes that Munby's biography "is her book as much as his," nevertheless he writes it from Munby's point of view only and states that her diaries and letters "can be sampled only briefly."[29]

I am in agreement with Stanley's efforts to shift attention away from the question of Munby's sexuality to Hannah; however, and quite surprisingly, this new emphasis is distressed by Stanley's insistence upon Hannah's ordinariness. Stanley states this thoroughly unconvincing perspective on the second page of her introduction:

> For me, it is precisely her "ordinariness" that makes Hannah so "extraordinary." She is an ordinary lower-class woman of the Victorian period; but her life, and her working life, is fully documented. The result is not only that she is "The most thoroughly documented housemaid of the Victorian age," but also the most thoroughly documented, thoroughly ordinary working-class woman of a period about which we still know all too little.[30]

Hannah is not ordinary. Her sexuality is extraordinary. As if, in an effort to keep her as clean as the floors that she scrubbed, Hannah (again, like a girl-child in Carroll's world, or the standard image of a Victorian mother) has been denied sexuality. Like a number of other scholars who are working on subjects of feminized fetishes (Emily Apter, Mary Kelly, Elizabeth Grosz, Mandy Merck), I want to, at the very least, grant Hannah some "perversions" of her own.[31] By considering Hannah's own auto-erotic tendencies and her love for such things as touching the hands of a bourgeois woman, or pushing her undressed body up an ash-ridden chimney, we will confront her sexuality. However, I am not interested in finding a name or a category for her sexuality: her performances of invisibility defeat such categorization. I am very interested in finding a language that sexuates her persistent invisibility. Her flesh represents more than hard work.

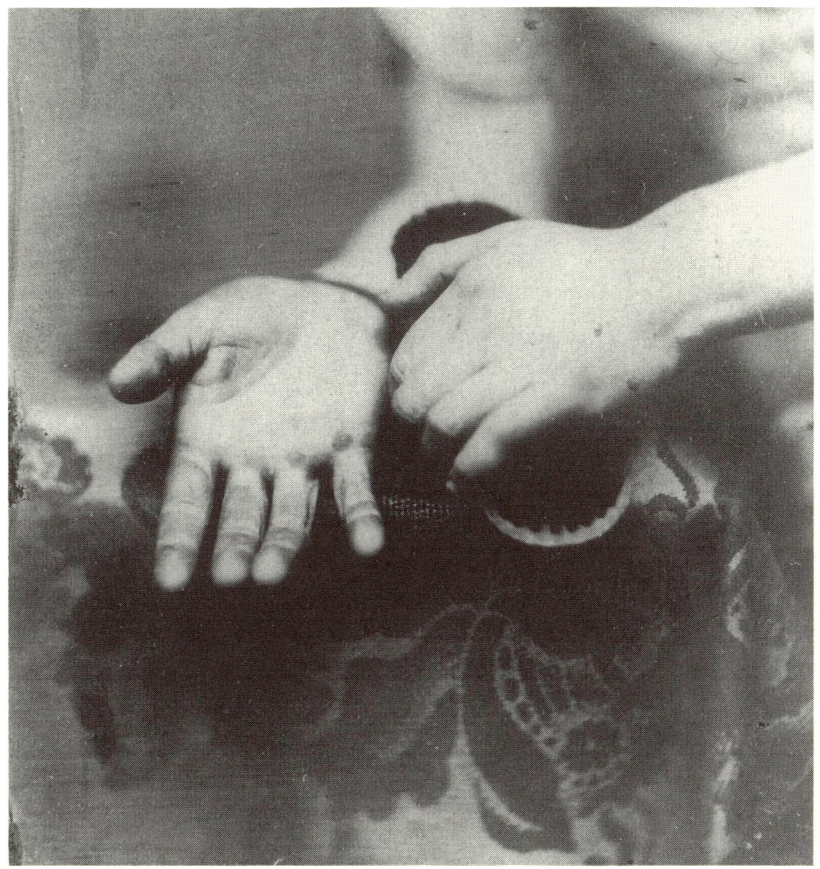

Figure 25. Fink, Hannah's hands, n.d.
(Master and Fellows of Trinity College, Cambridge)

Hands

My face was dirty (I'd been cleaning the dirty scullery out) & my arms black'd & my hands
*look'd swell'd & red, & begrimed with dirt—grener'd as we say in Shropshire. That is, the
cracks in our hands ingrain'd with black lead [used to clean grates around stoves, passage-
ways, etc.] & that, so that even scrubbing will not fetch it out, & in cold frosty weather one
dare not brush them. I had not worn gloves for years then, not even to see ladies in, so I was
without gloves to the lady at Mr Clark's that day. I saw Mrs Green & her daughter look
hard at my red hands.*—DIARIES OF HANNAH CULLWICK

There are many enigmatic photographs in the Munby Box, but probably
the one of only Hannah's hands (fig. 25) is the most enigmatic. This pic-

ture of her large, calloused hands represents Hannah's *different* sexuality synecdochically, perhaps not unlike the familiar trope of the uterus for female sexual difference in the nineteenth century.[32] As Laqueur writes of this pervasive figure: "The silent workings of a tiny organ weighing on the average seven grams in humans, some two to four centimeters long, and the swelling and subsequent rupture of the follicles within it, came to represent synecdochically what it was to be a woman."[33] When the uterus was in place, it represented an idealized maternal nature; when it wandered, it represented her hysteria. Hannah's swollen and ruptured hands, rough, strong, and big, represented her class and her servitude. Hannah's hands were out of control and stood in opposition to the tiny, smooth hands of a lady. Rather than hiding them, Hannah flaunted them, paraded them. They represented her sexuality, not only as signs of masochism but also as (tantalizing) signs of her remarkable difference. Her hands fingered between categories: though a woman, her hands marked her as masculine. In the Munby Box, which is filled with conventionally proportioned full-length, half-body and three-quarter body portraits, the photograph of Hannah's hands is nothing less than startling: they appear gigantic amongst a brigade of miniature women.

Recalling that Stewart describes the miniature as a space of order and containment—"a diminutive, and thereby manipulatable, version of experience, a version which is domesticated and protected from contamination"—the box functions as a miniature museum for housing Munby's collection of mostly white, mostly British, lower-class working women with a few exotic specimens thrown in for good measure (from France, Zurich, Constantinople, Venice, and Africa).[34] The specimens are often registered by height and other physical characteristics and by small stories of (anthropological-like) contact with the "other." Munby has inscribed the vitals and the tales of encounter, rather haphazardly in pen, on the back of the photographs. Most of the photographs are cartes de visite and are therefore quite small in scale. The Munby Box is a small, albeit dense, box, with little pictures of what were actually rather gigantic hardworking and hard-bodied women.

The workings of the miniature, whose very essence is that of containment and control, even managed to conquer the overwhelming scale of a truly gigantic woman from Nova Scotia (fig. 26). Miniaturized by the camera that shot her, she looks (in the context of the box) to be, roughly, the same size as the other women *pictured*. Munby's words on the back of

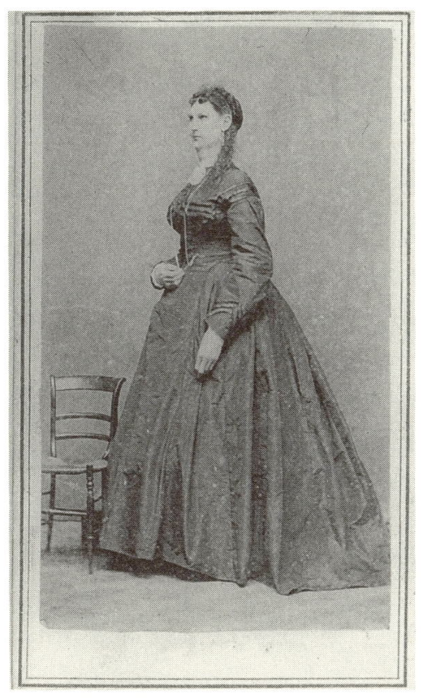

Figure 26. The "Gentle Giantess" of Nova Scotia, 1869. (Master and Fellows of Trinity College, Cambridge) Figure 27. The back of the carte de visite featuring the "Gentle Giantess" of Nova Scotia, 1869. Below her autograph, Munby has written the following: "The above is the autograph, written in my presence, of the 'Gentle Giantess' of Nova Scotia: her age, nineteen; her height, *eight feet one:* 'And I've not done growing yet, sir' said the stupendous maiden, looking down at me with a smile. Egyptian Hall: March 1869." (Master and Fellows of Trinity College, Cambridge)

the carte (written below her autograph) affirm his ease with this young woman, whose place in the collection he must have envisioned from the initial moments of their encounter. Though a novelty, she will always fit the part, the pull-out tray, the box. Munby wrote, with clear amusement, on the back of the carte below her signature: "The above is the autograph, written in my presence, of the 'Gentle Giantess' of Nova Scotia: her age, nineteen; her height, *eight feet one:* 'and I've not done growing yet, sir,' said this stupendous maiden, looking down at me with a smile. Egyptian Hall: March, 1869" (fig. 27).

In contrast to the Lilliputianized Gentle Giantess, Hannah's hands refuse containment and pop out of their small drawer as a grotesquerie from

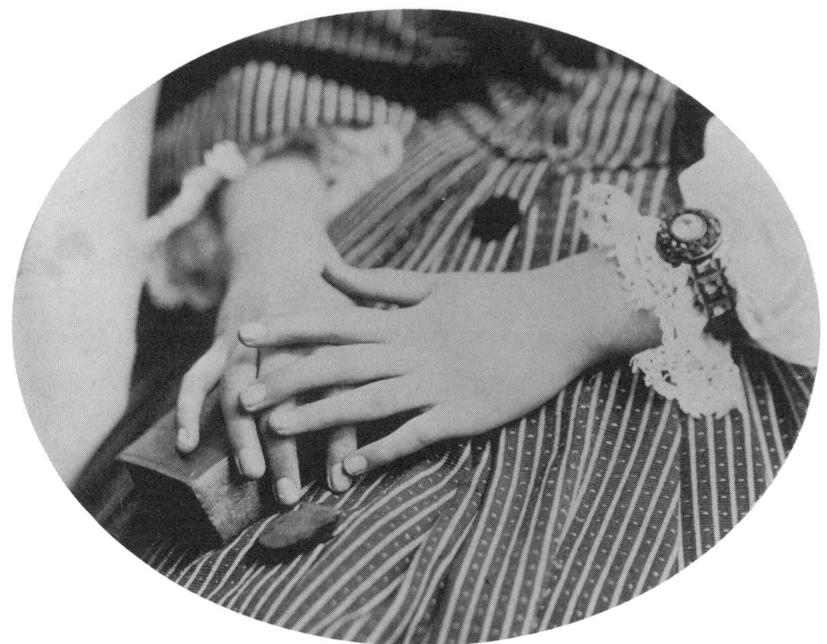

Figure 28. O. G. Rejlander, *Hands*, c. 1860.
(Gernsheim Collection, Harry Ransom Humanities Research Center,
The University of Texas at Austin)

the borders of Brobdingnag. Interestingly enough, I find that Hannah's big, disconnected hands mirror my own as I fondle the tiny pictures of hard-working woman that have been fetishistically frozen in a lovely miniature museum: a team effort by inspector Munby and the librarians of the Wren Library.

The unladylike nature of Hannah's massive hands readily comes through when one compares Mr. Fink's portrait of Hannah's hands to Rejlander's *Hands* (c. 1860, fig. 28).[35] We know that the hands in the Rejlander picture are those of a (young) lady's because all of the signs are there. She appears to be wearing a proper lady's daytime dress. She is holding a small but thickset book. Her fingers are long and slender and show no signs of labor. Her fingernails are highly manicured, extremely white and are as finely crafted as the white lace that finishes off her sleeves. (Her cuticles have been carefully and artfully pushed back.) She wears a decorative bracelet that could be a locket for holding a treasured snip of fine hair. Her lily-white hands, soft as down, are demurely closed away from the viewer. Her hands, which modestly cover her sex, may have been subjected to recipes for whitening and softening that were popular with the ladies of the period.[36]

The lady's hands are connected to her body, Hannah's are not: her body appears invisible, with only a trace of it to be seen, blurred and faded in the far right background of the picture. As a result, her hands take on the status of portraiture, as though they were a face, as though they, not her face, said it all.

We know that Hannah's hands are those of a *different* kind of woman, a working-class woman and a special one at that. Her fingers are blackened with dirt. While the lady may have taken pleasure in soaking her hands in honey, yellow wax, rose water, and myrrh, Hannah took pleasure in blackening hers with grime. And, because simple grime was never enough, Hannah used patches of black lead (that she would spit on) to literally draw on her skin. In order to build up the coarseness and texture of her hands, Hannah would clean grates without gloves.

Hannah's hands gesture together in a remarkable performance. Her right hand appears aggressive and proud as it parades its remarkable callouses. The left hand, a partner in crime, points at the right hand with four of its thick knuckles. The brush in Hannah's left hand is a stage prop that stands in remarkable opposition to the lady's small book. The book, which could hold recipes for femininity, mirrors the lady's hands as the brush (which could hold grime of all sorts) mirrors Hannah's hands. Porcelain hands versus Hannah's hands. The slave strap on Hannah's right hand (that she wore as a sign of her servitude to Munby, along with the small steel chain and padlock that went around her neck, to which only Munby had the key) is an unsettling costume that stands in remarkable contrast to the lady's jeweled bracelet.[37]

The photograph of Hannah's hands is entirely tactile. The Rejlander image is a picture of a different kind of touch: polished smoothness punctuated by fastidious bumps. For, even the raised elements of this picture (the facets of the bracelet, the book's tooled leather cover, the neat pleats of her dress, the soft lace at her sleeve) gently play into the picture's delicate surface. Even the photograph's oval format, without sharp edges, emphasizes smoothness. Because the overall image so closely mirrors the photographic paper's smooth surface, the hand of our eye glides across the picture's surface. The photograph feels as impenetrable as the lady it signifies. Differently, the *portrait* of Hannah invites overall fingering. Feel her callouses. Feel the silky brocade fabric with its raised floral design. Feel the leather wrist strap; imagine what it feels like to wear one. Feel the brush in her hand, in yours. Feel her muscular arms. As Hannah once said about her own hands (to Munby), "They are quite *hard* again—feel."[38]

I am always rather shocked at myself for seeing sexuality in this strange picture of hands. Why are Hannah's hands so sexual to me? Certainly, the diaries are partly responsible for this unexpected reading. Both Hannah and Munby wrote about hands as a sexual space that they enjoyed. Hannah often described the literal pain that she went through in order to gain admiration from Munby. For example, on one occasion she wrote: "It's to make my hands harder inside why I rub the brass with them whenever I can. It's anything but a pleasant feeling except that it's to make them more fit for M. to admire, for he likes a working woman's hands to be big & hard."[39]

And indeed, Munby does like a working woman's hands to be big and hard, as is exemplified in this passage from his diary:

> I passed a tallish young woman, evidently a servant, who was noticeable for the size of her *gloveless hands.* She seemed to be alone in the crowd, and (*with a view to her hands*) I asked if she meant to dance? No, she couldn't dance at all—only liked to look on: for which she was not sorry. So after a little chat we walked away, and I (still with a view to my hobby) proposed to rest on the bank near, under the trees. *She gave me her hand to help her up—and, oh ye ballroom partners, what a breadth of massive flesh it was to grasp!* She sat down by me, ready to talk, after the blunt fashion of such maidens, but not forward . . . . She was a maid of all work at Chelsea, it seemed. . . . I looked at her hands, and spoke my opinion of them. "How can you like them?" she says, like Margaret in the garden; "*they are so large and red, I'm ashamed of them.*" "They are just the hands for a servant," say I: "They show you are hardworking, and you ought to be proud of them. You wouldn't like them to be like a lady's?" "Yes I should! said she, bitterly: "and I should like to be a lady, and I wish my hands were like yours!" And she looked enviously at my hand, which was quite white and small by the side of hers . . . Her right hand lay, a large red lump, upon her light-coloured frock: it was very broad and square and thick—as large and strong & coarse as the hand of a sixfoot bricklayer . . . *the skin was rough to the touch, hard & leathery*

in the palm: there was nothing feminine about it in form or texture . . . and yet she was only nineteen.[40]

Munby's record of his encounter with a maid of all work from Chelsea is a texbook case of Freud's description of the fetish. Early on in Munby's story of yet another discovery, sexual intrigue is promoted by the fact that he spotted her hands secretly and voyeuristically, unaware that she was exposing herself, oblivious to the fact that she was "gloveless" (pantless). Munby is fixated on hands and seems to have fetishized them to stand in for the "castrated penis" (so the Freudian story goes). Even a Freudian skeptic would have to acknowledge that Munby's description of the young woman's hands (red, large, and hard) sounds very much like a description of an aroused man. Like Freud, Munby reads her sexual difference in relation to his own (she may not have a penis, but she has hands that mirror male genitals). Yet in a surprising turnaround, she reads his hands to be more like a lady's. This passage is a wondrous description of difference at play: it is arousing, comical, and definitely sexual.

Hannah describes another similar play of difference around marked and unmarked hands. Hannah's story is one of sexualized play, not between a masculinized woman and a feminized man, but between two (different) women. Hannah writes, "I've been busy cleaning windows & glasses this month, for the flies & the dust makes so much dirt. My hands are very coarse & hardish, but no more so than usual. Mrs. J. has very white hands & she often comes & lays her hands lightly on mine for me to feel how cold they are—*we* say it's to show the difference more than anything else."[41] I love this passage and the image of two women touching hands: one rough, hardened, reddened, large, maybe warm—the other soft, frail, white, and always cold. In this play of hands is a suggestion of an unexpected reciprocity. In Hannah's rough / delicate grasp is the possibility that her desire is not played out for Munby only.

Painting with Soot

On April 26, 1865, Hannah described an emphatically haptic and auto-erotic moment in which the reader senses *her* desire: a desire that has been consistently overlooked by Cullwickian scholars. Hannah is all alone; Munby is not there, but his presence is felt. She is undressed and has "got on a stool and up the chimney out o sight":

The soot was thick all around, and soft and warm and i lay in it and fetch'd a shower or two down wi my arms, and it trickl'd over like a bath—i stopped in the chimney and thought about Massa and how he'd enjoy seein me when i got down and all that, and wonder'd what he was doing and then i come down—it seem'd quite cold out o the chimney and i got into the water [in a bath] and wash'd me—it took me a good while to get clean and the water i made thick and black. i just put on my shift and petticoat and bundled my other clothes up and run into bed—[it was eleven o'clock] Massa wrote after and said at the very time i was in the chimney he was at a ball, and among ladies with white necks and arms and all so grand, and how he look'd at them and thought of me the while, and he could well imagine the contrast as he'd seen me so often.[42]

In this passage, Hannah's sensate body is emphasized through touch: the touch of the soot, "soft and warm," that she trickles over herself like a bath; the touch of the "cold" air that she feels once she is outside of the chimney; the touch of the blackened water that feels "thick"; the touch of light clothes (like shifts and petticoats) on her recently bathed body that has just jumped into bed.

For me, and I imagine for Hannah too, the fluidity between things is what makes this kind of play erotic: the flow between clean and dirty, between blackened then whitened skin, between the ladies at the ball and Hannah in her grimy tub, between Hannah's sexual play alone (onanistic, in that she touches herself with black soot, water, and white petticoats), and that with the others named (but not seen) in the scene. Desire and sexuality are markedly insistent and deviant, charged by the unsaid—in short, erotic.

While reading Hannah's words, my body is taken away (erotically) with the flow, "for my body does not have the same ideas I do."[43] We, Hannah and I, give ourselves away. In this fragment of Hannah's writing, and elsewhere in Hannah's body of work (the photographs and the diaries), and in my own writing, eroticism becomes a meaningful tool for the ways in which it breaks down categories (often spinning on the taboo), opens up dark (invisible) passages, compels my body to feel what the other has left behind.

What is left over from the story of the chimney crawl is all the black soot that touched her body and was shed like skin: a thick, black mucous that stayed in the tub. This rich "remainder," which gloved and lined her body, which communicated with the interior and the exterior of her body, calls into question any reversibility between black and white. No one is simply black, nor simply white—instead, they are metaphors for the body that are distinctly related to issues of class. Hannah painted herself as both black and white. When she was a lady, she painted herself white: whitening her dark, reddened hands with smart white gloves and, most certainly, dusting her face not with soot, but with the "Ophelia powders" so popular then.[44]

As in Hannah's bathtub story, residues of blackness can also be found floating around many of the soap advertisements that were popular later in the period: most notably an illustration for Pears' Soap that also features a bathing scene (fig. 29).[45] The point of the Pears' picture is that the wonderful soap, so powerful and pure, can wash a Negro white. The before and after pictures, with PEARS' SOAP blazoned in black and white between the two images, tells the consumer that blackness can be washed off in the bathtub: just like Hannah washed off her soot.

Yet, certainly unbeknownst to the advertisement's creator, the picture also suggests an indeterminable reciprocity between the races of the two children. In the top picture, one is somewhat surprised to see that it is a little white boy who stands in service to the little black boy in the tub. The white boy's servitude is reinforced by his work-apron. Save for their hair and the color of their skin, the two boys are quite similar in stature and shape—their facial features are different, but not remarkably so. But perhaps the most surprising aspect of this picture is that the soap in the white boy's hand is black, which suggests blacking up as much as scrubbing yourself white. Similarly, not only is race unfixed, but so is class. Conventionally it would be the white boy who has wealth and who is served; yet drawing from the picture itself, one would have to surmise that the owner of the lovely little slippers, which have been carefully stepped out of at the base of the tub, is the black boy—not the white boy who serves him. Likewise, the little aristocratic mirror and the elegant footstool also suggest refinement, ornament, leisure. Even the bathtub looks splendid: elegant, like Madame Récamier's "fainting couch" in Jacques-Louis David's famous portrait (1800). To whom do these lovely things belong?

By the time we get to the "after" picture, the joke is that the little blackened boy forgot to wash his face. Dumbfounded, he peers at himself in the mirror (held by the little white boy), with his arms outstretched,

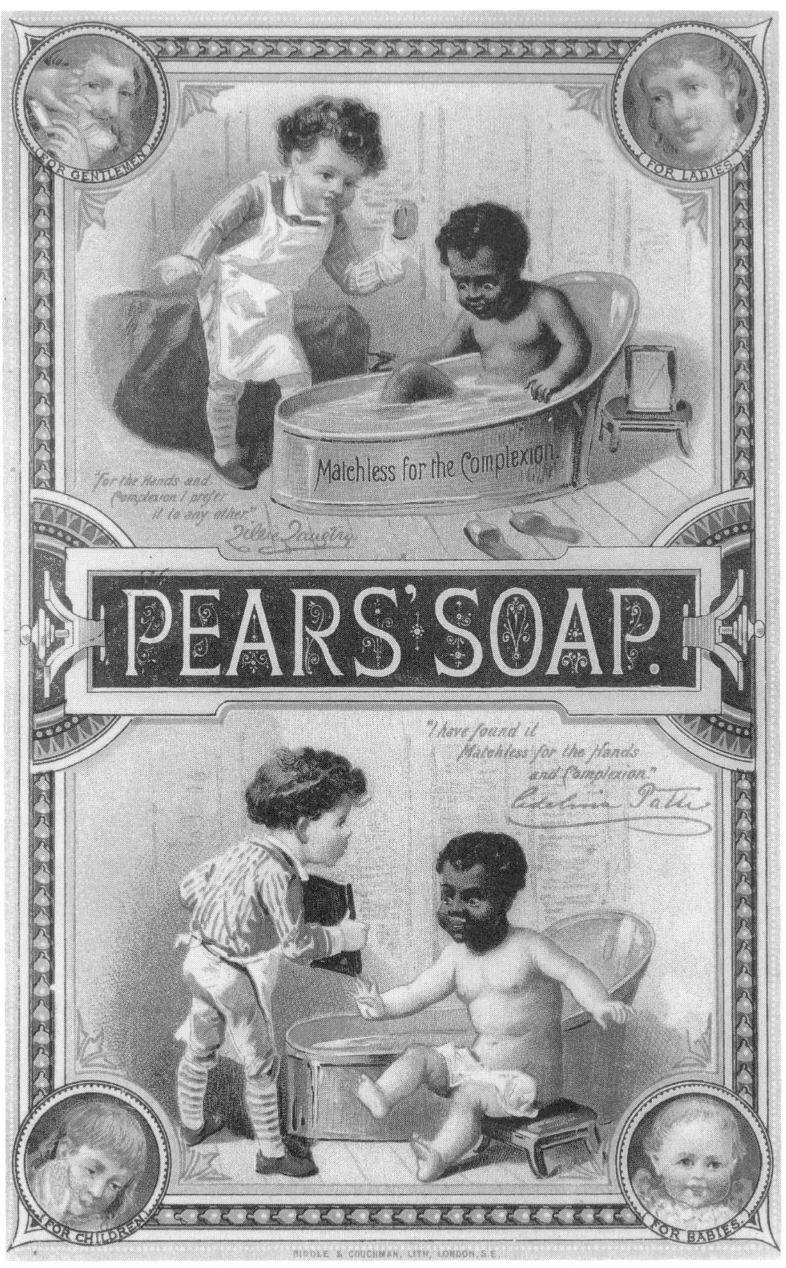

Figure 29. Pears' Soap advertisement, c. 1892. One of a number of soap advertisements from the later part of the Victorian period (c. 1885-1901) that used the image of a black child or adult being washed with the product. (John Johnson Collection, Bodleian Library, University of Oxford)

his right foot caught in a kick. Race (as manifested by the body of this half-white and half-black boy) has been visualized as even more uncertain. Could he, the once-black and now racially mixed boy, be the same race as the boy who holds the looking glass?[46] And what if he had washed his face? What race would he be then? Is he a "pickaninny" or not? The race of this child is invisible and as unfixed as black oil floating on water.

The image of the half-washed boy in the Pears' Soap advertisement reminds me of a passage from Munby's diary, in which we find a description of parts of Hannah's skin as figuratively painted extra white, while wearing her mistress's fancy dress (on the sly). Munby writes that, in the "ball dress of black gauze and lace . . . her neck and bosom, and even her shoulders, were bare. Dazzling white, they seemed, by contrast with her hardworking arms, which of course were also bare."[47] Whiteness, here, is a metaphor for the bourgeoisie (white mistress), against Hannah's darkened arms, which are a metaphor for the proletariat (black slave). By veiling Hannah's body with the materials of another class, her arms suddenly become "not white" as they perform in contrast to her suddenly "dazzling white" neck, bosom, and shoulders: Munby's passage unveils Hannah's whiteness and her darkness as culturally determined. As Peggy Phelan reminds us, "The same physical features of a person's body may be read as 'black' in England, 'white' in Haiti, 'colored' in South Africa, and 'mulatto' in Brazil. More than indicating that racial markings are read differently cross-culturally, these variations underline the psychic, political, and philosophical impoverishment of linking the color of the physical body with the ideology of race."[48] Likewise, in the Pears' Soap advertisement, the ideology of blackness is linked with dirtiness and ignorance: blacks could be white if they just washed, blacks do not even know enough to wash their own faces, or blacks need the white man to instruct them on how to be clean, civilized, and cultured; etc.[49] (As another Pears' advertisement boasts, Bishop Q. of Wangaloo, in Unpacific Seas, was better able to lead his "native flock" after he changed his "nigger face" to white with the help of a cake or two of pure Pears' Transparent Soap.)[50]

In a reversal of the Pears' Soap advertisements, Hannah seems to have spent much of her energy painting herself black, not only with soot and dirt but also with the black lead that she used to clean the grates that framed fireplaces. She literally used the black lead like makeup, as is indicated in the following passage from her diary, in which she describes a visit to Mr. Stodart's to have her likeness taken:

So I went one morning [to Mr. Stodart's] just as I was, but he was busy & the second time I went he let me in. I had slipp'd out without asking leave afore the lodgers' breakfast, & I was partly black wi' cleaning boots & grates & that. I had a dirty lilac frock on & old boots, & a coarse white apron on & my face & arms grimed, but I put a good *patch o' black lead* on my left arm to do 'em more with.

No one noticed me much in the streets, I think, & I got to Mr Stodart's & he took me up to his room smiling & said, "Well, you *are* dirty." But I said, "Oh no, sir, this is only what I am every day, but I want to be done thoroughly black like I am sometimes at work." *And I show'd him what the patch of black lead was for, me spitting on it & then daubing it on my arms & after all drawing them across my mouth and nose.*[51]

In a passage from Munby's diaries, we are presented with a related image of Hannah "made up." This time, she is somewhat selectively blackened. Her nose is "streaked" with soot or blacking and her lips are "disfigured" black. The dirty blackness is clearly alluring to Munby and he is prompted to kiss her.

As concerning those boots which my Hannah was cleaning: Her right hand held her blacking brush, her left was inside the boot; a streak of blacking or soot crossed her aquiline nose, another disfigured her sweet lips. The boot was still dirty: she stoaped and kissed it, and looking earnestly [?] at me, she licked off a flake. . . . Thereupon, black as her lips were I kissed them, in silence. For that act of hers was one of the signs between her and me, which preceded the great sign of all—her marriage.[52]

The racist ideology connecting Hannah's painting of herself black and being black is further reinforced in yet another advertisement of the late-Victorian period. This particular advertisement, for black lead itself, appeared in 1894, and is a continuation of the relentless relationship between servants, cleanliness, black bodies, white bodies, progress, and colonialism. The drawing shows a muscular "minstrel" leading a foot-race, complete with white challengers in the background (fig. 30). "No Dust!" is stamped across the chest of this champion as he runs through a space of racial puns. Below his picture, it is written that the *race* is "Black Led," a play on the "James' Dome Black Lead" that it is advertising. The figure's exaggerated lips, bright white teeth, and protruding eyes figure

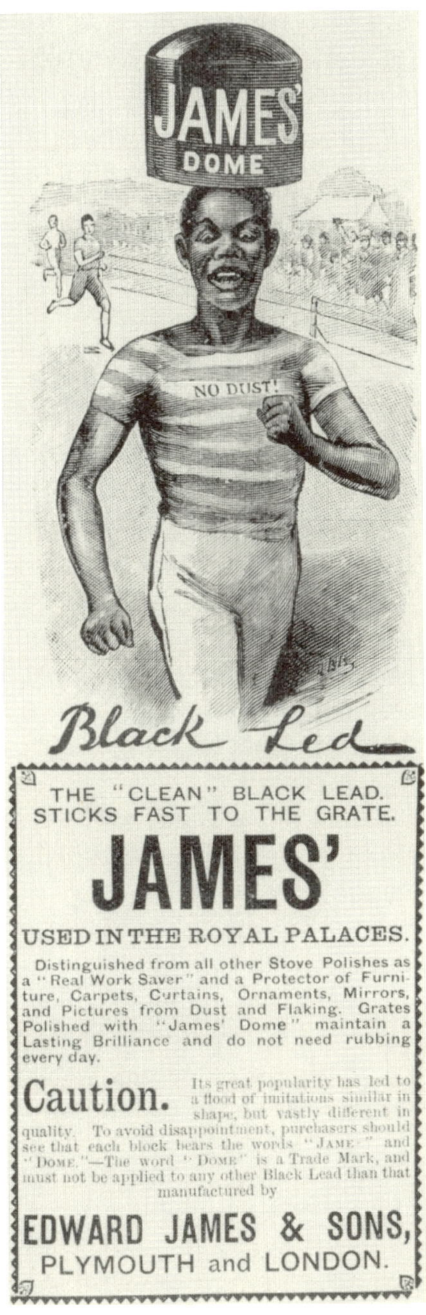

Figure 30. James' Dome Black Lead advertisement.
Illustrated Sporting and Dramatic News, 1894.
(Newspaper Library, The British Library)

him as racial stereotype, as minstrel. It is as if he too, like Hannah, has drawn on himself with black lead. What color then is this man? Could he be white like the women minstrels Munby drew in his journal? (Munby was fascinated by the fact that these "selfmade negresses" washed their black off every night.)[53]

Or more complicated yet, is the "No Dust" champion a black man who has painted himself as minstrel? After all, not all painted minstrels were white underneath. As Douglas A. Lorimer has written in his book *Colour, Class and the Victorians:*

> For the mid-Victorians the Negro remained an exotic and novel being, and they were prepared to accept even the exaggerated and farcical antics of the black minstrels as authentic. In 1866 [one year after Hannah's diary entry] Samuel Hague, an English entertainer and promoter, attempted to cash in on sympathy for the recently emancipated slaves and the popularity of the minstrel shows. He brought 26 ex-slaves from Georgia to Liverpool and staged a "genuine Negro" entertainment. Hague's audiences did not take to his attempt at realism, and soon the promoter had the ex-slaves like the white entertainers in the company put on the burnt cork. English audiences were thereby satisfied that they had seen the genuine article, the real black minstrel.[54]

In Hague's performance, African slaves (from America) must masquerade as minstrels in order to be seen as "genuine Negroes." Race, here, is assumed (as it is culturally determined) and worn as a mask. Similarly, as Joan Riviere demonstrated in her famous article from 1929, females often masquerade womanliness: through dress, through coquettish ways, through an embracement of maternality. Women masquerade as feminine in order to be seen as "genuine women."[55] Irigaray understands this masquerade of femininity as a loss to women. For,

> "femininity" is a role, and image, a value, imposed upon women by male systems of representation. In this masquerade of femininity, the woman loses herself, and loses herself by playing on her femininity. The fact remains that this masquerade requires an *effort* on her part for which she is not compensated. Unless her pleasure comes simply from being chosen as an object of consumption or of desire by masculine "subjects."[56]

This unfruitful kind of masquerade, in which the woman plays to masculine desire (without subversion),[57] is related to the notion of "passing": blacks who pass as white, gays and lesbians who pass as straight, even the poor who pass as middle class. As Phelan writes, "Passing performances *in general* seek to use one form of invisibility to highlight a usually privileged form of visibility."[58] Hannah seems to have broken this standard rule by refusing to privilege any form of visibility, so that it becomes impossible to determine what she is passing as: rather than highlighting any race, class, or even gender, she highlights invisibility.

Hannah, the champion of the *gaze of the invisible,* was able to paint on both the skin of a *whitened* lady and the skin of a *blackened* slave, as is represented in the other set of "before and after" pictures: Hannah as a lady (ready to sit for Gainsborough, 1874) and Hannah as a chimney sweep / slave (c. 1862).[59] Munby kept them side-by-side in a leather traveling mount that he probably took with him on his travels around Britain and abroad.

Starting with Hannah's hat and her slave scarf, we can begin to see many fits of unfixing standardized social roles. The pretty hat, appropriate for the times, might have been worn for an informal walk, or for a game of archery with other ladies. The tail of the hat is tasteful and flirtatious: long ribbons that trimmed the backs of hats were known to contemporaries as "Follow me Lads."[60] The slave scarf, bright against her darkened skin, plays to the Orientalist taste of the period and carries sexual connotations. It recalls the dark women found in paintings by the French painter Jean-Léon Gérôme, like the scarved black slave who bathes a white woman in *The Bath* (1880–85, fig. 31).[61]

Yet together the two pieces of millinery strangely echo each other, as if the scarf on the lady's head and the scarf on the slave's head were the same bit of silk. Both the lady and the slave are represented synecdochically by a similar (if not the same) object of female fetishization: a piece of clothing, a scarf, an object of tactile stimulation. (Freud was reluctant to grant women any perversions of their own, but he did admit that "all women . . . are clothing fetishists."[62] Lacan's teacher, Gaëtan Gatian de Clérembault, hypothesized that women fetishists required the tactile stimulation of pieces of cloth.)[63] Difference and sameness, like in the Pears' Soap advertisement, are entangled. Who is the opposite of who? What is being painted on? Class or race? Who is other to who? Are both women slaves?[64] Hannah, as slave, as newlywed to a bourgeois man, and as a maid of all

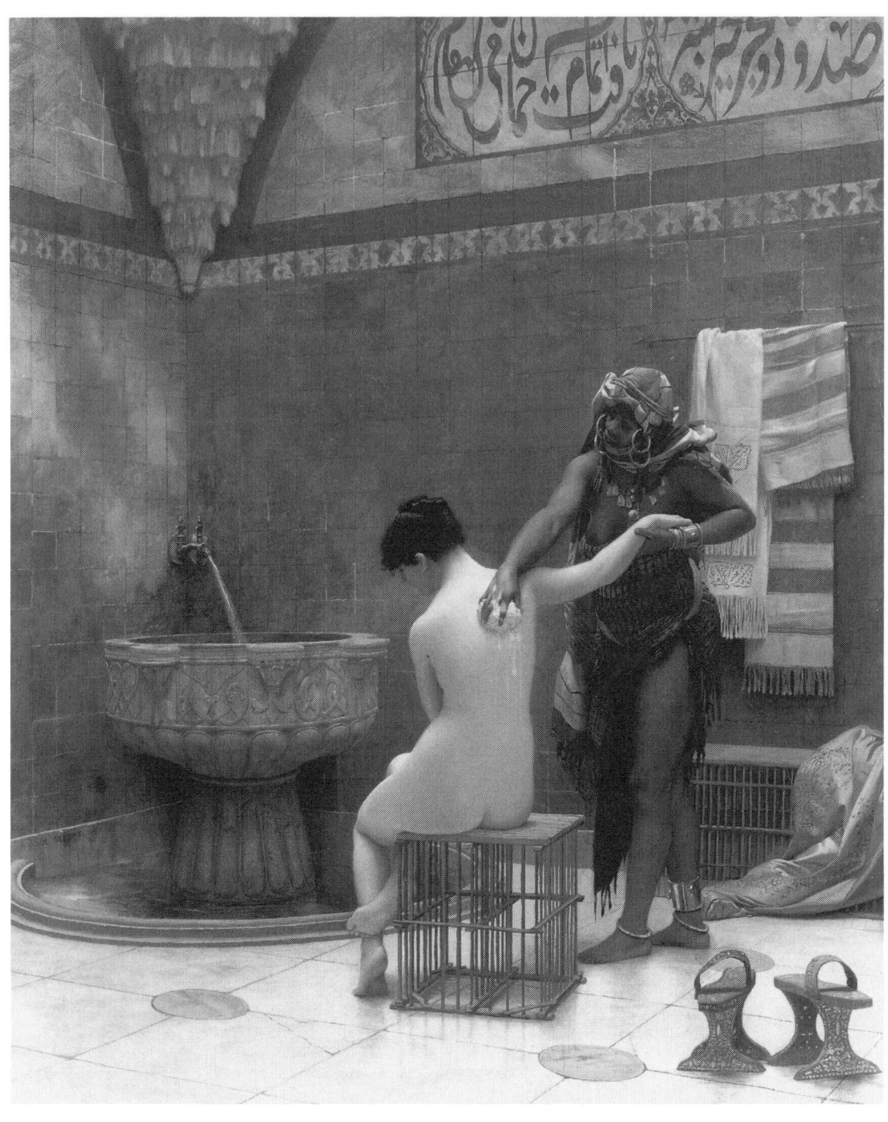

Figure 31. Jean-Léon Gérôme, *The Bath*, c. 1880-85. (Mildred Anna Williams Collection, The Fine Arts Museums of San Francisco)

work, made her class truly invisible. Munby saw Hannah's intriguing invisibility right from the beginning. On March 12, 1860, in the midst of calling her his Juno, while at the same time speaking of her lowly ways, Munby writes: "And so we get back to class distinctions: I love her, then, because she is *not* like her own class after all, but like mine!"[65]

Looking further at these pictures, we can see that the lady's dress is too tight; undoubtedly, it is being pulled by the girth of Hannah's biceps, which Munby measured at various times as "thirteen, fourteen, and once even eighteen inches round."[66] This is just one example of Hannah as a *misfit*. Consider also the image of her wearing a man's suit: now her clothes are too big. Her jacket is overly roomy, with sleeves large enough for two of her giant hands (fig. 23).

Three days after their wedding on January 18, 1873, Munby discloses that no matter whatever Hannah wears, the guise doesn't fit:

> We had good fare and warmth at the White Horse, & Hannah played her part [of the Lady] very fairly, by dint of natural sweetness. But now that she was drest in black silk, her shapely hands looked somewhat large and laborious, and her dear complexion somewhat coarse; whereas her face looks ladylike and her hands delicate, when she is in her own servant's dress. C'est sélon.[67]

What is particularly delightful about Hannah's guises is that the characters never quite fit the woman: there is a fascinating tension between convincing and not convincing. The photographs seem to confirm and almost take pride in the fact that Hannah had no looking glass.[68] They, the images, perform in the box as a seemingly endless series of almost-right theatrics that call identity into question. Rather than fixing her sexuality, her race, her class, or her gender, they unfix it: they render her (somebody called Hannah) invisible. Like Cindy Sherman's recent takeoffs on master paintings, the excitement lies not in the author's masterful deception, but in her masterful presentations of incongruities.

Hannah Not Only Painted Herself Black, She Also Painted Herself Celestial Rosyred

Investment in the look is not as privileged in women as in men. More than the other senses, the eye objectifies and masters. It sets at a distance, and maintains a distance. In our culture the predominance of the look over smell, taste, touch and hearing has brought

*about an impoverishment of bodily relations. The moment the look dominates, the body
loses its materiality.—Luce Irigaray*

"No gloves, no flowers! Massa, shall I do?"
She cries; "I have no looking glass, you know!"—Arthur Munby

Though Hannah had no looking glass, there are moments when she sees
herself looking at herself in a mirror.[69] Other times she knows people,
most often Munby, are looking at her. And at other times, she looks at
herself in photographs. Clearly, the visualizing of the self was a significant
part of Hannah's life. But I am arguing that when Hannah looked and/or
experienced herself being looked at, she experienced the gaze as an expanded constellation of the senses that included sight, but was not limited
by it. Hannah's performative life can be imagined as a fecund response to
Irigaray's assessment of the problem of the "predominance of the look."

Hannah, on a ride with identities, managed *not* to "impoverish bodily
relations," and managed not to "lose the materiality" of her body. Brushing up against Hannah, through the diaries and the photographs, signifies a
"Hannah" that is transmitted differently: invisible to the petrifying eye,
but rich in an invisibility that is comprised of criss-cross spectral move-
ments through color, gender, and class, through unsaid erotics, through
haptic autoeroticism. Though not consciously fighting the gaze (that we
have so thoroughly fetishized in critical theory), Hannah's imagination of
a different self (her invisible self) requires a scrambling of the senses,
which allows touch to feel sight and sight to feel touch: as in a blush, when
your burning neck can feel yourself being looked at; or, when you see
someone else blushing and can see their hot cheeks feeling your look.
Hannah always seems to feel her body feeling.

Irigaray cites (and sites) touch, admittedly essentially, all over the female body.[70] Though this is not the place to debate the intricacies, useful-
ness, and liabilities of Irigaray's essentialist tactics, her emphasis on the
tactile female body is useful for this project of liberating Hannah's invisibility. Irigaray, rather shockingly and famously, situates the female body
in a state of autoeroticism, always *in touch,* with itself. "As for women,
she touches herself in and of herself without any need for mediation, and
before there is any way to distinguish activity from passivity. Women
'touches herself' all the time, and moreover no one can forbid her to do
so, for her genitals are formed of two lips in continuous contact. Thus,
within herself, she is already two—but not divisible into one(s)—that

caress each other."[71] This stuff makes me blush, but I am attracted to the notions of a self-caress. It is a useful entryway into the less morphological uses of touch that Irigaray finds in the female body, specifically women's use of language, cast by touch:

> "She" is indefinitely other in herself. This is doubtless why she is said to be whimsical, incomprehensible, agitated, capricious . . . not to mention her language, in which "she" sets off in all directions leaving "him" unable to discern the coherence of any meaning. Hers are contradictory words, somewhat mad from the standpoint of reason, inaudible for whoever listens to them with ready-made grids, with a fully elaborated code in hand. For in what she says, too, at least when she dares, *woman is constantly touching herself* [emphasis added]. She steps ever so slightly aside from herself with a murmur, an exclamation, a whisper, a sentence left unfinished . . . . What she says is never identical with anything, moreover; rather, it is contiguous. *It touches (upon).*[72]

This is classic Irigaray, with her emphasis on the fact that women often speak differently than men, and when they do their language is often fragmented, contradictory, spoken from many lips.[73] Such voices have been oppressed and repressed, by being categorized as hysterical; but Irigaray and other French feminists (especially Hélène Cixous) have celebrated it as a language of fecund feminine difference.

The Victorian era, the Golden Age of (female) Hysteria, twists on the fact that the Victorian period was also the Golden Age of Women's Writing.[74] Hannah's performative roles reflect some of the hysterical multiplicity that was a part of seemingly all women's lives in the Victorian period: ranging from those who were labeled "hysterical" for merely speaking their mind to those who were clinically ill.[75] The latter performed hysteria under especially debilitating and serious constraints in unexceptional spaces: as a way of fulfilling the masculine ideal of femininity as the fainting, weak, frail woman; to escape the caged life assigned to them; or to become stars in the clinic.[76] Hugh Welch Diamond, the pioneer of psychiatric photography in England, even photographed his patients as Ophelia-types (with shawls draped over their shoulders, and in one instance a crown of wild weeds on her head) or in staged settings reminiscent of the Victorian "art" photography of Cameron or Robinson.[77] The complicated relationship between acting and hysteria was culturally acknowledged: that is why the Victorian actress Ellen Terry visited a London asylum to prepare herself to be mad on stage.[78] So, while George Eliot and Mrs. Gaskell were publishing their novels as never before, women were both culturally inscribed as hysterical and writing their own bodies as hysterical: woman's body was a contested site, a tabula rasa. Changing from costume to costume, Hannah "steps so slightly aside from herself with a murmur [in a man's suit], an exclamation [as a blackened slave], a whisper [in a lady's dress], a sentence left unfinished [in a man's suit]." She "*touches (upon)*" many identities, but her relationship to them is never more than "contiguous." Hannah *looks* different.

In the following passage (from Munby's diary), we find a representation of Hannah's own body-rich gazing that took place when "Massa" paid her a visit. Because the diary entry is not Hannah's, but Munby's, it feels further from the actuality of what we might perceive to be Hannah's real experience. For despite the fact that Hannah's diaries were written so that Munby could read them, one is inclined to see her as a more reliable narrator of her own life than Munby: after all, her words came from her own hand; they are contiguous with her. This entry from Munby's diary is additionally suspect because it was written some forty years after the actual event. (Munby wrote the diary entry on Saturday, January 11, 1890, but Michael Hiley has reasoned that the incident took place in the late 1850s.)[79] However, as should already be clear, my intention is not to get at a single kernel of truth. I am more interested in Munby's text as part of a complex representation that registers their bizarre charades (with Munby as the straight man) as part of a reciprocal endeavor. As in the earlier quote in which Munby lost it over a young woman's gloveless hand ("oh ye ballroom partners, what a breadth of massive flesh it was to grasp!"), Munby is again hilariously melodramatic, every bit as much of an actor as his cohort. And Hannah is playfully erotic as she looks different(ly) in her Mistress's mirror:

> She was then a general servant in a tradesman's well to do family at Kilburn; and one day, I went to see her, at her own suggestion, in her master's house, for the family were all absent, and she wished to show me her work, and the places where she worked. She showed me the kitchen she had to scour; the big kitchen grate that she blacked, the chimney that she swept, the scullery where she cleaned

the sink, the hole in which she cleaned the boots and knives; and the scenes of many another sordid but necessary task. And she took me upstairs and showed me her attic, a little bare room, with a blue-check quilt on the bed, and one chair, and a common washing stand in the corner, with jug and basin; "what I never use," said she, "for you know I always wash me at the sink." *There was no looking glass in the room; she seldom used one.* Then as we came downstairs, she opened, by way of contrast, the door of her mistress's luxurious bedroom. On the bed lay a ball dress, of black gauze and lace, with crimson garniture; and this made me wish to see for once how Hannah would look in a lady's condition. I told her to put on the ball dress. She hesitated to profane the Missis's things by touching them, much more, by wearing them; but to please me, she consented. She took off her own servant's dress and put on that of her mistress. It was too short and too narrow for her, and it would not meet her healthy rustic waist; still, she was able to wear it; and, seeing a rose in the room, I brushed out her bright hair in a lady's fashion, and placed the rose within it. Thus she stood before me to be looked at; smiling and slightly blushing; feeling awkward and strange, in that unknown garb, but not looking awkward at all, but most graceful I gazed on her in a kind of rapture: so lovely a figure she was, so ladylike, so sweet, that I longed "to take her away from her slavery," and make her a lady indeed. "And now, dear," at last I said, "turn round, and look at yourself." She wondered what I meant; for she had forgotten, that behind her stood a large cheval glass, capable of showing her from top to toe. But she turned round, and saw herself reflected at full length in the mirror. The effect of this revelation was startling. It was not her beauty, that struck; nor yet the sight of herself in a garb she had never worn before: but now for the first time she noticed that her neck and bosom, and even her shoulders, were bare. Dazzling white, they seemed, by contrast with her hard-working arms, which of course were also bare: but *in an instant, they were suffused, like her face, with one universal blush—celestial rosyred. Love's proper hue.* She shut her eyes, turned sharply from the glass, and suddenly flung herself into my arms—"that I might rather feel than see the beating of her heart." "Oh Massa," she whispered, "I am naked!"

Never before had I felt so strongly the need of self control in her presence: never, before or since, have I been filled with a more passionate ardour of love and reverence for that pure and innocent soul, who had trusted herself so utterly to me. I soothed and comforted and at length released her.[80]

Part of the sexual charge of this melodramatic performance rests on touch: it was taboo for Hannah to try on her mistress's black and crimson dress because her lower-class body would debase the same fabric that would later rub up against an upper-class body: Hannah "hesitated to profane the Missis's things by touching them." There were cultural laws against such touching. The breaking of this prohibition was layered in eroticism.

Eroticism between Hannah and Munby is shot all over the scene of this crime: through the usual cross-class sexual play; through all of the looking (he has watched her dress and undress, and he has made her look in the mirror while he gazes at her gazing at herself); he has made her disobey the authority of her Missis; he has made her wear something that makes her look more naked than being naked; and the secrecy of the act, which it found out would probably lead to Hannah's dismissal, gives it a pornographic air.

However, I think that the most erotic aspect of this scene lies in the fact that it was really Hannah and her employer that were made intimate by this act. (Not that this would not turn Munby on too.) The eroticism of the moment is intensified by the fact that the two women share skin (without the Missis ever knowing it, a seduction of a quiescent body). After all, when women share clothes, it is often a sign of deep intimacy. Wearing your friend's dress, especially one that is cut close to the body, makes you acutely aware of the other's body, her size, her smell.[81]

Looking at a pair of photographs, which are also in the Munby Box, will help us to play out the intimacy that can take place between two women moving in and out of one dress. The first picture features two girls, paper mill workers from Dartford, sitting side by side: one in light-colored dress, the other in mostly dark clothes (1863, plate 13). They are rigidly posed; their faces look serious; the photographer's camera has kept its distance. Switching over to the companion picture, we see that the camera has moved in on the girl who was formerly on the left. Her face is now full of pleasure; the girl who was on the right is no longer in the picture (1863, plate 14). The lone girl, or rather the girl who appears to be alone, is smirking, ready to burst into laughter. (Her facial expression strikes me as an amplification of the look on Mary Hillier's face in *Fervent in Prayer*, plate 4) What's so funny? What secret is she sharing with the photographer? A closer look reveals that this girl must have persuaded her friend to lend her the dark, rather stylish bodice and her clean pinafore. (A beaded necklace has also appeared.) "As she is a size larger than the bodice, she has to put her right hand to her stomach to prevent the fastenings bursting open and she is trying throughout the exposure to stop her laughing—perhaps she is having to hold her breath to save herself from disaster."[82] She seems to be taking pleasure in the fact that when others see you wearing another woman's dress, they know that you share a familiarity, a knowledge of the other woman's body that makes a show of your own. Here, giggles and flirtations are the result; she may be blushing. The mise-en-scène of this picture is akin to Hannah's: in both an other woman's tight dress becomes an erotic showing and sharing of skin.[83] Admittedly, it is a bit of a skin flick for me too. As I write, I discover that the little puffs and folds of skin that poke out between the fastenings of the paper mill girl's bodice become my *punctum,* "a skin that I share" with her, in that they erotically pierce me . . . as does my own imagination of Hannah's "rustic waist" in "black gauze and lace."[84]

But there is still more erogenous touching to consider in the story: it was also erotic for Munby to brush out her "bright hair," which, of course, entails touching it in a most agreeable way. As Elisabeth G. Gitter writes in "The Power of Women's Hair in the Victorian Imagination," "The combing and displaying of hair, as suggested by the legends of alluring mermaids who sit on rocks singing and combing their beautiful hair [a popular theme in Victorian painting], thus constitute a sexual exhibition. And the more abundant the hair, the more potent the sexual invitation implied by its display, for folk literary, and psychoanalytic traditions agree that the luxuriance of the hair is an index of vigorous sexuality, even of wantonness."[85] As Gitter points out, the brushing of a woman's hair has long been a sign of sexual exchange—with the hair signifying a range of complex meanings from "the exclusively female power to weave the female web" to "a glittering symbolic fusion of the sexual lust and the lust for power that she embodies"—but for the Victorians, who saw to it that a woman restrained the sexuality of her hair through chignons and other elaborate (pinned-up) styles of the period, the brushing out of a woman's hair meant letting her sexuality out.[86]

Carroll, Munby's contemporary who was driven not by working-class women but by bourgeois little girls, played out sexual desires through bowers of girl-hair. The comparison between Carroll and Munby is apt: Hudson wrote a biography on both and draws comparisons between the two. In his book on Munby, Hudson writes: "Munby's compassionate feeling for working women was comparable to his contemporary Lewis Carroll's intense concern for little girls; Munby's inner compulsion culminated in his secret marriage no less surely than Carroll's crystallized in the *Alice* books."[87] However, unlike Munby, Carroll's diaries rarely contain anything that even suggests erotic inclinations.[88] Thus, much has been made of his explicitly erotic statement—a rarity among his own volumes of books, diaries, and letters: "I can imagine no more delightful occupation than brushing Ellen Terry's hair."[89] A similar charge comes through another lovely portrait of Irene MacDonald by Carroll. This time the mise-en-scène has shifted from the secluded room of an odalisque to that of a Victorian girl's bedroom. The camera has caught Irene in her delicate nightdress, flaunting hair that looks wild, slept in, and untamed (plate 15). (Lucky for Carroll, all little girls, because of their presumed innocence, wore their enticing hair down all of the time. In fact, when they reached an age that required them to pile their hair on top of their heads, he quickly broke off his relationships with them.) Taming such a mane appears to be an impossible job for the cumbersome hairbrush that is oversized in her girl-hand. Irene's pouting face has the picture's title written all over it: *"It Won't Come Smooth"* (1863). The staging of this little girl suggests that she is pleading for help with all of her lovely hair. Like Munby in Hannah's hair (though with a different end in mind), it is not difficult to imagine Carroll fiddling with Irene's hair in preparation for the closing of the (camera's) shutter. Like Carroll and the other "other Victorians," Hannah and Munby were familiar with the codes of hair brushing: the two were partners in this eroticism. In a moment of haptic foreplay, leading up to the consummation of their looking, Hannah's came smooth.

But the most erotic touch of all comes near the end of the performance, with Hannah closing her eyes, shutting out sight itself, like a long erotic kiss, in order to *feel*: "She shut her eyes, turned sharply from the glass, and suddenly flung herself into my arms—'that I might rather feel than see the beating of her heart.'" This passage is charged from looking, especially the kind of looking that produces shame that you can see: a blush.

Faced with the concept of the blush again, how are we to read Hannah's blushing? As indicated by a host of authors of the period, from Charles Darwin to Charles Dickens, it was usually the woman who blushed. As Darwin informed them, "The relaxation of the muscular coats of the small arteries, by which the capillaries become filled with blood" was a feminine thing.[90] In the previous chapters, I demonstrated how the period's representations of ideal womanhood (as in the purely innocent little girl or the angel in the house) were suspended between a blush and a nonblush: they were cultural manifestations of creatures who could not possibly exist. Perhaps this is why Hannah once said, when considering the possibility of marriage, "For I never feel as if I *could* make up my mind to that—it is too much like being a *woman* [emphasis added]."[91] Hannah, far from an angel in the house and far from girlhood, must have blushed differently. Unlike Georgina Podsnap, she did not speak with her cheeks out of social ineptness. Nor did Hannah blush out of shame.

For, while the looking-glass blush seems to suggest shame, it also seems to defeat shame through its performance.[92] The shameful and shameless blush mirrors Hannah's other *becoming* identities (woman, slave, black, white lady, etc.), which read simultaneously as both real and false personages. So that when she *makes* (not fakes) blushes, one senses that she is neither ashamed nor not ashamed. In "Shame and Gender: Contribution to a Phenomenology of Oppression," Sandra Lee Bartky demonstrates how women are especially prone to "*rituals* of self-shaming undertaken in order to bear more easily [an anticipated] shame."[93] Embedded in "ritual" are descriptive words such as "prescribed," "system," "custom," "ceremonial act": all of which play the "ritual of self-shame" as performance. Hannah, in a sense, saw shame coming and grabbed it before it was inflicted on her: that way, she could take pleasure in performing it upon herself.

In a series of acts that were almost always based on shame, Hannah (who eventually learned to speak French, who read philosophy and Anne Thackeray's "Village on the Cliff," who planned to read Samuel Richardson's *Clarissa,* and who recited Shakespeare while cleaning the floor) must have been at least imperfectly conscious of her role as performer.[94] Hannah must have known (at least subconsciously) that the black and crimson ball dress would not fit, that it would enhance (rather than diminish) her fantastic biceps, that it would make a strange spectacle of her, that it would unfix the categories of lady and servant. And she (I think) must have known that a good blush (all the way into her arms!?) would induce plenty of passion in herself and in Munby. Just thinking about such a moment of anticipated shame must have made her turn rosyred.

For although the conduct books and the English novels of the period, which feature the modest woman as a subject for the narrative, often stress the pleasure affected on others when a young woman diffuses crimson on her cheek, there is no reason for us to believe that it could not (and did not) also give pleasure to women as well.[95] The sexologist Havelock Ellis emphatically states, "There can be no doubt that the blush is sexually attractive"—yet he also speaks of the sexual blush as "an irradiation of sexual erethism that . . . may contain an element of pleasure."[96] Similarly, Ellis writes about the blush that comes when "a woman is pumped full of compliments" as also being "accompanied by pleasure," partly because she feels it to be attractive, and partly because this "general rosiness" and "erection of spinal organs" seems to feel pretty good.[97] Arguably, when Ellis writes about erect spinal cords, he must be speaking of the pleasure he takes when he sees a girl blush (he even suggests that we consider an erection to be a "blushing of the penis").[98] But I do think that Ellis is getting at the often overlooked pleasure that a woman might take from performing a blush. In short, when that supposedly "innocent blush predictably plays before a room," it can feel good, not only to the audience but also to the spectacle.[99]

Hannah (herself) writes provocatively about blushing when she describes the circumstances around the taking of the Magdalene picture:

> And then the young man [the photographer by the name of Mr. Stodart] said he would like to take me again in other ways [he had just taken her, blackened—"cleaning a pair o' boots in one & another like blacking the grate") & that he wasn't so busy now if I could come—one to be done as Magdalene, & I shd want nothing to wear but a white skirt. Massa said that Mr Fink (the one as took me for him in London once) wanted me to be done as *Una*—what that is I hardly know. Well, I went again & was done. I had to strip off my servant's things—to my shift, what I hardly liked, but still I knew there was no harm in that, & Mr S. was a serious sort o' man & we

neither of us laugh'd or smil'd over it. He took me in a kneeling position as if praying, with my hair down my back & looking up. The side face was good for it, but the *hands* was too big & coarse he said, so it wouldn't do as a picture. And so it's best for me to be done as a drudge what I am, for my hands & arms are tho' chief to *me,* to get my living with, & I don't care about my face if Massa likes it.

But Mr S. gave me one or two of the Magdalenes on cards . . .

When I was stripp'd for the Magdalene I was little confused, having my steel chain & padlock round my neck, for Mr. S. said, "Oh take that chain off." I said, "I canna, sir." He said, "Is it lock'd" *I blush'd a bit* as I said, "Yes, & I've not got the key." "Ah, there's some mystery about that," he said. And so it was done wi' the chain on, but as I said the hands was too big, & the position too stiff to look well. But I kep' the cards he gave me, & he also gave me a likeness of himself in colours, & he's exceedingly good-looking I think, & I've put him in my album. I paid Mr S a good bit for the picture, having 3 or 4 different ones.[100]

In this text, rather than suffusing her face and arms in "celestial rosy-red" (as she did in Munby's story), she blushes just "a bit." Her tiny coloring comes out when Mr. S. learns that she has not got the key to the locked steel chain and padlock around her neck. (We know, along with Hannah, that only Munby had the key. We may blush, too.) This blush, as before, feels playfully deliberate and for show. She punctuates the story (seemingly without shame) when she almost eagerly adds: "& I've not got the key." She wore the chain with pride; after all, one imagines that she could have arranged to have the chain taken off (the Magdalene picture was planned before she arrived at the studio). But like her hands and arms, the chain is a big and clunky part of her own complex self-representation of invisibility. Both her hands and her chain undo the religiosity of Magdalene. Both fight against Magdalene's supposed helplessness. Both besmirch the purity of her white gown. Both play into her exposed breasts, which are not feminine at all, but are as firm and as startingly masculine as the thick chain and her thick hands.

The picture of Hannah as Magdalene is indicative of the Victorian interest in representing the other Mary: the unchaste Mary Magdalene. Hannah's portrait of 1864 is one instance in the plethora of representations of Magdalene, a topos well established in narrative forms by the

1850s.[101] We have already seen Hillier as a suggested Magdalene in several of Cameron's Mary pictures. There are many more, such as *The Kiss of Peace,* which depict Hillier dramatically as a Magdalene-type through an emphasis on the infamous hair. My personal favorite is one that, despite its title, *The Angel at the Tomb* (1869, plate 16), is read as a Magdalene picture because of this focus on hair. Mike Weaver describes Hillier's incredible hair as "tousled and tangled as never before in the history of art."[102] Differently, Hannah's greasy hair sticks close to her head, with tired strands catching themselves on her shoulders and neck, while others fall uninterestingly down her back.

I think that the picture of Hannah as Magdalene is extremely erotic, but not in the conventional sense of Cameron's beautiful pictures of Mary Hillier as Mary Magdalene. Like Spenser's Una from his *Faerie Queen,* Hannah is sexually charged through a display of black and white.[103] Hannah's hair serves as a black veil over exposed, very white, sexually ambiguous breasts. The whiteness of her breasts bring color to my face. The image is further eroticized, because, unlike the hair of Hillier, Hannah's hair looks like it really did take part in Mary Magdalene's sensual performance of anointing the feet of Jesus with the musky smelling spikenard, only to wipe his feet dry with her own lovely hair. One is reminded of the fact that Hannah performed similar acts of eroticism through her habit of washing Massa's feet, a ritual that she appears to have taken great pleasure in. Furthermore, Hannah's hands, large, with featherlike fingers, take on the character of strange, displaced angel wings: they are both heavenly, manly, grotesque, and beautiful—they must have looked very erotic to Munby. And her eyes are not cast up to God, but hold their look, without shame, on the other person in the room: Mr. S.

Interestingly enough, the name "Mary" was itself an invisible name for female servants in the Victorian era. So it is not surprising that Hannah was also referred to as Mary.[104] (The fact that Cameron's own maid was actually named Mary and posed as both the Virgin Mary and Mary Magdalene is an intriguing part of this extension of the invisibility of "Mary.") One of the most humorous uses of "Mary" to signify the commonly undifferentiated maids of the period, occurs in *Alice in Wonderland,* when Alice finds herself to be shrunken to the size of a rabbit and then mistaken by the White Rabbit as his housemaid: "Very soon the Rabbit noticed Alice as she went hunting about, and called out to her in an angry tone, "Why, Mary Ann, what *are* you doing out here? Run home this moment, and fetch me a pair of gloves and a fan! Quick, now!"[105] Alice shared with Hannah (even if for only a brief period) the invisibility of being a servant named Mary.[105] And like Alice (and the ever-cleaning Wendy), Hannah's adventures took place in a netherland.

Smarting My Eyes

. . . in a certain way nothing is as sensitive, especially to touch, as my sight.—Luce *Irigaray*

Hannah's pictures annihilate us by refusing categorization, which then undoes our subjectivity. Hannah's pictures are in our eyes, but they are not controlled by us: they do not accept us, even as we suck them in with our eyes. As Lacan has remarked, "The picture is in my eye. But I am not in the picture."[107] Of course, all pictures do this, but I think that Hannah's photographs exaggerate this annihilated relationship; for although her pictures can be framed in various ways, they never seem to contain Hannah, not even in a mythic sense. She remains invisible.

Lacan's two-line statement of annihilation ("The picture is in my eye. But I am not in the picture.") was sparked by his famous recollection of being at sea with some fisherman. While staring at a bit of flotsam that had floated by—a sardine can—one of the fishermen exclaims to Lacan: "*You see that can? Do you see it? Well it doesn't see you!*"[108] The fisherman's statement, riddled with irony, is poking fun at Lacan. The fisherman is illustrating how Lacan is "rather out of place in the picture," out on a fishing boat in the middle of the sea.[109] For among "those fellows who were earning their livings with great difficulty," Lacan "looked like *nothing* on earth"—not unlike the flotsam floating on the surface of the waves.[110] The "joke" disturbed Lacan. For, seeing himself as the fishermen saw him, as a bit of garbage, as nothing, was annihilating.[111]

It is in this double way that even an inanimate object, such as the picture of Hannah's hands, or the Munby Box itself, actually gazes back at us, but in such a way as to *overlook* the viewer. It is annihilating. As a result, our gaze within its constructed socialization (as primary, as the only true sense) always falls short. We can't see Hannah, but she gazes back at us.

The gaze that Hannah gives the viewer is her expanded gaze, her *gaze of the invisible,* which is "forever organized or disorganized, around an impossibility of seeing [*un impossible à voir*]. Insurmountable other of the visible, not reducible to its invisible other side. It is a question of another world [a nether world], another landscape, a *topos* or a locus of the irreversible."[112] That is why in the empty frame with the accompanying note that tells us that Hannah has gone to get kitchen beer, we can take pleasure in the fact that she is not there. For she is also "not, not there." Invisible to the naked eye, she can be touched in the netherplaces of another landscape that destabilizes the reversibility of black and white, upper class and lower class, man and woman.

I close the box and take off my white gloves, which are covered with a black soot that is impossible to see. Knowing that the box never *really* contained her, knowing that her ashes will never rest, knowing that I can never wash her off, I know that I love her and that she can never be mine. I take pleasure in this annihilation. I blush an invisible blush.

CONCLUSION
After-Time

The long grass rustled at her feet as the White Rabbit hurried by—the frightened Mouse splashed his way through the neighboring pool—she could hear the rattle of the teacups as the March Hare and his friends shared their never-ending meal, and the shrill voice of the Queen ordering off her unfortunate guests to execution—once more the pig-baby was sneezing on the Duchess's knee, while plates and dishes crashed around it—once more the shriek of the Gryphon, the squeaking of the Lizard's slate-pencil, and the choking of the suppressed guinea-pigs, filled the air, mixed up with the distant sob of the miserable Mock Turtle.

So, she sat on, with closed eyes, and half believed herself in Wonderland, though she knew she had but to open them again, and all would change to dull reality.—Lewis Carroll, ALICE'S ADVENTURES IN WONDERLAND

I am at the end of this book. I am in its "after-time" (a term that Alice's older sister uses to describe that time after "child-life").[1] Like Carroll—and his tales of an Alice who never grows past "seven and a half, exactly" and who never fully wakes from her Wonderland and Looking-Glass worlds—I feel a similar desire to suspend my stories as a never-ending tea party, as a never-ending dream, "ever drifting down the stream—lingering in the golden gleam."[2] I am uneasy about the closing of this book; I take no pleasure in the prospect of going out—"bang!—just like a candle!"

> "He's dreaming now," said Tweedledee: "and what do you think he's dreaming about?"
>
> Alice said "Nobody can guess that."
>
> "Why about *you!*" Tweedledee exclaimed, clapping his hands

triumphantly. "And if he left off dreaming about you, where do you suppose you'd be?"

"Where I am now, of course," said Alice.

"Not you!" Tweedledee retorted contemptuously. "You'd be no-where. Why you're only a sort of thing in his dream!"

"If that there King was to wake," added Tweedledum, "you'd go out—bang!—just like a candle!"[3]

The dream—Alice's dream, the Red King's dream, my dream—is over, rather *almost* over. But "she sat on, with closed eyes, and half believed herself in Wonderland, though she knew she has but to open them again and all would change to dull reality." But (because of my lack of eagerness to push the Dormouse all the way into the teapot and put a lid on it) let's not open our eyes just yet, at least not all of the way. Instead, let's go "traveling the wrong way," like Alice did on the Looking-Glass train, back to the beginning.[4] "Living backwards!" Alice repeated in great astonishment. "I never heard of such a thing!"[5] Through Hannah, through Mary, through Alice, through me (performing Alice), we land back on the title of the book: *Pleasures Taken*. Stay put for a little while.

Pleasures Taken

"Pleasures Taken" suggests the act of taking pictures: we like to photograph what we take pleasure in—children, our friends, our lovers, our-selves. Sometimes, we take pictures, or have pictures taken, of our-selves for the pleasure of a lover, as Hannah did; these are gifts from the "original."

In less-formidable settings, some photographs can be understood as pictures "taken" (stolen) from the original. For example, in the mystical sense of Balzac's proposition that a thin layer of skin is taken with each photograph. Or, as in recent critical texts that have addressed the cam-era's power *to take,* by passing off a regime of interests in the guise of truth. (Allan Sekula, John Tagg, Sander Gilman, Martha Rosler, and Abigail Solomon-Godeau are but a few of the authors who have examined this complex issue.) The object (an actual woman, a specific child, a real man) taken is shot—dressed in precision, taken as the truth—and given as evidence through our confidence in the mechanical. Although I acknowledge the political relations that these texts highlight and frame, and without in any way undermining the significance of their contributions or reducing their various approaches to one, this book is a different road taken. A road that changes direction by focusing on invisible sites of pleasure. For example: the girl's own sexuality, its scrawl, in Carroll's photographs, or Cameron's scratchy maternal pleasures, beyond motherhood, or Hannah's irregular pleasure in chimneys and photographic studios.

But not so invisible is the hands-on pleasure that is taken from the photograph's unique status: its reproducibility, availability, and general pocket-size. Photographs give pleasure in being small and private, protected by the leaves of the photo album (as many of Carroll's and Cameron's still are). Photographs can be as easily swept away as they can be accessed—whether their subjects are mundane or profane or something in between. An album of photographs, tucked in a bureau drawer, stashed on a shelf, or protected by a glass cabinet, was not uncommon in the Victorian middle-class home. With the opening of such books, the pictures are ours to take in and to take on. We perform with them and they perform with us.

Pleasures Taken: Performances of . . .

"Performance" names my own refusal to give into transitivity and the pleasure that I take in the intransitivity of the actual photographs, in the nature of photography itself, and in the construction of my own writing.

The photographs that I have discussed are intransitive in the sense that they feature subjects-objects who strike back at us with "the will and the force of the sitter"—just who is taking who becomes a moot point. Irene MacDonald's half-closed eye and schoolgirl signature (fig. 11), Mary Hillier's "remarkable smirk," caught before the break of laughter while supposedly fervent in prayer (plate 4), and the absent picture of Hannah fetching beer (fig. 24) are torn not from the wooden stretchers of painting, but from the planks of the stage. The intransitive quality of all such (portrait-oriented) photographs, especially those caught in between the covers of this book, registers them as free from exclusive authors. In this (con)text, neither Carroll nor MacDonald, nor Cameron, nor Hillier, nor Hannah, nor Munby, nor any professional or amateur photographer can be said to be playing the leading role of director; rather, it is a drama performed by a cast of subject-objects.

It is in this way that my own writing echoes the photographs that I am discussing. As part of the book's after-time, I read and write the work aloud: an attempt at "vocal writing."[6] (Barthes writes, "If it were possible to imagine an aesthetic of textual pleasure, it would have to include: *writing aloud*."[7]) I imagine writing it aloud to those I love and to those I hate and to those that I am not too sure about. I listen for and grapple with that indistinguishableness that fascinates me: it is, not only, there between the photographic subject-objects of this book, but it is also, deliberately, there between the text and me. I am neither in the text nor outside the text, but *of* the text . . . like Hillier in *The Bereaved Babes / The Mother Moved!* (plate 9), who is neither inside nor outside the picture, but *of* the picture. Such indistinguishableness also figures the pleasure of Barthes's *Pleasure of the Text,* in which the text is oddly inscribed (by the book's title and through the style of its writing) as "of the text." *Du texte* (in French) "is both objective and subjective genitive; the text is both object and subject of pleasure."[8]

Pleasures Taken: Performances of
Sexuality and . . .

Sexuality glimmers under the skin of these photographs: thinly and briefly, but relentlessly, like the pulsating and scattered light of a firefly, like a flash of skin where the garment gapes. Flash back to where Alice Liddell's tiny bare shoulder pokes through a ripped shirt (fig. 12); where a loose shawl nearly falls below Mary Hillier's must-be-beautiful breast, but doesn't (plate 8); where Hannah's white hand begins to emerge from within the clutches of velvety blackness and beyond the too-long sleeve of a man's suit (fig. 23). Between the pages of this book, sexuality is a ribbon bookmark, a lost strand of tangled hair, a tear in the page, a papercut in a finger that traces its own fissure along the marbled bodies of Carroll's girl-children—along Cameron's iridescent babies, girls, and mothers—and back and around (underhandedly) along Hannah's "grener'd" palms, cracked and "ingrain'd with black lead . . . so that even scrubbing will not fetch it out." Such staging of sexuality—sexuality made to appear as disappearance—is seductive. These pictures have seduced me, and I, admittedly, have seduced them to my own pleasure.[9]

*Pleasures Taken: Performances of Sexuality
and Loss in Victorian Photographs*

The pleasure in what D. A. Miller refers to as Barthes's "embrace of a certain privation" is freely taken and re-given to the readers of my book, through a style that performs "the novelesque without the novel."[10] In other words, I take part-objects from novels—and here I would include history and theory, which is more often than not based on the same narrative structure as the novel—in order to sew a text of my own. I seek "a way of cutting, of perforating discourse *without rendering it meaningless.*"[11] "Narrativity is dismantled yet [I hope, I desire that] the story is still readable."[12] It is the pleasure that I take in tearing at the seams of more traditional academic garments. It is the pleasure that I take in wearing someone else's dress or trousers, only to poke out between its fasteners, like the paper mill girl that I adore. I pursue small things, dislodged from the whole, like buttons popped. The buttons, or a thread, or a bead, or a piece of satin lining, are the remainders left over from the plots of the big stories (histories, theories); but they make a text(ure) that I can wear, one that houses, rustles, and touches my own privation—a privation, which is, of course, much different than that of Barthes.

Privation is another term for loss or absence. Privation is, I think, a rather beautiful word, which hushes itself through its own sound and connoted (private) secrecy, and is able to blanket its harsher meaning of "the state of being deprived." For Miller, Barthes's "privation" was his homosexuality, which his cultural milieu afforded no proper place for. *Bringing Out Roland Barthes* develops what even Barthes's most ardent critics have refused to see: Barthes's gay sexuality. Miller, tenderly and convincingly, and even at times with displeasure, finds provocative and (often) sad glimmers of it in a host of Barthes's books—especially, of course, *Incidents,* but also *A Lover's Discourse, S / Z, Roland Barthes by Roland Barthes, Camera Lucida,* and *Empire of Signs.* Miller writes about this "once thought to be" invisible sexuality of Barthes, as if discovering a series of lost photographs that had been lovingly and shamefully tucked between the pages of these books—for the very purpose of giving evidence, of being found out—for promoting a discourse that could take place (possibly) only after Barthes's death . . . not unlike Munby's collection of photographs and diaries, which were kept secret until long after the deaths of both Hannah and her "Massa."

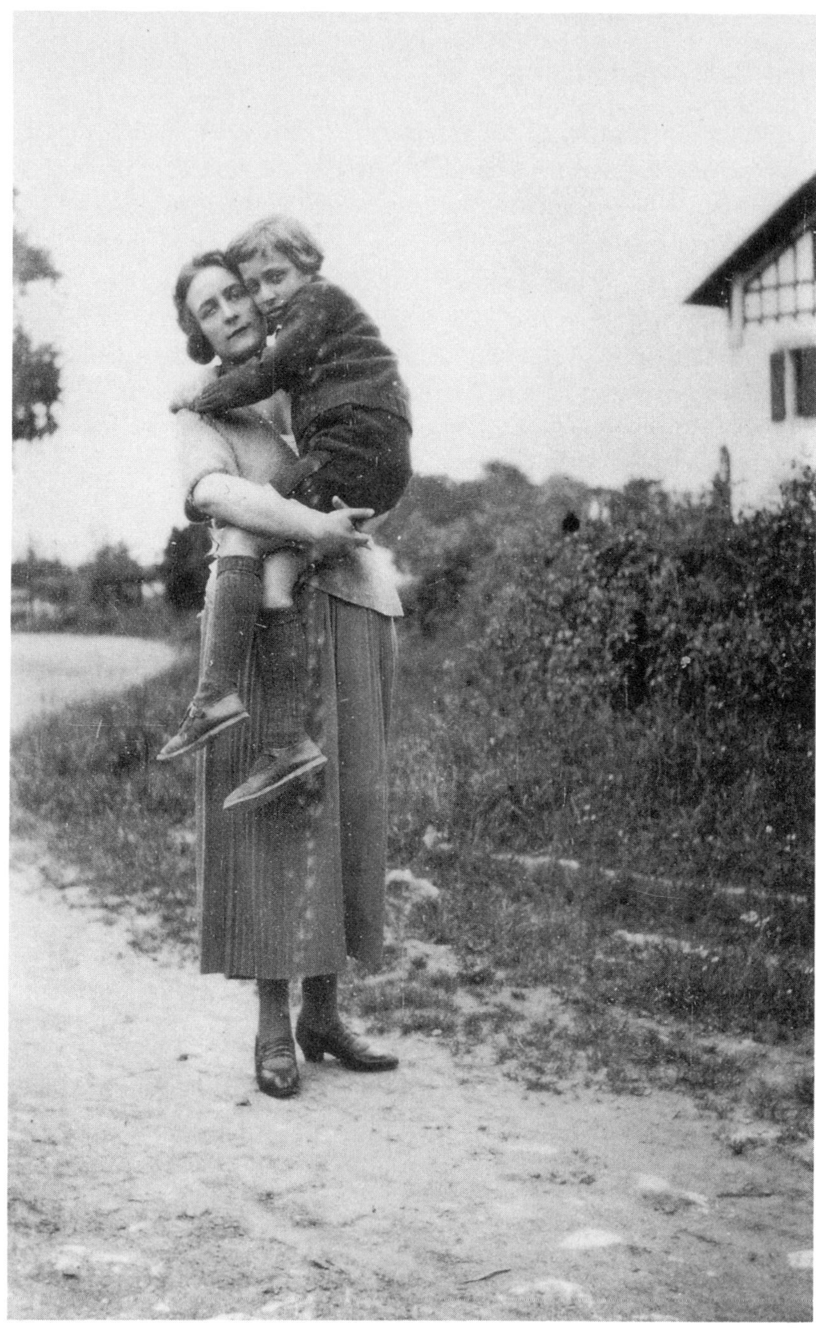

Figure 32. *"The Demand for Love"* (Roland Barthes with his mother, Henriette) c. 1923. (Courtesy of Éditions du Seuil, Paris)

But, *Pleasures Taken* is emphatically written from my privation. My intention is not to play Barthes. However, I do like playing in the same theater. Much to my own astonishment, and with secret (if not also guilty and perverse?) pleasure, it is really with his mother that I catch myself playing.

My own privation as a mother comes poignantly through when I come face to face with Barthes's beautiful mother, Henriette, in a famous photograph of the two (fig. 32). She is holding the not-yet "Barthes," the young (but not tiny) Roland, cheek to cheek. The picture appears, with a caption, "The demand for love," in *Roland Barthes by Roland Barthes*.[13] These words, which rest below the photograph, are simply said—but they seem to strike out at the reader, like an unsolicited confession. They are an invisible tear through the heart of the picture.

In looking at this image, I feel, in my own arms, the weight and the demand of a child who is growing and who is losing—losing what is labeled as childhood innocence, while growing to know things. This child must now already know death. (I dread that moment of knowledge, that turn that every child takes.) I see it in the eyes of Barthes-as-a-child and his mother, in the eyes of one of my two children, in my own eyes. The demand for love helps the mother of Barthes and the still-child-Barthes block what they both know, what my older child knows, what I know. Henriette willingly holds him despite his good size and long, trim legs: she might even demand it. It helps her to imagine that he doesn't know. (People are always telling my children that they are too big to be carried.)

Miller, as a gay man, whose text is an "album of moments in an imaginary 'homosexual encounter,' " which unclosets Roland Barthes (with love and all the frustration that comes with love), reads the photograph differently from the way I do:[14]

Consider . . . the photograph of Barthes as a child being held by his mother. The universalization attempted by his Lacanian caption— "The demand for love"—hardly succeeds in pacifying the scandal of this amazing image, in keeping it from being read (no less, or less certainly, than anything in Mapplethorpe) as the image of a certain gay male body. His ungainly lower limbs betray the boy, and not just because, as Barthes says of studio portraiture, "every ideal image, every social promotion begins by getting rid of the legs." They are too long for short pants, and too long to justify what the boy nonetheless evidently persists in wanting: to be carried by his mother. "But isn't it time he stood on his own two feet?" etc.[15]

For Miller, the part that has been left out is "the image of a certain gay male body." For me, the part that has been left out is different. For me, what is left out is the mother's privation. My privation. Whereas Miller's "phantasm of interlocution" is Barthes, and Barthes's "phantasm of interlocution" is his mother, my "phantasm of interlocution" is close to that of Barthes, but different. Like Barthes, I too am touched by his mother; I too encircle my arms around her neck and imagine the perfume of her rice powder (a smell for which I have no referent, but one in which I take pleasure in imagining). But, unlike Barthes, I partake in this touching and smelling as a mother. (I recognize that my pleasure verges on the auto-erotic.) I write of myself as a mother—as a mother who is drawn to the sexuality of Cameron's maternal space, as a mother who remembers her own child-sexuality and who now sees it in her own children, as a mother whose privation is a desire to be demanded—demanded for love. To "like the demand," Barthes tells us is to have a "maternal appetite."[16] (Like Hannah?)

For me the writer is not, as she is for Barthes, "someone who plays with his mother's body." When I write, I play with my own body, my own maternal body, in "order to glorify it, to embellish it, or in order to dismember it."[17] I play with (Barthes's) mother's body—the body that Miller describes as being at the (broken) heart of Barthes—not as a child, but as another mother. As a result, and with a strange conscious neurosis, Miller's writing on Barthes's "problem" with his mother, gives me pleasure:

> Worst of all, the adult Barthes, far from having the sense to be ashamed of his prolonged dependency, matter-of-factly proffers and "assumes" this evidence of his body's id, just as, with great and deliberate simplicity, he will later mourn his mother's death in perfect indifference to all charges of "overattachment." In fact, every image of Barthes, whether fully grown or all alone, materially reinscribes his mother in the characteristically dejected posture of his body, always ducking and drooping, as though always wanting, but never any longer able, to drop in her arms.[18]

I read this and find my arms are open and waiting, a site of privation, a site of desire.

A keepsake of a golden splash, a splash of river water, a white lace handkerchief, Lewis Carroll's white gloves, Evelyn Hatch printed and painted on curved glass, a strand of Cameron's (or Hillier's) hair, scratches in emulsion, kisses between women printed on paper, a halo, a child at a breast that has no milk, a wooden box, borrowed white gloves, a note from Hannah, thirteen-and-one-half-inch biceps, a heated blush—all are palpable fragments of the "novelesque without the novel" that I will never cease desiring . . . writing.

NOTES

Introduction: Pictures and Conversations

1   Alice Pleasance Liddell was a real child-friend of Carroll's who is treated more fully in chapter 1.

2   Lewis Carroll, *Through the Looking-Glass,* in *The Annotated Alice,* 269.

3   Lewis Carroll, *Alice's Adventures in Wonderland,* in *The Annotated Alice,* introduction and notes by Martin Gardner (New York: Meridian, 1960), 57.

4   Ibid., 72.

5   The date was 4 July 1862. The story was written down at Alice's request and given to her on 26 November 1864, as a Christmas present. This copy, entitled *Alice's Adventures Underground,* contained Carroll's own illustrations, and ended with an oval portrait (taken by Carroll) of Alice herself. *Alice's Adventures in Wonderland,* with illustrations by John Tenniel, was first published by Macmillan in 1865.

6   "We 'Other Victorians' " is the title of Michel Foucault's introduction to *The History of Sexuality,* trans. Robert Hurley (Pantheon: New York, 1978); originally published as *Historie de la Sexualité,* Vol. 1, *La Volenté de savoir* (Paris: Gallimard, 1976). The title of Foucault's introduction is particularly important to my concerns in that it is derived from Steven Marcus's book *The Other Victorians: A Study of Sexuality and Pornography in Mid-Nineteenth-Century England* (New York: Basic Books, 1964). Marcus's "other Victorians" are, of course, the prostitute, the hysteric, the pimp, etc. Foucault is interested in the ways in which "those 'other Victorians' . . . seem to have surreptitiously transferred the pleasures that are unspoken into the order of things that are counted. Words and gestures, quietly authorized, could be exchanged there at the going rate. Only in those places would untrammeled sex have a right to (safely insularized) forms of reality, and only to clandestine, circumscribed, and coded types of discourse. Everywhere else, modern puritanism imposed its triple edict of taboo, nonexistence, and silence" (p. 4). Similarly, Foucault imagines our current discourse to be in a similar "insularized" space; our

insistent discussion of sex (supposedly out in the open) is just as much a "repressed" discourse as the one that we have imagined that the Victorians spoke.

7   Anthony Lane wrote in a review of *Howard's End,* "Rule No. 1 of Merchant-Ivory productions: the past is free of wear and tear" (*New Yorker,* 15 November 1993, 114).

On a related note, Griselda Pollock has suggested a similar relationship between the representation of women in Victorian high art (Pre-Raphaelite painting and drawing) and our popular culture (film, advertisements). In both representational spaces she sees women represented through a fetishization of large eyes, narrow noses, and bee-stung lips, with an emphasis on sameness rather than difference. The look of these women, something that she calls "the cult of the beautiful face," is remarkably similar, both then and now. See *Vision and Difference: Femininity, Feminism and the Histories of Art* (London: Routledge, 1988). Pollock's writing prefigures what was yet to come: an overwhelming fetishization of Victorian culture itself that began in the 1990s. Suddenly, our bookstores and gift shops and even "Victoria's Secret" display postcards and/or calendars featuring women's faces as imaged by Dante Gabriel Rossetti, Edward Burne-Jones, et al.

8   As James R. Kincaid has written, "Photographing children before they slip away, before that 'bloom' can no longer be caught, is a need felt by Lewis Carroll, by J. M. Barrie, and, judging by the television and magazine advertisements of film companies like Kodak and Polaroid, by nearly everyone today." *Child-Loving: The Erotic Child and Victorian Culture* (New York: Routledge, 1992), 227–28.

9   Karin Calvert, *Children in the House: The Material Culture of Early Childhood* (Boston: Northeastern University Press, 1992), 7.

10   Peter Wollen, "Fire and Ice," *Photographies* 4 (1984). As quoted by Christian Metz, "Photography and Fetish," *October* 34 (Fall 1985): 84. Amy Ruth Buchanan has effectively used this dramatic phrase of Wollen's to discuss the child-images produced by a fascinating photographer of our times, Ralph Eugene Meatyard. See Buchanan, "Death, Decay, Masks and Play: Ralph Eugene Meatyard's Family Pictures," (Honors thesis, University of North Carolina, 1993).

11   Of course, the movie also shares this indexical relationship with photography. As Christian Metz has written, "Film and photography are close to each other, both are *prints* of real objects, prints left on a special surface by a combination of light and chemical action." "Photography and Fetish," 82.

12   Roland Barthes, *Camera Lucida: Reflections on Photography,* trans. Richard Howard (New York: Farrar, Straus and Giroux, 1981), 6. Originally published as *La chambre claire* (Paris: Éditions du Seuil, 1980).

13   Barthes, *Camera Lucida,* 53.

14   Ibid.

15   Ibid., 69–71.

16   Kincaid, *Child-Loving,* 279.

17   J. M Barrie, *Peter and Wendy,* vol. 9 of *The Works of J. M. Barrie, Peter Pan Edition* (New York: Charles Scribner's Sons, 1930), 253. In later editions the novel has been misleadingly retitled *Peter Pan. Peter Pan, or the Boy Who Would Not Grow Up* is the title of the play developed from the novel.

18   Barrie, *Peter and Wendy*, 37.

19   Barrie, "A Dedication" to *Peter Pan, or the Boy Who Would Not Grow Up*, in *The Uniform Edition of the Plays of J. M. Barrie* (New York: Scribner's Sons, 1928), xxix. As cited in Kincaid, *Child-Loving*, 278.

20   Kincaid, *Child-Loving*, 278.

1   Dream-Rushes: Lewis Carroll's Photographs of Little Girls

1   Vladimir Nabokov, *The Annotated Lolita*, edited, with preface, introduction, and notes by Alfred Appel Jr. (New York: McGraw-Hill, 1970), 54–55. Without drawing any conclusions, it is notable that it was Nabokov who translated *Alice in Wonderland* into Russian in 1923. Several authors have written about the literary connections between Carroll's writing and that of Nabokov. See, for example, Elizabeth Prioleau, "Humbert Humbert Through the *Looking-Glass*," in *Twentieth Century Literature* 21, no. 4 (December 1975), 428–37.

2   Helmut Gernsheim, *Lewis Carroll, Photographer* (New York: Dover, 1969), 18.

3   Morton Cohen, *Lewis Carroll, Photographer of Children: Four Nude Studies* (New York: Potter, 1978), 4, 30.

4   Here is one example of Carroll's banter, written to Gertrude Chataway on 13 April 1878 (Morton N. Cohen and Roger Lancelyn Green, eds. *The Letters of Lewis Carroll* [New York: Oxford University Press, 1979], 305–7):

> My dear Gertrude,
>
> As I have to wait here for 1/2 an hour, I have been studying Bradshaw (most things, you know, ought to be studied: even a trunk is studded with nails) and the result is that it seems I could come, any day next week, to Winchfield, so as to arrive there about 1: and that, by leaving Winchfield again about 1/2 past 6, I could reach Guildford again for dinner. The next question is *how far is it from Winchfield to Rotherwick?* Now do not deceive me, you wretched child! If it is more than 100 miles, I can't come to see you, and there's no use talking about it. If it is less, the next question is, *how much less?* These are serious questions, and you must be as serious as a judge in answering them. There mustn't be a smile in your pen, or a wink in your ink (perhaps you'll say "there can't be a *wink* in *ink:* but there *may* be *ink* in a *wink*"—but this is trifling: You mustn't make jokes like that when I tell you to be serious) while you write to Guildford and answer those 2 questions. You might as well tell me at the same time whether you are still living at Rotherwick—and whether you are at home—and whether you get my letter—whether you're still a child, or a grown-up-person—and whether you're going to the sea-side next summer—and anything else (except the alphabet and the multiplication-table) that you happen to know. I send you 1.0000000 kisses, and am
>
> Your loving friend,
> C. L. Dodgson

5   James R. Kincaid, "Alice's Invasion of Wonderland," *PMLA* 88, no. 1 (January 1973): 93.

6   Cohen, *Lewis Carroll, Photographer of Children,* 5.

7   Ibid., 31.

8   Michel Foucault, *History of Sexuality* 1:24.

9   Cohen, *Lewis Carroll, Photographer of Children,* 6–7.

10   Ibid., 5.

11   I use the date 1879 on the authority of the *Oxford English Dictionary,* although it is actually not until the fourth edition of *Clinical Lectures* (1889) that the passage that uses and discusses the word "sexuality" appears.

12   J. Matthews Duncan, *Clinical Lectures on the Diseases of Women,* 4th ed. (London: J. and A. Churchill, 1889), 223.

13   Sigmund Freud, "The Sexual Life of Human Beings" standard ed., vol. 16 (London: Hogarth Press, 1953–74), 311.

14   Pollock, *Vision and Difference,* 127–28.

15   Freud, "Sexual Life of Human Beings," 312.

16   Gernsheim, *Lewis Carroll, Photographer,* 65.

17   Three of the four nudes have been painted over. The fourth is actually a watercolor *only*; probably made from laying a piece of watercolor paper over one of Carroll's photographs. The photograph of Evelyn is the most *photographic* and the most sexually explicit.

18   Cohen, *Lewis Carroll, Photographer of Children,* 32.

19   Not only is the girl-sexuality of the photograph taboo—but also the painting over of the scientifically (as opposed to artistically) produced photographic image. Images like this one of Evelyn Hatch were uncharacteristic of Carroll's work; for he preferred his photographs to be clean, sharp, precise, and free of artistic blurs.

20   Nina Auerbach, "Falling Alice, Fallen Women, and Victorian Dream Children," in *Romantic Imprisonment: Women and Other Glorified Outcasts* (New York: Columbia University Press, 1986), 168. The essay first appeared in a special issue of *English Language Notes* 20, no. 2 (December 1982), and then later in *Soaring with the Dodo,* ed. Edward Guiliano and James R. Kincaid (Charlottesville: University Press of Virginia, 1982).

21   Nina Auerbach, *Woman and the Demon: The Life of a Victorian Myth* (Cambridge: Harvard University Press), 1982.

22   Nina Auerbach, Introduction, to *Romantic Imprisonment* (New York: Columbia University Press, 1986), xx.

23   Ibid., xxi.

24   Rozsika Parker and Griselda Pollock, *Old Mistresses: Women, Art and Ideology* (New York: Pantheon, 1981). See especially chapter 4, "Painted Ladies," 114–33.

25   Ibid., 116.

26   Nancy Armstrong has dealt with the very interesting and conflicting ideas of occidentalism that arose during this period of orientalism, as reflected in the anxieties found in *Alice's Adventures in Wonderland* (and elsewhere), as well as in a selection of

Victorian photographs. Nancy Armstrong, "The Occidental Alice," *Differences* 2, no. 2 (1990):3–40.

27   Hélène Cixous, "Introduction to Lewis Carroll's *Through the Looking-Glass* and *The Hunting of the Snark*," *New Literary History* 13, no. 2 (Winter 1982): 234.

28   Laurel Bradley, "From Eden to Empire: John Everett Millais's *Cherry Ripe*," *Victorian Studies* 34, no. 2 (Winter 1991): 187.

29   Granted, pubic hair has rarely been shown in any female nudes before the twentieth century; the genital region is traditionally concealed by a hand, or a fan, or by the twisting of the body. But in these paintings of the Victorian nude, the smooth, hairless pubic region, clean as a whistle, is flaunted.

30   "My mind has been considerably exercised this season by the exhibition of Alma-Tadema's nude Venus . . . [there might] be artistic reasons which justify such public exposure of the female form . . . In the case of the nude of an old master much allowance has been made . . . for old masters it might be assumed knew no better . . . but for a living artist to exhibit a life-size, life-like, almost photographic representation of a beautiful naked woman strikes my inartistic mind as somewhat if not very mischievous" (The Bishop of Carlisle as quoted in Christopher Wood, *Olympian Dreamers: Victorian Classical Painters, 1860–1914* [London: Constable, 1983], 115).

31   Abigail Solomon-Godeau, "The Legs of the Countess," *October* 39 (Winter 1986): 103.

32   John Ruskin's failed marriage is one of the most famous of such *animal* stories told. Ruskin, an acquaintance of Carroll, Alice's famed art teacher (who appears in *Alice* as the Old Conger Eel, the "drawling master" who taught "drawling," "stretching," and "Fainting in coils"), is another often cited player in the Victorian "cult of the little girl." Ruskin, a man of letters who wrote many letters to young girls, fell in love with the "unmarked" Effie Gray (who later, in fact, became Effie Millais) when she was thirteen. She, like Alice, was also a recipient of her own fairy tale, Ruskin's *King of the Golden River.* Despite their early love, the relationship turned sour when the two were finally wed and Ruskin was faced with Effie's matured body. Though we cannot be certain that his "disgust" for Effie's body came as a result of her womanly curves and a spot of pubic hair, Mary Lutyens has reached this conclusion. (Mary Lutyens, *Effie in Venice* [London: John Murray, 1965], see esp. 20–21). Ruskin soon divorced Effie Gray and later fell in love with a ten-year-old girl named Rose La Touche.

      Stranger still was Ruskin's long and drawn-out epistolary seduction of Kate Greenaway, the children's author and illustrator. Surprisingly, his interest was not in *her* but in her insipid drawings of little "dollies." (The same critic who brought Turner his fame!) Embarrassingly enough, Ruskin even requested the drawn girls to be sent without clothes(!): "As we've got so far as taking off hats, I trust we may in time get to take off just a little more—say mittens—and then—perhaps—even shoes! and—(for fairies) even . . . stockings—and then— . . . Will you—(it's all for your own good—!) makes her (a drawing of a sylph) stand up and then draw her for me without a cap—and without her shoes,—(because of the heels) and without her mittens, and without her—frock and frills? And let me see exactly how tall she is—and how—round. It will be so good of and for you—And to and for me" (Rodney Engen, *Kate Greenaway* [New York: Schocken, 1981], 93–94).

33 See especially the essays by Laqueur, Poovey, and Schiebinger in *The Making of the Modern Body: Sexuality and Society in the Nineteenth Century,* ed. Thomas Laqueur and Catherine Gallagher (Berkeley and Los Angeles: University of California, 1987), as well as Elaine Showalter, *The Female Malady* (New York: Pantheon, 1985).

34 For example, John Pudney (more of a good storyteller than a reliable narrator) writes the following before launching into the topic of Carroll's there/not-there sexuality (a trait that Carroll is often assigned, as if he too were a girl-child): "Alice was the first and greatest of these love affairs with maidens, unformed women, little girls of nursery age, creatures in whose presence he lost his stammer, smelled the breeze across the cornfields of Daresbury and found the reality of Wonderland" (*Lewis Carroll and His World* [New York: Charles Scribner's Sons, 1976], 67–68).

35 When Lewis Carroll stammered, he pronounced his real name as Mr. Do-Do-Dodgson. According to Gardner, this is the explanation behind the Dodo character who appears amongst the "queer-looking party" at the Caucus-race. *The Annotated Alice,* 44 n. 7. Introduction and notes by Gardner.

36 Speculation over why Carroll gave up photography in 1880 is rife. Cohen has argued that Carroll abandoned his favorite hobby for two reasons: the victory of the new dry plate process over the wet collodion process that Carroll preferred, and Carroll's desire to devote more time to scholarship in order to finish his many projects before he died (Cohen, *Lewis Carroll, Photographer of Children,* 22–25). Gernsheim, in contrast, contends—after discussing the situation with many of Carroll's models in their old age—that "despite his precaution of photographing girls in the nude only in the presence of the mother or another adult woman, a scandal did develop in Oxford in 1880, which decided Lewis Carroll to abandon his hobby altogether. This bears out my feeling that the reason for his decision lay outside the field of photo-technique" (Gernsheim, *Lewis Carroll, Photographer,* v).

37 Deborah Gorham, "The 'Maiden Tribute of Modern Babylon' Re-Examined: Child Prostitution and the Idea of Childhood in Late-Victorian England," *Victorian Studies* 21, no. 3 (Spring 1978): 353–79.

38 The age of consent was raised to thirteen in 1875. Prior to that year, the age of consent had been twelve, which reflected legislation of the thirteenth century.

39 Monique Witting, "The Category of Sex," *Feminist Issues* 2, no. 2 (Fall 1982): 64–68.

40 Similarly, Judith Walkowitz has explored Josephine Butler's campaign against the Contagious Diseases Acts, in which Butler fought against the inevitability of prostitution as a cultural institution while still maintaining, importantly, that women had a right not to be harassed and even to choose to prostitute themselves. Walkowitz's discussion of Butler demonstrates what Foucault has suggested—that sexuality was *not* repressed in the Victorian world but was in fact at the center of their

discourse. See Judith Walkowitz, *Prostitution and Victorian Society: Women, Class and the State* (Cambridge: Cambridge University Press, 1980).

41 Gorham, " 'Maiden Tribute of Modern Babylon' Re-Examined," 363–64.

42 Wittig, "Category of Sex," 67.

43 Barthes, *Roland Barthes by Roland Barthes,* 132.

44 Louis Marin, *Utopiques: jeux d'espaces* (Paris: Les Éditions de Minuit, 1973), 27–28. The translation is from Louis Marin, *Utopics: The Semiological Play of Textual Space,* trans. Robert A. Vollrath (Atlantic Highlands, N.J.: Humanities Press International, 1990), 12. (Originally published by Humanities Press in 1984, under a slightly different title: *Utopics: Spacial Play.*)

45 I owe this phrase to Eva-Lynn Jagoe.

46 Carroll and many other critics of the day were very critical of Cameron's technique (a topic I elaborate on in chapter 2); they felt that she was not being *true* to the medium. (However, Carroll was a great fan of Lady Hawarden's *clear* photographs.) Gernsheim writes of one of the occasions when Carroll and Cameron met: "In August 1864, when he [Carroll] was on holiday at Freshwater, Isle of Wight, they spent a happy evening at Mrs. Cameron's house looking at each others' photographs. She had then been photographing for only a few months, but characteristically already spoke of her pictures 'as if they were a triumph in art,' as Lewis Carroll records with a touch of mockery, adding more critically, 'Some are very picturesque, some merely hideous. *She* wishes she could have had some of *my* subjects to do *out* of focus—and *I* expressed an analogous wish with regard to some of *her* subjects" (i.e., to do them in focus).

47 Of course, the same is true for Carroll. His distaste for naked little boys and his penchant for naked little girls comes through in many of letters. As he wrote in one: "I confess I do *not* admire naked boys in pictures. They always seem to me to need *clothes:* whereas one hardly sees why the lovely forms of girls should *ever* be covered up!" (Cohen and Green, eds., *Letters of Lewis Carroll,* 947). It seems that utopic childhood is almost always gendered feminine—even in complicated cases like Barrie's *Peter Pan.* The fact that Peter is usually played by a young woman in the movie and stage productions is but one general example of this tendency to gender childhood as feminine. Interestingly enough, Barrie's own photographs of the "real" little Peter (Davies) and all of his brothers were often nudes shot from the back. See the photographs in Andrew Birkin's *J. M. Barrie and the Lost Boys* (London: Constable, 1979).

48 Carroll Smith-Rosenberg, *Disorderly Conduct* (New York: Oxford University Press, 1985).

49 Carroll, *Through the Looking-Glass,* 256–57.

50 Consider the following letter written by Carroll to one of his few child-friends to remain a friend past puberty: "I always feel specially grateful to friends who, like you, have given me a child-friendship and a woman-friendship. About nine out of ten, I think, of my child friendships get ship wrecked at the critical point, 'where the stream and river meet,' and the child-friends, once so affectionate, become

uninteresting acquaintances, whom I have no wish to set eyes on again" (Stuart Dodgson Collingwood, *The Life and Letters of Lewis Carroll* [London: T. F. Unwin, 1898], 367–69).

51 Roland Barthes, "The Photographic Message," in *Image / Music / Text,* trans. Stephen Heath (New York: Hill and Wang, 1977), 19.

52 Barthes writes: "The photograph is literally an emanation of the referent. From a real body, which was there, proceed radiations which ultimately touch me, who am here; the duration of the transmission is insignificant; the photograph of the missing being, as Sontag says, will touch me like the delayed rays of a star" (*Camera Lucida,* 80–81).

53 Barthes, *Camera Lucida,* 3.

54 Ibid., 31 and 32.

55 Ben Maddow, *Faces* (Boston: New York Graphic Society, 1977), 22. As quoted in Jan B. Gordon and Edward Guiliano, "From Victorian Textbook to Ready-Made: Lewis Carroll and the Black Art," in *Soaring with the Dodo,* 12.

It is notable that Carroll was a great fan of the theater and was a close friend of Ellen Terry; a few Carroll scholars have suggested that they were romantically inclined toward each other. In any case, it was through Terry that Carroll gave support to many girl-actresses.

56 Gernsheim, *Lewis Carroll, Photographer,* 13.

57 Similarly, Auerbach reads Carroll's photograph of Alice Price "caught" holding a doll face to face as a mockery of proper motherhood; she comments, "The pensive sensuality of the child's pose, the erotic hunger of her expression, become more apparent to us as we look, until the doll becomes less a thing to nourish than a thing to eat" (Auerbach, *Romantic Imprisonment,* 167).

58 Metz, "Photography and Fetish," 81.

59 Phyllis Greenacre, "The Character of Dodgson as revealed in the Writings of Carroll," in *Aspects of Alice,* ed. Robert Phillips (London: Victor Gollancz, 1972), 316.

60 Jeffrey Stern, *Lewis Carroll's Library* (Charlottesville: University Press of Virginia, 1981), 79.

61 Susan Stewart, *On Longing: Narratives of the miniature, the gigantic, the souvenir, the collection* (Baltimore: John Hopkins University Press, 1984), 65.

62 Metz, "Photography and Fetish," 84.

63 Cixous, "Introduction to Lewis Carroll's *Through the Looking-Glass* and *The Hunting of the Snark,*" 240.

64 Ruth Bernard Yeazell, "Podsnappery, Sexuality, and the English Novel," *Critical Inquiry* 9 (December 1982): 343.

65 Carroll, *Through the Looking-Glass,* 247.

66 Metz, "Photography and Fetish," 82.

67 Ibid., 83.

68 Ibid., 84.

69 Cohen and Green, eds., *Letters of Lewis Carroll,* 1007.

70   Cohen, *Lewis Carroll, Photographer of Children,* 29. (This letter is omitted from Cohen's *Letters of Lewis Carroll.*)

71   While Rejlander also photographed "simulated" poor children, they were represented sentimentally and without the sexuality of Carroll's "Beggar Alice."

72   Gillian Wagner, *Barnardo* (London: Weidenfeld and Nicolson, 1979), 140.

73   The situation is not that different from Stead's own manipulation of Eliza Armstrong in order to write the sensational "Maiden Tribute of Babylon."

74   Stern, *Lewis Carroll's Library,* 174.

II To Make Mary: Julia Margaret Cameron's Photographs of Altered Madonnas

1   Those familiar with the photography of the period may be reminded of the photographs of Hannah Cullwick, a Victorian maid of all work, collected by (but not taken by) her secret lover, eventual husband, and sometimes employer, Arthur Munby. See chapter 3.

2   Cameron began photography in 1864.

3   Gernsheim, *Julia Margaret Cameron,* 84.

4   Ibid., 82.

5   Mike Weaver, *Whisper of the Muse: The Overstone Album and Other Photographs,* exhibition catalog for the J. Paul Getty Museum, Malibu, 1986. Almost all of the Madonna photographs discussed in this chapter can be found in the Overstone Album. Weaver shares with Gernsheim some doubts about the "greatness" of these early Mary pictures: "The photographs in the Overstone Album come from the first eighteen months of Mrs. Cameron's work and are not yet of the very highest quality" (15). Weaver's concerns are partly technical, as are Gernsheim's (Cameron's blurry, messy photographs were quite unorthodox); the *beauty* of Cameron's "careless" technique is a topic that is addressed throughout this chapter.

6   Gernsheim, *Julia Margaret Cameron,* 21.

7   Ibid. The "beggar girl," to whom Gernsheim refers, was Mary Ryan. Ryan eventually became one of Cameron's parlormaids and photographic models, not unlike Hillier herself.

8   Gernsheim, *Julia Margaret Cameron,* 38.

9   Ibid., 21.

10   Virginia Woolf, realizing the effective and overblown stage directing performed by her Aunt Julia (Cameron was Woolf's great aunt), has captured Cameron's antics in a play, *Freshwater: A Comedy,* ed. with a preface by Lucio P. Ruotolo (New York: Harcourt Brace Jovanovich, 1976).

The following excerpt from the play is worth quoting (11–12). It gives a good sense of Cameron's performative life, with great attention to historical detail, even if it is told with exaggerated irony. The scene is set in a studio. Mrs. Cameron has been washing Mr. Cameron's head. Ellen Terry, the famous Victorian actress, has been posing for the painter George Frederick Watts as Modesty at the feet of Mammon. Mrs. Cameron has suddenly gotten the urge to photograph Terry with

Tennyson, with Terry playing the part of Tennyson's Muse. Terry is questioning the newly assigned role of Muse, because she still feels herself to be Modesty. Mary is, of course, Cameron's maid, Mary Hillier:

> MRS. C.: Yes. But now you're the Muse. But the Muse must have wings. [MRS. C. *rummages frantically in a chest. She flings out various garments on the floor.*] Towels, sheets, pyjamas, trousers, dressing gowns, braces—braces but no wings. Trousers but no wings. What a satire upon modern life! Braces but no wings! [MRS. C. *goes to the door and shouts:*] Wings! Wings! Wings! What d'you say, Mary. There are no wings? Then kill the turkey! [MRS. C. *shuffles among the clothes. She exits.*]

11 Cameron's maiden name was Pattle, and as the story is always told, all of the Pattle sisters were beauties, save for Julia Margaret, who more than made up for it through her eccentricities and talent.

12 Laura Troubridge, *Memories and Reflections* (London: Heinemann, 1925), as quoted in Gernsheim, *Julia Margaret Cameron,* 30.

13 Anne Thackeray, letter from Freshwater to Walter Senior, Easter 1865, as reproduced in Hester Thackeray Ritchie, ed., *Thackeray and His Daughter: The Letters and Journals of Anne Thackeray, with Many Letters of William Makepeace Thackeray* (London: Harper and Brothers, 1924), 138. Thackeray later became Lady Ritchie, and was the eldest daughter of William Makepeace Thackeray. The Thackerays ran in the same intellectual circles as the Camerons. For more on the relationship between the Thackerays and the Camerons, see Hardwicke Knight, "Anne Isabella Thackeray and Julia Margaret Cameron," *History of Photography* 7, no. 3 (July–September 1983): 247–48 and Ann Wilsher and Benjamin Spear, " 'A Dream of Fair Ladies': Mrs. Cameron Disguised," *History of Photography* 7, no. 2 (April–June 1983): 118–20. Although the latter article is quite informative in terms of a Cameron-like character that appears in Anne Thackeray's novel *From an Island* (1877), the essay is not about Cameron's lived disguises within a *performative* life, as its title might suggest.

14 Gernsheim, *Julia Margaret Cameron,* 41.

15 The common use of the phrase "angel in the house," is, of course, indebted to Coventry Patmore's famous verse-sequence, *The Angel in the House.* The first part of the book was published in 1854, with subsequent parts published in 1856, 1860, and 1863. In its entirety, *The Angel in the House* is a long (and very dull) narrative of the courtship and marriage of Honoria, "whose unselfish grace, gentleness, simplicity and nobility reveal that she is not only a pattern Victorian Lady but almost literally an angel on earth." Sandra M. Gilbert and Susan Gubar, *The Madwoman in the Attic: The Woman Writer and the Nineteenth-Century Imagination* (New Haven, Conn.: Yale University Press, 1979), 22. Honoria, selfless and dedicated to the male gender, reinforces Patmore's sentiments that "Man must be pleased; but him to please / Is woman's pleasure." Coventry Patmore, *The Angel in the House* (London: George Bell and Sons, 1892), 73. In an age of religious doubt, the period's embracement of the "angel in the house" enabled characters like Honoria to become objects of worship and "patterns" for Victorian ladies at home. And indeed,

Honoria is like a (displaced) virgin in her purity and "vestal grace," even after marriage (*Angel in the House,* 205). For, even after having been "won" by her husband, Honoria is still so pure that she still does not really belong to him: she belongs to the heavens. As Honoria's husband confesses, ". . . this Temple keeps its shrine / Sacred to Heaven; because, in short, / She's not and never can be mine" (*Angel in the House,* 206).

16   Julia Margaret Cameron, from a letter to Sir John Herschel (31 December 1864). As quoted in Gernsheim's *Julia Margaret Cameron,* 14.

17   The question as to whether Cameron's pictures were intentionally out of focus or merely a result of her inexperience and / or what Gernsheim has called her "slovenliness" (*Julia Margaret Cameron,* 73) has been hotly debated since her first exhibitions. Gernsheim is particularly critical of the early photographs from 1864–65 (her pictures improved *technically* later in her career, though the wooliness would always remain) and has "established that the softness of Mrs. Cameron's early photographs was largely due to her faulty lens and slapdash manipulation" (*Julia Margaret Cameron,* 70). In the end, Gernsheim concludes that the blurs, the blotches, and the cracks that appear in her pictures cannot be read as intentional and cannot be seen as adding to the beauty of her pictures. Though a great lover of Cameron, Gernsheim writes with near irritation that "it was a great misfortune that Mrs. Cameron's manual dexterity did not equal her artistic vision. Technical virtuosity by itself is certainly not enough, but equally one can hardly acclaim as a masterpiece a work, however artistic, that falls short of reasonable technical quality. The carelessness with which Mrs. Cameron sometimes handled her pictures unfortunately does not add to our appreciation of them" (*Julia Margaret Cameron,* 72–73).

Clearly, my feelings are radically different from Gernsheim's. Nearly all of the images that I discuss in this chapter are from the early years (1864–65) and suffer the most from what Gernsheim as termed "misfortunes." These early Madonna pictures are the photographs I have always been the most drawn to; they are the ones that, for me, are by far the most beautiful.

All things considered, I find debates over artistic intentionality to be extremely tiresome, both for their unanswerability and for the ways in which they detract from the finished work. The question of intentionality is by no means particular to photography: it has always been a "problem" in the discipline of art history. (However, because photography is more connected to science than other visual mediums, it is more vulnerable to suspicions based on technical grounds.) One must not overlook the fact that women and other "naïves" have been historically read as more unconscious of what they are up to. Possibly Cameron's own son summed up my feelings best, nearly a century ago, when he said that "in photography, as in other art, the process is nothing, the final result everything." Marie A. Belloc, "Interview with Mr. H. Hay Herschel Cameron," *Woman at Home* 4 (1896–97): 586.

18   Gernsheim, *Julia Margaret Cameron,* 70.

19   In particular, Dante Gabriel Rossetti's *Beata Beatrix* (1864–70) is often read as

being influenced by Cameron's picture of Mary Hillier entitled *Call, I follow, I follow—let me die* (c. 1867). The connection is plausible, given the fact that Rossetti was quite enthusiastic about Cameron's portraiture. For more on the reciprocity between Cameron's work and the Pre-Raphaelites, see Michael Bartram, *The Pre-Raphaelite Camera: Aspects of Victorian Photography* (Boston: Little, Brown, 1985), esp. 129–33.

Cameron's influence on photography itself is most clearly felt in the work of some of the American pictorial photographers, whose style and subject choices often relate to Cameron. Gertrude Käsebier immediately comes to mind, specifically soft-focus, blurry images such as *Blessed Art Thou Among Women* (1899), *The Manger* (c. 1899), *The Heritage of Motherhood* (c. 1905), and *Mother and Child Wearing Kimonas* (c. 1900), etc. Like Cameron, Käsebier made the subject of mother and child a prominent theme in her oeuvre and in her life. "A woman," she said, "never reaches her fullest development until she's a mother" (as quoted in William Innes Homer's catalog essay for *A Pictorial Heritage: The Photographs of Gertrude Käsebier* [Wilmington: University of Delaware and the Delaware Art Musem, 1979], 26–27). Also of interest would be the images by the pictorialist Imogen Cunningham of her artist friend Clare Shepard cast as the Goddess or Adored One. An image like *The Dream* (c. 1910), alternately titled *Nei-san-Koburi,* gives evidence of Cunningham's enthusiasm for Pre-Raphaelite painting and literature. This frontal portrait calls to mind an image such as Rossetti's *Beata Beatrix,* and thereby through proximity Cameron's *Call, I follow, I follow—let me die.* Also of interest is the fact that Cameron took a picture entitled *The Dream* (1869), known also as *Daydream,* that is a hazy portrait of her maid / model (Mary Hillier). Indeed, both artists share in their *Dreams* a proclivity toward displaying beautiful women shimmering in a foggy light that registers their respective models as mysterious objects of a secular / divine religion. Of final interest is the work of the pictorialist F. Holland Day, whose fuzzy close-up photographs of himself as Christ prove to be interesting companions of Cameron's close-up pictures of Madonnas and Madonna-types. While F. Holland Day also *pictured* women (some, such as *Mother Nursing Child* [1905], were heavily influenced by his friend Gertrude Käsebier), he is better known for his pictures of beautiful young men cast as types taken from the Bible and Greek myths, with others simply cast as their stunning selves. Indeed, Day's lovely and erotically charged pictures of feminized masculinity can be seen as mirroring Cameron's pictures of young women, which are not without their own (veiled) erotic charges.

20   See Richard A. Cohen's introduction to *Face to Face with Levinas,* ed. Richard A. Cohen (Albany: State University of New York Press, 1986), 7.

21   Emmanuel Levinas, *Otherwise Than Being or Beyond Existence,* trans. A. Lingis (The Hague: Martinus Nijhoff, 1981), 90.

22   Nadar addresses this in his discussion of Balzac and the daguerreotype: "According to Balzac's theory, all physical bodies are made up entirely of layers of ghostlike images, an infinite number of leaflike skins laid one on top of the other. Since Balzac believed man was incapable of making something material from an apparition, from

something impalpable—that is, creating something from nothing—he concluded that every time someone had his photograph taken, one of the spectral layers was removed from the body and transferred to the photograph. Repeated exposures entailed the unavoidable loss of subsequent ghostly layers, that is, the very essence of life." Nadar, "My Life as a Photographer," trans. Thomas Repensek, *October* 5 (Summer 1978): 9.

23   The ways in which the veiled hand exaggerates touch was pointed out to me by Jo DeDecker.

24   Metz, "Photography and Fetish," 84.

25   Mark Taylor, *Altarity* (Chicago: University of Chicago Press, 1987), xxviii.

26   Wendy Martin, "Anne Bradstreet's Poetry: A Study of Subversive Piety," in *Shakespeare's Sisters,* ed. Susan Gubar and Sandra M. Gilbert (Bloomington: Indiana University Press, 1979), 19–31.

27   See Londa Schiebinger, "Skeletons in the Closet: The First Illustrations of the Female Skeleton in Eighteenth-Century Anatomy," in *Making of the Modern Body,* 42–82. Schiebinger notes that what had begun in the eighteenth century as a "flood of medical literature on sex differences did not subside in the course of the nineteenth century" (63). And that "man" (white and European) continued in the nineteenth century to be the measure of all others: women, children, and primitives. It was in 1829 that skeletons of man, woman, and child were brought together (by John Barclay) for the first time "for sake of comparison." Barclay argued that woman's distinguishing characteristic was her enlarged pelvis.

28   Thomas Laqueur, "Orgasm, Generation, and the Politics of Reproductive Biology," in *Making of the Modern Body,* 1–41. The verse that Laqueur quotes is as follows:

> though they of different sexes be,
> Yet on the whole they are the same as we,
> For those that have the strictest searchers been,
> Find women are but men turned outside in. (2)

29   Stephen Heath, *The Sexual Fix* (London: Macmillan, 1982), 29.

30   Sigmund Freud, "Femininity," in *The Standard Edition of the Complete Psychological Works,* ed. James Strachey (London: Hogarth Press, 1953–74), vol. 22, 117–18.

31   Julia Kristeva, "Stabat Mater," in *The Kristeva Reader,* ed. Toril Moi (New York: Columbia University Press, 1986), 161.

32   Bram Dijkstra, *Idols of Perversity: Fantasies of Feminine Evil in Fin-de-Siècle Culture* (New York: Oxford University Press, 1986), 19.

33   "Alone of all her sex" refers to Marina Warner's book, *Alone of All Her Sex: The Myth and the Cult of the Virgin Mary* (London: Weidenfield, 1976). Warner's text demonstrates the complex uniqueness of the Madonna: a singular feminine figure who stands without sexuality and without death and therefore stands alone among women.

34   Catherine Clément, *The Lives and Legends of Jacques Lacan,* trans. Arthur Goldhammer (New York: Columbia University Press, 1983), 83.

35   See Auerbach, *Woman and the Demon,* 70–72. Significantly, Auerbach has observed

that it was in the nineteenth century that painters began regularly portraying angels as female. Auerbach argues that the Victorian cult of the "angel in the house" can be associated with the disappearance of God, with its theological imagery arising in part from a displacement of traditional metaphors for the sacred onto the secular figure of the woman. Though she offers scant evidence for her claim that there were no visual representations of female angels before the nineteenth century, it is true that our contemporary associations of the angel with the feminine / female (quiet, demure, nonthreatening) suggest the validity of her case. Indeed, recent angels are in striking contrast to the "original" archangels, such as Gabriel, who were representations of strength and mobility. (Gabriel, from Hebrew, means "God is [my] strength.")

36   Queen Victoria wrote the following to her eldest and pregnant daughter, Victoria, in 1858: "I had 9 times for 8 months to bear those above-named enemies and misery [aches, sufferings, enjoyments to give up, constant precautions to take] (besides many duties) and I own it tried me sorely; one feels so pinned down— one's wings clipped—in fact, at the best . . . only half oneself." Erna Olafson Hellerstein, Leslie Parker Hume, and Karen M. Offen, eds., *Victorian Women: A Documentary of Women's Lives in Nineteenth-Century England, France, and the United States* (Palo Alto, Calif.: Stanford University Press, 1981), 209.

37   Cameron even photographed Emily Peacock as *The Angel in the House* for Patmore in 1873. Patmore himself wrote a (mostly enthusiastic) article on Cameron's pictures, in which he indicated that "Mrs. Cameron was the first person who had the wit to see that her mistakes were her success, and henceforward to make her portraits systematically out of focus." Coventry Patmore, "Mrs. Cameron's Photographs," *Macmillan Magazine* 13 (January 1866): 230.

38   Hellerstein, Hume, and Offen, eds., *Victorian Women*, 123. Gernsheim, *Julia Margaret Cameron*, 78.

39   For an excellent discussion of the maternal conflict represented by Berthe Morisot, see Linda Nochlin, "Morisot's *Wet Nurse:* The Construction of Work and Leisure in Painting," in Nochlin's *Women, Art and Power: And Other Essays* (New York: Harper and Row, 1988), 37–56.

40   Julia Margaret Cameron, "Annals of My Glass House" (1874) (Gernsheim, *Cameron,* 180). "Annals of My Glass House" (1874) was never completed. It was first published, posthumously, in a catalog that accompanied an exhibition of Cameron's work shown at the Camera Gallery, London, April 1889. "Annals of My Glass House" was later reprinted in *Photographic Journal* (London) (July 1927): 296–301. The text is reprinted in Helmut Gernsheim's *Julia Margaret Cameron, Her Life and Photographic Work* (New York: Aperture, 1975) and Mike Weaver's *Julia Margaret Cameron, 1815–1879* (London: Herbert Press, 1984). The manuscript of the "Annals" is in the collection of the Royal Photographic Society of Great Britain, Bath, England.

41   Kristeva, "Stabat Mater," 178.

42   Rosalind Krauss, "Tracing Nadar," *October* 5 (Summer 1978): 33–34.

43   In "Annals of My Glass House," Cameron writes enthusiastically about the memory

of photographing Annie as *My First Success:* "I was half-way through a beautiful picture when a splutter of laughter from one of the children lost me that picture, and less ambitious now, I took one child alone, appealing to her feelings and telling her of the waste of poor Mrs. Cameron's chemicals and strength if she moved. The appeal had its effect, and I now produced a picture which I called 'My First Success.' I was in a transport of delight. I ran all over the house to search for gifts for the child. I felt as if she entirely had made the picture. I printed, toned, fixed and framed it and presented it to her father that same day" (Gernsheim, *Julia Margaret Cameron,* 181).

44   Dan Meinwald, *Memento Mori: Death in Nineteenth-Century Photography,* exhibition catalog for the California Museum of Photography, University of California, Riverside, 1990, 8.

45   Cameron as far as I know, photographed an *actual* deceased child only once: *Study of a Dead Child* (1869). In this picture, sleep is suggested because the child is in bed—the child more than likely died in bed—but there is no artful play with the medium that allowed Cameron to speak her captivating language of contradictions. The stonelike body appears almost grotesque: the feet have mysteriously become oversized; likewise the body has become stretched.

46   I thank Amy Ruth Buchanan for introducing me to the work of Sally Mann.

47   Postmortem photographs in the Victorian period were meant to be viewed privately within the confines of the family. To view a photograph of a person's deathbed outside of the family was generally taboo; the only exception being the deathbed of a prominent person. Paintings of deathbed scenes were seen as acceptable because "they represented the pathos of the situation as a universal experience. When represented in a photograph, however, the same scene—and the same pathos—was perceived as specific to the family depicted" (Meinwald, *Memento Mori,* 5). That is why Henry Peach Robinson's photograph of a young girl dying in the presence of her family, entitled *Fading Away* (1858), proved so controversial. As Meinwald writes, "While it was known that the photograph has been stage-managed, objections were made because it was perceived to be an intrusion upon a private scene" (*Memento Mori,* 5).

48   Kincaid, *Child-Loving,* 7.

49   Although the gender of this child is not absolutely clear, it was characteristic of Cameron, as was briefly discussed in chapter 1, to represent male figures with female models. In addition to Cameron's staging of girls as Jesus and John the Baptist, she also had Hillier pose as *The Angel at the Tomb* (1869), who according to the biblical narrative is male.

50   Emmanuel Levinas, *Totality and Infinity,* trans. Alphonso Lingis (Pittsburgh: Duquesne University Press, 1969), 261.

51   Susan Rubin Suleiman, "Writing and Motherhood," in *The (M)other Tongue,* ed. Shirley Nelson Garner, Claire Kahane, and Madelon Sprengnether (Ithaca, N.Y.: Cornell University Press, 1985), 357. The Barthes quote is from *The Pleasure of the Text,* trans. Richard Howard (New York: Farrar, Straus and Giroux, 1975), 17. Originally published as *Le Plaisir du texte* (Paris: Éditions du Seuil, 1973).

52   Barthes, *Camera Lucida,* 68–69.

53   At times, this semiotic *breaches* "the boundaries of the symbolic in privileged moments of social transgression, when, like the repressed, it seeks to intervene into
the symbolic to subvert its operations." Elizabeth Grosz, *Sexual Subversions, Three
French Feminists* (Sydney: Allen and Unwin, 1989), xxi. Kristeva sees this interven-
tion in the writing of Mallarmé and Joyce, in Bellini's use of color, etc. (I will
address the relationship among Bellini / color / maternality—according to Kristeva—and Cameron's Madonnas later in this chapter.) I am arguing that this inter-
vention takes place in the work of Cameron. Those familiar with Kristeva's work
understand that this is in itself a "breach," for, according to her, it is men who best
articulate this maternal *jouissance*. Kristeva suggests that because a girl is never
really able to resolve her oedipal relation to her mother, she is never able to
articulate her distance from (or even her sameness with) the maternal body. As a
result, it is the male who, in a privileged relationship with the symbolic, is able
both to speak the "symbolic" and to rupture it. Because of his absolute differentia-
tion from the maternal body, he can recall and re-represent the maternal space,
without being consumed by it. "It is consistent with Kristeva's claim that certain
men, in the privileged moment of the rupturing of their oedipal and symbolic
unity, are able to name, evoke, reinscribe the maternal space-time and pleasure
where women cannot" (Grosz, *Sexual Subversions,* 82). Is it any wonder that Irigaray
(and other feminists) regards Kristeva's position as antifeminist and phallocratic?

54   Kristeva, "Stabat Mater," 166.

55   Ibid., 171.

56   Ibid., 166–67.

57   Leon Roudiez relates Kristeva's notion of *jouissance* to *j'ouïs sens* in his introduction
to the English translation of Kristeva's *Desire in Language:* "In Kristeva's vocabu-
lary . . . "jouissance" is total joy or ecstacy . . . [and] through the working of the
signifier, this implies the presence of meaning (*jouissance* = *j'ouïs sens* = I heard
meaning), requiring it by going beyond it." Leon Roudiez, introduction to Julia
Kristeva's *Desire in Language: A Semiotic Approach to Literature and Art,* ed. Leon S.
Roudiez, trans. Thomas Gora, Alice Jardine, and Leon S. Roudiez (New York:
Columbia University Press, 1980), 16. Kristeva's *jouissance* thereby pushes at the
borders of signification through sonorous joy (along with chromatic joy, haptic joy,
olfactic joy, etc.).

     On a related note, Kaja Silverman, through Kristeva, has explored the ways in
which filmmakers have challenged and rethought the *male gaze* through an emphasis
on a different way of seeing that emphasizes sound. See Kaja Silverman, "The
Fantasy of the Maternal Voice," in *The Acoustic Mirror: The Female Voice in Psycho-
analysis and Cinema* (Bloomington: Indiana University Press, 1988), 101–40. For
example, Silverman uncovers the complexities of the melodious (female / maternal) "voice-off" (the term used to describe the "voice-over" in the script) in Peter
Wollen's and Laura Mulvey's groundbreaking film *Riddles of the Sphinx* (1976) as a
space of maternal *jouissance*. Silverman's introduction to the book poignantly states,
"It has somehow escaped theoretical attention that sexual difference is the effect of
dominant cinema's *sound* regime as well as its visual regime, and that the female

voice is as relentlessly held to normative representations and functions as is the female body" (viii).

58   Kristeva, "Stabat Mater," 167.

59   Gernsheim, *Lewis Carroll, Photographer,* 60. This quote is also referenced in chapter 1: see 41 n. 43.

60   H. P. Robinson, *Pictorial Effect in Photography* (1869), as cited in Gernsheim, *Julia Margaret Cameron,* 68.

61   Weston J. Naef, preface to the J. Paul Getty Museum's catalog for the exhibition *Whisper of the Muse,* 12.

62   Anne Thackeray, "A Book of Photographs," in *Toilers and Spinsters* (London: Smith, Elder, 1876), 363. Thackeray is actually quoting the words of a painter who remains nameless in her essay.

63   The image is of two feminized blond creatures representing the type-characters of Jesus and John: "*The Double Star* proposes him [John] as the last person in the Old Testament and Jesus as the first in the New now brought into perfect typological register. They are not twins but the doubles of each other." Mike Weaver, "A Divine Art of Photography," in *Whisper of the Muse,* 31. But, as Weaver has also pointed out, the John and Jesus are also doubles of many of Cameron's images of women kissing each other: *The Salutation* (1864), *The Kiss of Peace* (1869), and *Flos and Iolande* (1864). See Weaver, "Divine Art of Photography," 37. The relationship of *The Double Star* with these other pictures of women kissing women brings the gender of John and Jesus into question, creating a play between male and female, as Cameron has done on other occasions. *The Double Star* is both a kiss between John and Jesus and a kiss between Mary and Elizabeth, a metaphorical double-kiss, as might have happened during "the salutation." ("And it came to pass, that, when Elizabeth heard the salutation of Mary, the babe leaped in her womb; and Elizabeth was filled with the Holy Ghost; and she spoke out with a loud voice; and said, Blessed art thou among women, and blessed is the fruit of thy womb, And whence is this to me that the mother of my Lord should come to me?" Luke 1:41–43.) This mirroring effect allows the children of *The Double Star* "to leap" into the space of Cameron's Madonna pictures.

64   Christina Rossetti did meet Cameron on at least one occasion in 1866, as is documented in the following passage, taken from a letter to her brother William Michael Rossetti: "Mrs Cameron called one day . . . with a portfolio of her magnificent photographs, of which she kindly presented five to Mamma, Maria, and self. Maria and I returned her visit at Little Holland House, where we saw the gigantic Val [Prinsep], Mr Watts, Mrs Dalrymple, and got a glimpse of Browning . . . I am asked to go down to Freshwater Bay, and promised to see Tennyson if I go; but the whole plan is altogether uncertain, and I am too shy to contemplate it with anything like unmixed pleasure." Georgina Battiscombe, *Christina Rossetti: A Divided Life* (London: Constable, 1981), 139.

65   Christina Rossetti, "Goblin Market," in *Goblin Market and Other Poems* (London: Macmillan, 1865), 1. The first edition was published in 1862.

66   Ibid., 9–10.

67 Ibid., 25.

68 Ibid., 11.

69 Kristeva's "Giotto's Joy" and "Motherhood According to Giovanni Bellini" are both collected in *Desire in Language*.

70 Kristeva, "Motherhood According to Giovanni Bellini," 243.

71 The version of this photograph, at George Eastman House, is inscribed to Mary Frazer Tyler (later the second Mrs. Watts): "My best photograph, sent with a kiss to the beautiful artist and dear friend Marie."

72 Because there are no attributes to specifically identify either woman, one could easily reverse their identities. Weaver, in fact, does reverse my reading ("Divine Art of Photography," 37). Gernsheim reads the picture as a representation of Keats' "St. Agnes' Eve" (*Cameron*, 191).

73 Weaver illustrates this beautifully through a number of pictures that signify Hillier as both a Virgin-type and a Magdalene-type. See "Divine Art of Photography," esp. 39–50.

74 Although there is no indication of genital love between Hillier and other women, or Cameron and other women, I think that Cameron's camera-eye certainly caught the artist's love and desire for all things beautiful, including Hillier herself. Cameron's *picturing* of the love between women may have been left unquestioned by her contemporaries (just as Clementina Hawarden's representations of similarly sexualized same-sex love between young women was also left undisputed) because of the range of sensual activities that were permitted in the private spaces between women. Smith-Rosenberg illustrates this complex relationship of women's love for other women in nineteenth-century America in her chapter "The Female World of Love and Ritual: Relations Between Women in Nineteenth-Century America" (*Disorderly Conduct*). There, she sums up this private ("homosocial") space that everyone could see, but very few took notice of as follows: "At one end of the continuum lies committed heterosexuality, at the other uncompromising homosexuality; between, a wide latitude of emotions and sexual feelings. Certain cultures and environments permit individuals a great deal of freedom in moving across this spectrum. I would like to suggest that the nineteenth century was such a cultural environment. That is, the supposedly repressive and destructive Victorian sexual ethos may have been more flexible and responsive to the needs of particular individuals than those of the mid-twentieth century" (76).

75 This was pointed out to me by Joseph Lucchesi.

76 For example, it is certain that Gernsheim has misidentified the model in *The Dream* and in *The Angel at Sepulchre* as Cyllene Wilson. The profiled noses could belong to no other than Mary Hillier. See Gernsheim, *Julia Margaret Cameron*, 151–52.

77 My association of smell with the maternal is in contrast with its typical valuation, the most famous example probably being the long and fetid footnote in Freud's "Civilization and its Discontents" in which he elaborates on "the fact that '*inter urinas et faeces nascimur* [we are born between urine and faeces]." Freud, "Civilization and its Discontents," In *The Standard Edition of the Complete Psychological Works* (London: Hogarth Press, 1953–74), vol. 21, 106.

78   Though hardly a historian, the sexologist Havelock Ellis devotes a chapter to smell in his *Studies in the Psychology of Sex* (1905); there he continually associates the (animalistic) odor of musk with women, the Chinese, the black, etc. Havelock Ellis, *Sexual Selection in Man,* vol. 4 of *Studies in the Psychology of Sex* (Philadelphia: F. A. Davis, 1928). For a cultural history of smell in France, see Alain Corbin, *The Foul and the Fragrant: Odor and the French Imagination* (Cambridge: Harvard University Press, 1986). Originally published as *Le Miasme et la jonquille: L'odorat et l'imaginaire social XVIIIe–XIXe siècles* (Paris: Aubier Montaigne, 1982). Of related interest, Hans J. Rindisbacher has written a useful book that examines literary olfaction over the past 150 years, with a focus on Italian, German, French, Russian, and English texts: *The Smell of Books: A Cultural-Historical Study of Olfactory Perception in Literature* (Ann Arbor: University of Michigan Press, 1992). Barthes uses the phrase "the texture of perfume" to describe the voice of Proust in "Odors," in *Roland Barthes by Roland Barthes,* trans. Richard Howard (New York: Hill and Wang, 1977), 135.

79   This picture is not included in any of the book-length studies or major catalogs on Cameron's work.

80   Mike Weaver, "The Photographer of the Sublime," in *Cameron,* 137.

81   Weaver does not discuss "touch" in Julia Margaret Cameron's work, nor does he discuss Charles Cameron's notion of "touch" beyond the quote provided in my text.

82   Charles Hay Cameron, *An Essay on the Sublime and Beautiful* (1835). Copies of the treatise, as part of his *Two Essays,* are housed in the Bodleian and British Libraries. My quote can be founded in Weaver, "Photographer of the Sublime," 137.

III   Touching Netherplaces: Invisibility in the Photographs of Hannah Cullwick

Note: Whenever possible, I have quoted from the diaries of Hannah Cullwick and Arthur Munby as they are reproduced in published texts. In other cases I have referred to the numerical ordering of the Munby and Cullwick papers established by the Library of Trinity College, Cambridge.

1   Leonore Davidoff, "Class and Gender in Victorian England" in *Sex and Class in Women's History,* ed. J. L. Newton, M. P. Ryan, and J. R. Walkowitz (London: Routledge and Kegan Paul, 1983), 57.

2   A maid of all work did everything, including the lowliest of jobs. Hannah took pride in the fact that she could do everything, doing her jobs with her own peculiar strength and enthusiasm, which included "boot cleaning, knife cleaning, cleaning the silver and plate covers of serving dishes, cleaning and trimming oil lamps; emptying 'slops' and cleaning toilets, drawing and carrying water; dressing, washing and looking after infants and children of employers, their relatives and friends; gutting and plucking game birds and other fowl, gutting and skinning hare; keeping and balancing household account books, estimating what provisions were required when these were daily released from lock stores by 'the Missis,' ordering from tradesmen and tradeswomen; answering the bell to visitors, carrying boxes and hampers to and from railway stations, carrying visitors' luggage up and down stairs,

escorting ladies of the family to and from social functions to protect them; laying and waiting at table, cooking elaborate as well as plain food, preserving fruit in season, making marmalade; making cushions from plucked feathers, sewing clothes for employers' charities, replacing the linen covers of their religious tracts and attending their charitable bazaars." Liz Stanley, ed., introduction to *The Diaries of Hannah Cullwick: Victorian Maidservant* (London: Virago, 1984), 5.

3   Stanley, ed., *Diaries of Hannah Cullwick,* 17. It seems that Hannah was always ambivalent about the institution of marriage. She rarely wore the wedding ring Munby gave her. After Munby presented the marriage license to Hannah, she wrote, "I car'd very *very* little for the license of being married either. Indeed, I've a certain dislike to either, they seem to have so little to do with our *love* & our union . . . I like the life I lead." Once married, Hannah became ill and was forced to move back to the country to "rusticate" herself.

4   By Munby's request the diaries and photographs "were locked up until 1950 by which time, as he had foreseen, the shock and degradation of such a story would have died away." Davidoff, "Class and Gender in Victorian England," 31.

5   Stanley, ed., introduction to *Diaries of Hannah Cullwick,* 4.

6   Stanely, ed., *Diaries of Hannah Cullwick,* 274.

7   Arthur Munby, as cited by Derek Hudson in his *Munby: A Man of Two Worlds: The Life and Diaries of Arthur J. Munby 1828–1910* (London: Gambit, 1972), 134.

8   However, it appears that Hannah briefly describes the circumstances of the photograph in her diaries. See Stanley, ed., *Diaries of Hannah Cullwick,* 91.

9   Levinas, *Otherwise Than Being or Beyond Existence,* 90.

10   Heather Dawkins, "Politics of Visibility, Domestic Labour and Representation: The Diaries and Photographs (1853–74) of Hannah Cullwick," *Parallelogramme* 10, no. 4 (April–May 1985): 47–50. This is an early article by Dawkins. Later she wrote a much more substantial and very useful article in which the error was rectified: "The Diaries and Photographs of Hannah Cullwick," *Art History* 10, no. 2 (June 1987). Davidoff, "Class and Gender in Victorian England."

11   After completing this chapter, I received a copy of Griselda Pollock's recent article on the photographs and drawings of women coal miners that are contained in the Munby archives at Trinity College. Pollock's orientation is from a very different perspective than mine. While my writing, as the reader will soon see, focuses on Hannah (her desire and her sexuality and my erotic relationship to it)— Pollock's focuses on Munby and other male artists and writers (of the same period) who were fascinated with "the complex of dirt, bodies, sex, and labor as it seemed to be presented to the bourgeois tourist by the mining industry and its communities" ("The Dangers of Proximity: The Spaces of Sexuality and Surveillance in Word and Image," *Discourse* 16, no. 2 [Winter 1993]: 19). But, like me, Pollock also gives a brief personal narrative that focuses on her experience of entering the wondrous Wren Library and being presented with the box ("a large chest"). She too indulges in the oddness of wearing white gloves, in order to inspect the dirty women represented. It was a pleasure to read about her similar experiences. And it was through her article that I better understood why I first

began telling the story of my white gloves and the box: it gives me authority; it proves that I was there. For early on, when I first presented a version of this paper to Chicago art historians, my respondent was surprised to learn that I had actually spent a lot of time with the box. I was shocked that this was not clear to him, and I was possibly even more shocked at the fact that my voice (for him) was not credible unless I had worn the archivist's gloves and leafed through the "real" material. So, by the time that I got to the University of North Carolina, Chapel Hill, later that year (1990) and delivered my story of Hannah again, you can bet that my tale of the gloves, the box, and the men who brought it all to me was there. I performed it with all of the authority I could muster. (The title of the lecture was "A Utopic 'Play' Of Difference: Hannah Cullwick, Victorian Maid-of-All-Work, Monster of Inexhaustible Beauty." It was also delivered that same year at SUNY–Binghamton and at Lower Links, Chicago.)

12   Luce Irigaray, "The Invisible of the Flesh: A Reading of Merleau-Ponty, *The Visible and the Invisible,* 'The Intertwining—The Chiasm,' " in *An Ethics of Sexual Difference,* trans. Carolyn Burke and Gillian C. Gill (Ithaca, N.Y.: Cornell University Press, 1993), 182. Originally published as *Éthique de la différence sexuelle* (Paris: Les Éditions de Minuit, 1984).

13   Maurice Merleau-Ponty, *The Visible and the Invisible, Followed by Working Notes,* ed. Claude Lefort, trans. Alphonso Lingis (Evanston, Ill.: Northwestern University Press, 1968). Originally published as *Le Visible et l'invisible* (Paris: Éditions Gallimard, 1964).

14   Ibid., 263.

15   Ibid., 257.

16   Jacques Lacan, *The Four Fundamental Concepts of Psycho-Analysis,* ed. Jacques-Alain Miller, trans. Alan Sheridan (New York: W. W. Norton, 1977). Originally published as *Le Seminaire de Jacques Lacan, Livre XI, Les quatre concepts fondamentaux de la psychanalyse* (Paris: Éditions du Seuil, 1973).

17   Ibid., 84.

18   Merleau-Ponty, *Visible and the Invisible,* 261. Jacques Lacan, "The Mirror Stage as Formative of the Function of the I as Revealed in Psychoanalytic Experience," in *Écrits: A Selection,* trans. Alan Sheridan (New York: W. W. Norton, 1977). Originally published as *Écrits* (Paris: Éditions du Seuil, 1966).

19   Lacan, *Four Fundamental Concepts,* 80.

20   Ibid., 80–81.

21   Irigaray, "Invisible of the Flesh," 175.

22   Ibid., 159.

23   Ibid., 184.

24   Michel de Certeau, *The Writing of History,* trans. Tom Conley (New York: Columbia University Press, 1988), 251. See also de Certeau's specific response to Maurice Merleau-Ponty, "The Madness of Vision," *Enclitic* 7, no. 1 (Spring 1983): 24–31.

25   "Sexuate" is Irigaray's invented term for a language that points toward a sex that is beyond reversibility, that bathes in the remainder of reversibility. See "Invisible of

the Flesh," 184. Irigaray also uses the term, less poetically, to define laws ("sexuate rights") she imagines for future societies. These laws do not seek to give women equality with men; instead, they are interested in keeping differences intact and respecting the rights those differences entail, through law. (The new laws that Irigaray lists address rights to virginity, rights to motherhood, rights to human dignity, rights to media coverage directed at women, etc.—an extremely varied and, at times, seemingly outrageous list indeed.) The bottom line is that Irigaray does not believe in the reversibility that lies underneath the concept of "equal rights." However, despite differences in tone (between sexuating language and sexuating law), the concept remains the same: men's language (including judicial law) cannot simply be reversed and applied to women. See "The necessity for sexuate rights," and "How to define sexuate rights?" *The Irigaray Reader,* ed. Margaret Whitford, trans. David Macey (Oxford: Basil Blackwell, 1991). "The necessity for sexuate rights" originally published in Irigaray, *Je, Tu, Nous* (Paris: Grasset, 1990). "How to define sexuate rights?" originally published in Irigaray, *L'Oubli de l'air chez Martin Heidegger* (Paris: Les Éditions de Minuit, 1983).

26   Hannah and Munby are well-known figures in Victorian studies, and a number of works have addressed this odd couple. I have already cited several texts: the article by Davidoff, the two articles by Dawkins, the biography on Munby by Hudson, and Hannah's diaries as edited by Stanley. Peter Stallybrass and Allon White address Cullwick in "Below Stairs: The Maid and the Family Romance," in *The Politics and Poetics of Transgression* (Ithaca, N.Y.: Cornell University Press, 1986), 149–70. Michael Hiley has compiled a very useful collection of writings and photographs that address and extensively picture Victorian working women (with less theorization than the aforementioned accounts): *Victorian Working Women: Portraits from Life* (London: Gordon Fraser, 1979). Interestingly enough, Hiley actually grants Hannah the most sexuality of her own—not through his own writing but simply by virtue of including two erotic passages from the diaries that the major critical texts have left out (see notes 42 and 80). Also of interest is Liz Stanley's "Biography as Microscope or Kaleidoscope?: The Case of 'Power' in Hannah Cullwick's Relationship with Arthur Munby," *Women's Studies International Forum* 10, no. 1 (1987): 19–31. And, Julia Swindells's "Liberating the Subject? Autobiography and 'Women's History': A Reading of *The Diaries of Hannah Cullwick,*" in *Interpreting Women's Lives: Feminist Theory and Personal Narratives,* ed. Personal Narrative Group (Bloomington: Indiana University Press, 1989), 24–38. Though this latter essay was published five years after Stanley's edited volume of Hannah's diaries and two years after Dawkins's second essay on the diaries and photographs, Swindells still credits Munby as the photographer, which is indicative of how much easier it is to see Munby as the one who called "all the shots" in this relationship.

27   Stanley, ed., *Diaries of Hannah Cullwick,* 306, 26 (respectively).

28   Much has been made about the fact that Munby's own nursemaid was also named Hannah (Carter). She took care of the Munby family for twenty-eight years.

29   Stanley, ed., introduction to *Diaries of Hannah Cullwick,* 7.

30   Ibid., 2.

31   It is interesting to consider why Hannah's own sexual orientation has not been considered, whereas Munby's has been the site of explicit *perversions,* including homosexuality. Interestingly enough, *mere* silence on Hannah as a sexual subject has registered her as a heterosexual, while Munby can be easily envisioned as a repressed homosexual. What kind of heterosexual is she? And does she fit that space any better than she fits the space of homosexual? Why have her own complex performances not led the theorists and historians to consider her as queer? Could she not be a queer man gloved in a woman's body? For more on an expanded understanding of queerness, see Eve Kosofsky Sedgwick's extremely useful texts on the subject, especially *Epistemology of the Closet* (Berkeley and Los Angeles: University of California Press, 1990) and *Tendencies* (Durham, N. C.: Duke University Press, 1993).

32   In the Munby Box the hands are paired with a photograph of Hannah as an elderly woman, and together they are accompanied by a note in Hannah's hand. The note reads: "Dearest Massa / I have been a hardworking servant forty two or three years & I have been yours thirty years or more, and I am still your faithful wife & loving servant. / Hannah, 1884—."

33   Laqueur, "Orgasm, Generation," 28.

34   Stewart, *On Longing,* 69.

35   Rejlander "may have been the first photographer to specialize in details of the human form, taken for the use of figure painters." Edgar Yoxall Jones, *Father of Art Photography: O. G. Rejlander, 1813–1875* (Greenwich: New York Graphic Society, 1973), 74. Interestingly enough, Rejlander had a maid, "Frizzlewig," who served as his model. Though Fink's photograph of Hannah's hands is undated, it appears to be contemporary with Rejlander's portrait of the Lady's hands. Coincidentally, Hannah had visited Rejlander, and several of the portraits in the Munby Box are by him. I thank Ann Paterra for guiding me to *Hands.*

36   The conservation of fine aristocratic hands was a major preoccupation for many bourgeois women of the period. Etiquette books supplied recipes for the whitening and the softening of hands. One book, written later in 1889, entitled *Rules of Etiquette and Home Culture,* gives the following recipe: "Melt together, in a dish over boiling water, four ounces of honey, two ounces of yellow wax and six ounces of rose water. Add one ounce of myrrh while hot. Before going to bed, rub this thickly over the skin . . . A good way to keep the hands white is to wear at night large cloth mittens filled with wet bran or oat meal, tied closely at the wrists." I am indebted to Kelly Baum for presenting me with this and other useful insights on the maintenance of the bourgeois Victorian woman's hands.

37   Hannah originally wore the leather wristband to support an ailing wrist, but it was later transformed into a sign of her servitude to Munby. Munby writes the following about it in his diary: "The leather strap and buckle such as navvies use, which she wore on her right-wrist, night and day, for the years, was another such sign [of her commitment to Munby]. It was the only bracelet she has ever had; and when it was worn out by constant soaking in pails and tubs, she came to me for another,

and I kept the old one as a relic. As she never wore gloves, this wrist strap and her large ruddy hands—so different from her ladylike face—made her an object of curiosity. . . . Her fellow servants rallied her about the strap, but without effect, and when her mistress spoke of it, she answered truly enough, 'I sprained my write Ma'am, wi' lifting tubs, when I was a scallion' " (Munby 75, 11 January 1890, 50–51). The diary goes on to describe how the wristband horrified one of her employers. But Hannah, who always insisted on her personal freedoms, refused to take it off and was soon terminated. As Hannah once wrote, "I was *born* to serve, & not to order" (Stanley, ed., *Diaries of Hannah Cullwick,* 85). Hannah's insistence on wearing the slave band stands in interesting contrast to the fact that, once she was married, she very rarely wore her wedding ring. In regards to the chain, I was surprised to learn that Munby also (if secretly) decorated his body with "signs," for he "always kept and wore the little key" (Munby 75, 11 January 1890, 57).

38   Hannah as quoted by Munby in his diary, as cited by Hudson, *Munby,* 71.

39   Stanley, ed., *Diaries of Hannah Cullwick,* 66.

40   Munby as quoted in Hudson, *Munby,* 71; emphasis added.

41   Stanley, ed., *Diaries of Hannah Cullwick,* 111.

42   Hiley, *Victorian Working Women,* 32. The drama of the chimney story is further expanded upon when Munby writes about another soot "bath" performed by Hannah (Munby 75, 11 January 1890, 78–81). Notice how in this case, part of the charge of the moment stems from the spectacle of Hannah's dirty and lowly image before upper-class ladies. The ladies have just been confronted with a small disaster, a "fall of soot" and Hannah has been employed to clean it up. Munby recounts the story as told to him by Hannah:

> Kneeling on the hearth, she plunged her bare arms into the soot, and gathered it up by armfuls into her pails. "I soon got as black as black," she told me; "it was warm work an' the soot fled all over my face an' arms and neck, an stuck on wi' sweat. Those ladies sat and looked on; exclaiming to me another "How dreadful! I'm sure I could not *bear* to touch soot!" But they gave a reluctant admiration to the black creature before them. "Oh, Hannah! How *can* you do it so well?" "Why Ma'am," said Hannah, looking up, "I enjoy it! It's a good piece of work, and there's nothing so soft as soot; an' the smell's refreshing—like what ladies call *salts.*" "I thought," said she to me afterwards, "when they see how well I did it, they'd of ask'd me if I'd bin up chimneys; an' then I should ha' told'em. But they didn't, so of course I couldna speak."

43   Barthes, *Pleasure of the Text,* 17. The full sentence reads, "The pleasure of the text is that moment when my body pursues it own ideas—for my body does not have the same ideas I do." The quote is symptomatic of an erotics of reading that is carried by *The Pleasure of the Text,* in which Barthes gives himself away to the reader.

44   One of the most well known was "Lily Powder," which was made by Queen Victoria's own *perruquier:* Mr. Willie Clarkton. See Neville Williams, *Powder and

Paint (London: Longmans, Green, 1957), 105. I am indebted to Anna Snoderly for this reference.

45   Although direct evidence of intimate physical contact between Hannah and Munby is limited, they did bathe each other and there are also diary entries that discuss pleasurable kissing.

46   The philosopher and performance artist Adrian Piper (who *looks* white and claims her black identity) has suffered and theorized the issue of just who is black and who is white in series of works going back to the late 1960s. In her article "Passing for White, Passing For Black," *Transition* 58, 4–32, she reveals the great efforts that whites have gone to to keep racial purity intact. In the end, it becomes quite clear that all of us are either passing for white or passing for black, and that whiteness and blackness is a social condition.

47   Hiley, *Victorian Working Women*, 28–29.

48   Peggy Phelan, *Unmarked: Politics of Performance* (New York: Routledge, 1992), 8.

49   See Jean and John Comaroff, "Medicine, Colonialism, and the Black Body," in *Ethnography and the Historical Imagination* (Boulder, Colo.: Westview Press, 1992), esp. 224–25.

50   See the *Illustrated London News*, 14 May 1887, 557. There are endless examples of such racial ideology in the advertisements put out by Pears. One of the most famous and clearest (in terms of cleaning up the other) features a drawing of "Soudan natives" looking at a huge rock that has been inscribed with giant white letters that spell out "Pears Soap is the Best." The top of the advertisement reads: "The Formula of British Conquest." See the *Illustrated London News,* 27 August 1887, 249. A most disturbing aspect of these advertisements is the fact that they are printed right next to "real" news stories of British colonialism and racial conquest.

51   Cullwick, *The Diaries of Hannah Cullwick,* 75; emphasis added in last sentence of each paragraph.

52   Munby 75, original manuscript, Trinity College Library, Cambridge. Diary entry for 11 January 1890, 48–49.

53   The following passage from Munby's diary, 1883, speaks to this fascination:
> Passing through Scotland Yard about noon, I saw a large crowd, in the street, & heard the banjos of some Ethiopian Serenaders. But there were surely female voices as well as male: and going up, I was astonished to see that two of the five "niggers" were young women. Yes: there were two young women, drest in fantastic ballet costume, and with shining black faces & necks & hands. Their heads were bare; their hair decked with network and rolls of scarlet cloth: they wore pink calico jackets, petticoats of spangled blue, ending a little below the knee: and red stockings and red boots. One of them came up to me, when the singing was over, with her tambourine; and earned a sixpence for her courage in blackening her face.
>   . . . They wash the black off every night.
>   I remarked to her that this was the first time that I had ever seen female niggers (except one, & that long ago) singing in the open street. "Yes Sir," she

said "it's a new thing; but we mean to stick to it." I watched these two selfmade negresses going through the crowd by turns, collecting money after the performance. They did it very quietly and simply; appealing in silence— with not even a smile, for the lampblack varnish disguised whatever good looks they had, so smiles would have been useless. (Hudson, *Munby,* 157–59)

54   Douglas A. Lorimer, *Colour, Class and the Victorians: English Attitudes to the Negro in the Mid-Nineteenth Century* (Leicester: Leicester University Press, 1978), 88.

55   Joan Riviere, "Womanliness as Masquerade," *International Journal of Psychoanalysis* 10 (1929): 303–13.

56   Luce Irigaray, *This Sex Which is Not One,* trans. Catherine Porter with Carolyn Burke (Ithaca, N.Y.: Cornell University Press, 1985), 84. Originally published as *Ce Sexe qui n'en est pas un* (Paris: Éditions de Minuit, 1977).

57   Irigaray assigns the term "mimicry" to the masquerade of femininity that is performed consciously as a subversive act in order to uncover the masculinist standards that exploit her sex. One of the best (recent) examples of this is the California news reporter who managed to mimic femininity all the way up to the winning of the Miss California Beauty Pageant; after being crowned, she announced her other identity.

58   Phelan, *Unmarked,* 96; emphasis added.

59   As has been pointed out by Dawkins ("Diaries and Photographs of Hannah Cullwick," 182), there are two copies of Hannah as slave / chimney sweep, the original has been captioned as "Hannah as a slave." There is another traveling mount that once contained Hannah as a wholesome working girl (with a pretty bonnet, a lovely shawl, a beautiful big basket, a bright white apron) *and* as fashionable young Lady (with beautifully expose shoulders, flowers in her hair, ribbons on her wrists).

60   Madeleine Ginsburg, *Victorian Dress in Photographs* (New York: Holmes and Meier, 1983), 58.

61   For an excellent discussion of Gérôme and orientalism, see Linda Nochlin, "The Imaginary Orient," in *The Politics of Vision: Essays on Nineteenth-Century Art and Society* (New York: Harper and Row, 1989), 33–59.

62   Sigmund Freud, "Freud and Fetishism: Previously Unpublished Minutes of the Vienna Psychoanalytic Society," ed. and trans. Louis Rose, *Psychoanalytic Quarterly* 57 (1988): 159.

63   For more on women, clothing, and haptic fetishes, see Emily Apter, "Splitting Hairs," in her *Feminizing the Fetish: Psychoanalysis and Narrative Obsession in Turn-of-the-Century France* (Ithaca, N.Y.: Cornell University Press, 1991), 99–123. See also Yolande Papetti, Françoise Valier, Bernard de Fréminville, and Serge Tisseron, *La passion des étoffes chez un neuro-psychiatre, G. G. de Clérembault (1872–1934)* (Paris: Éditions Solin, 1987).

64   See Monique Wittig's useful and lucid insights on the relationship between race, gender, and slavery in "The Category of Sex" *Feminist Issues* 2, no. 2 (Fall 1982): 64–68.

65   Munby as cited by Hudson, *Munby,* 54. The question of Hannah's class is, indeed,

very complicated. Despite the fact that Hannah worked as working-class woman her entire life—doing unbelievably difficult labor at incredibly low wages—I still have trouble registering her as *simply* lower class. After all, her lower-class life was shaken by such things as a trip to France, or the wearing of fine clothes. And though she did not receive money from Munby, except as a paid maid, there is a difference in the fact that he was (since the beginning of their relationship) always looming in the background as a possible crutch. So although Hannah was certainly lower class and led a very hard life, her class situation was substantially different from that of other women who were also maids of all work, in more class-isolated situations. One could argue that she "passed" as lower class and she "passed" as upper class. This is a touchy issue: no one would ever want to underestimate Hannah's life struggles; yet it is curious that other scholars have not seen the rough edges around the issue of her class.

66   Davidoff, "Class and Gender in Victorian England," 48.

67   Munby as quoted in Hudson's *Munby*, 320.

68   Both of their diaries appear almost to flaunt this fact.

69   The first epigraph is from an interview of Luce Irigaray in *Les Femmes, la pornographie et l'érotisme,* ed. M.-F. Hans and G. Lapouge, as quoted in Griselda Pollock, *Vision and Difference* (London: Routledge, 1988), 50. The second epigraph is from a sonnet that describes Hannah and Munby's wedding day (Hudson, *Munby*, 318). This is one of at least thirty-six sonnets that Munby wrote to Hannah, which he had placed in an envelope some thirty years after their marriage. Interestingly enough, most of them were copied in Hannah's handwriting.

70   Discussions of Irigaray's essentialism are abundant. The following is a short list of texts that I have found useful on the topic: Diana Fuss, *Essentially Speaking: Feminism, Nature and Difference* (New York: Routledge, 1989); Eléanor Kuykendall, "Toward an Ethic of Nurturance: Luce Irigaray on Mothering and Power," in *Mothering, Essays in Feminist Theory,* ed. Joyce Trebilcot (Totowa, N.J.: Rowman and Allanheld, 1984); and Carolyn Burke, "Irigaray Through the Looking Glass," *Feminist Studies* 7, no. 2 (Summer 1981): 288–306. Burke provides a relatively early (American) entry into Irigaray that manages to feel its way past the usual pronouncement of essentialism. Burke insists on distinguishing "analogy" from "morphology," stressing that Irigaray promoted the latter. Accordingly, then, the "lips" of "When our lips speak together" should not be reduced to an anatomical specification, rather their figure should be used to suggest another mode (not another model). In this morphological space, Irigaray's lips imply plurality and a mode of being "in touch" that differs from the phallic mode of discourse. The lips that speak together play upon the vaginal lips and the lips that encircle our mouths—and the lips that speak between women—and they also suggest a language that sounds different, as when you hum with your lips together. Luce Irigaray, "When Our Lips Speak Together," in *This Sex Which is Not One.*

71   Irigaray, "This Sex Which is Not One," in *This Sex Which is Not One,* 24.

72   Ibid., 28–29.

73   In her first book, *Le Langage des déments* (The Hague: Mouton, 1973), Irigaray

discovered that male schizophrenics were better able to articulate their condition through traditional language, whereas female schizophrenics tended to speak their condition through the body.

74   Elaine Showalter, *The Female Malady: Women, Madness and English Culture, 1830–1980* (New York: Pantheon, 1985). See especially chapters 2 and 3, "The Rise of the Victorian Madwoman" and "Managing Women's Minds."

75   As Showalter writes, "It is certainly possible to see hysteria within the specific historical framework of the nineteenth century as an unconscious form of feminist protest, the counterpart of the attack on patriarchal values carried out by the women's movement." Yet, as Showalter goes on to explain, one should not romanticize it, nor essentialize an "equation between femininity and insanity. Rather, it must investigate how, in a particular cultural context, notions of gender influence the definition and, consequently, the treatment of mental disorder" (*Female Malady*, 5).

76   The documented cases of women who were suspected of performing their roles for notoriety mostly come out of the French clinic, Salpêtrière, run by Jean-Martin Charcot: the much photographed Augustine is the most famous. "Because the behavior of Charcot's hysterical stars was so theatrical, and because it was rarely observed outside of the Parisian clinical setting, many of his contemporaries, as well as subsequent medical historians, have suspected that the women's performances were the result of suggestion, imitation, or even fraud. In Charcot's own lifetime, one of his assistants admitted that some of the women had been coached in order to produce attacks that would please the *maître*. Furthermore, there was a dramatic increase in the incidence of hysteria during Charcot's tenure" (Showalter, *Female Malady*, 150–51).

77   Showalter, *Female Malady*, 87.

78   However, Ellen Terry "found the madwomen much 'too theatrical' to teach her anything" (Showalter, *Female Malady*, 92). For more on the relationship between madness, Ophelia, and Ellen Terry, see Nina Auerbach, *Ellen Terry: Player in Her Time* (New York: W. W. Norton, 1987), esp. 238–41.

79   It is difficult to tell when the incident actually occurred. "Munby mentions it in his diary entry for Monday 2 February 1863, saying it happened 'once, long ago' " (Hiley, *Victorian Working Women*, 135 n. 14).

80   Munby as quoted in Hiley, *Victorian Working Women*, 28–29; emphasis added.

81   I am in no way suggesting that this erotic sharing of garments does not take place between two men, or between a man and woman: it does.

82   Hiley, *Victorian Working Women*, 64.

83   Of course, the situation between the paper mill girls is also radically different than Hannah's, because they are of the same class.

84   Here I am invoking Barthes's understanding of how he connects to a person in a photograph (the referent), which he sees as the equivalent of sharing skin. Barthes writes that the light in the photograph, "although impalpable, is certainly here a carnal medium, as skin that I share with him or her who was photographed" (*Camera Lucida*, 81).

85   Elisabeth G. Gitter, "The Power of Women's Hair in the Victorian Imagination," *Publication of the Modern Language Association of America* 99, no. 5 (October 1985): 938.

86   Gitter, "Power of Women's Hair," 936 and 943. It is difficult to imagine what Munby meant by brushing her hair out in a lady's fashion; possibly after brushing it, he pulled it back in some "fashion," though it is difficult to believe that it truly would have been a lady's fashion.

87   Hudson, *Munby*, 3.

88   However, much has been made of the missing diaries, which many feel contains evidence of his love for Alice Liddell, the "real" Alice of Wonderland fame.

89   Carroll, as cited in Morton N. Cohen, "The Actress and the Don," in *Lewis Carroll: A Celebration, Essays on the Occasion of the 150th Anniversary of the Birth of Charles Lutwidge Dodgson,* ed. Edward Guiliano (New York: Clarkson N. Potter, 1982), 2. The Carroll quote comes from one of a number of diaries that are now mysteriously missing. By 1930, four of Carroll's thirteen volumes of diaries had disappeared. Whether they were lost or intentionally destroyed by members of Carroll's family (to cover up any dark shadows in his life) is a matter of debate. In any case, Langford Reed, who published a biography on Carroll in 1932, managed to get a hold of the missing diaries before their disappearance; Reed's text is Cohen's source for the Ellen Terry quote. See Langford Reed, *The Life of Lewis Carroll* (London: W. & G. Foyle, 1932), 90.

90   Charles Darwin, *Expression of the Emotions in Man and Animals* (London: John Murray, Albemarle Street, 1890), 328. The first edition was published in 1872. Interestingly enough, the volume contains photographs by Rejlander (some even of Rejlander), demonstrating a range of expressions from grief to joy.

91   Stanley, ed., *Diaries of Hannah Cullwick,* 170.

92   Webster's first definition of the blush is "to become red in the face especially from shame."

93   Sandra Lee Bartky, "Shame and Gender: Contribution to a Phenomenology of Oppression," *Center for Twentieth-Century Studies Working Papers,* Working Paper no. 7 (Fall–Winter 1989–90): 8; emphasis added.

94   Probably the most shocking act of shame was the fact that Hannah licked Munby's boots clean.

95   Ruth Bernard Yeazell has thoroughly analyzed this topic in *Fictions of Modesty: Women and Courtship in the English Novel* (Chicago: University of Chicago Press, 1991). See especially the chapter "Modest Blushing," 65–80.

96   Havelock Ellis, *Studies in the Psychology of Sex,* 7 vols. (Philadelphia: F. A. Davis, 1928), vol. 1, "The Evolution of Modesty," 74, 73. The latter quote of Ellis's references the work of Stanley Hall, "A Study of Fears," *American Journal of Psychology,* 1897. Ellis first published his "Evolution of Modesty" in 1899.

97   Ellis, *Studies in the Psychology of Sex,* 74.

98   Ellis, *Studies in the Psychology of Sex,* 73.

99   This notion of a blush that "plays before a room" is Yeazell's. See *Fictions of Modesty,* 69.

100   Stanley, ed., *Diaries of Hannah Cullwick,* 76–77; emphasis added.

101   Dawkins, "Diaries and Photographs of Hannah Cullwick," 180.

102   Weaver, *Whisper of the Muse,* 39.

103   Mr. Fink and Mr. Stodart were both seeing the play of oppositions in Hannah when they suggested that she model as Una and Magdalene, respectively. Mr. S's suggestion that Hannah wear only her white "shift," which was then coupled with her head of black hair, suggests not only the metaphorical symbols embodied in Mary-Magdalene, but also a character like Spenser's Una. Una with her white lamb, her white ass that she rides, and her physical whiteness is self-contradicted by her black stole, her veiled face, and sadness. In fact, "Her sadness (. . . identifies her fleetingly with Mary Magdalene) . . . [as it signifies] the Fall of Man with its consequent veiling of truth." A. C. Hamilton, gen. ed., *The Spenser Encyclopedia* (London: Routledge, 1990), 705.

104   Stanley, ed., introduction to *Diaries of Hannah Cullwick,* 32.

105   Carroll, *Alice's Adventures in Wonderland,* 55–56.

106   For an interesting analysis of Alice and class, especially her anxiety about the lower class, see Armstrong's "Occidental Alice."

107   Lacan, *Four Fundamental Concepts,* 96.

108   Ibid., 95.

109   Ibid., 96.

110   Ibid.

111   What is usually overlooked in Lacan's sardine story is the double annihilation that class difference performs. Even if Lacan could somehow (magically) escape the all-discriminating annihilation of vision itself, he would still never be part of the Fisherman's Netherworld. Lacan's eyes and his class keep him perpetually *out:* out of the space of the frame, out of the sardine can, out of the working class.

112   Irigaray, "Invisible of the Flesh," 153.

Conclusion: After-Time

1   This rather haunting term can be found in the final (and very long) sentence that concludes *Alice's Adventures in Wonderland,* 164. The sentence is as follows: "Lastly she pictured to herself how this same little sister of hers would, in the after-time, be herself a grown woman; and how she would keep, through all her riper years, the simple and loving heart of her childhood; and how she would gather about her other little children, and make *their* eyes bright and eager with many a strange tale, perhaps even with the dream of Wonderland of long ago; and how she would feel all their simple sorrows, and find pleasure in all their simple joys, remembering her own child-life, and the happy summer days."

2   Carroll, *Through the Looking-Glass,* 251 and two lines from "A Boat, Beneath A Sunny Sky," the poem that closes *Through the Looking-Glass,* 345.

3   Carroll, *Through the Looking-Glass,* 238.

4   Ibid., 218.

5   Ibid., 247.

6   Barthes, *Pleasure of the Text,* 66.

7   Ibid. Barthes continues to define this as follows: "*Writing aloud* is not phonological but phonetic; its aim is not the clarity of messages, the theater of emotions; what it searches for (in a perspective of bliss) are the pulsional incidents, the language lined with flesh, a text where we can hear the grain of the throat, the patina of consonants, the voluptuousness of vowels, a whole carnal stereophony: the articulation of the body, of the tongue, not that of meaning" (66).

8   Jane Gallop, *Thinking Through the Body* (New York: Columbia University Press, 1988), 101. I am also indebted to Gallop for her sensitivity to the word "of" as it relates to her desire (and Barthes's desire) to let sexuality out of art and writing (rather than keeping it contained within a painting, a photograph, a text). See her published lecture, "The Prick of the Object," also in *Thinking Through the Body,* 149–60.

9   This paragraph on sexuality has been highly influenced by Barthes's description of erotic zones in *Pleasure of the Text,* 9–10. Most notably, his idea of the erotic as "skin flashing between two articles of clothing," which is a "staging of an appearance-as-disappearance" (10).

10 D. A. Miller, *Bringing Out Roland Barthes* (Berkeley and Los Angeles: University of California Press, 1992), 48.

11 Barthes, *Pleasure of the Text,* 8.

12 Ibid., 9.

13 Barthes, *Roland Barthes by Roland Barthes,* 34.

14 From the back cover of *Bringing Out Roland Barthes.* I am attracted to the word "album"; as indeed, as I have already suggested, this short text reads like a series of photographic moments, in which Barthes is seen in a different light.

15 Miller, *Bringing Out Roland Barthes,* 32–33.

16 Barthes, *Pleasure of the Text,* 25–26. Here Barthes is speaking of liking the demand of a "prattle-text."

17 Ibid., 37.

18 Miller, *Bringing Out Roland Barthes,* 32–33.

BIBLIOGRAPHY

Apter, Emily. *Feminizing the Fetish: Psychoanalysis and Narrative Obsession in Turn-of-the Century France*. Ithaca, N.Y.: Cornell University Press, 1991.

Armstrong, Nancy. "The Occidental Alice." *Differences* 2, no. 2 (1990): 3–40.

Auerbach, Nina. *Woman and the Demon: The Life of a Victorian Myth*. Cambridge: Harvard University Press, 1982.

———. *Romantic Imprisonment: Women and Other Glorified Outcasts*. New York: Columbia University Press, 1986.

———. *Ellen Terry: Player in Her Time*. New York: W. W. Norton, 1987.

Barrie, J. M. *Peter and Wendy*. Vol. 9 of *The Works of J. M. Barrie, Peter Pan Edition*. New York: Charles Scribner's Sons, 1930.

———. *Peter Pan, or The Boy Who Would Not Grow Up. The Uniform Edition of the Plays of J. M. Barrie*. New York: Scribner's Sons, 1928.

Barthes, Roland. *The Pleasure of the Text*. Translated by Richard Howard with a note on the text by Richard Miller. New York: Farrar, Straus and Giroux, 1975. Originally published as *Le Plaisir du texte* (Paris: Éditions du Seuil, 1973).

———. "The Photographic Message." In *Image / Music / Text,* translated by Stephen Heath. New York: Hill and Wang, 1977.

———. *Roland Barthes by Roland Barthes*. Translated by Richard Howard. New York: Hill and Wang, 1977.

———. *Camera Lucida: Reflections on Photography*. Translated by Richard Howard. New York: Farrar, Straus and Giroux, 1981. Originally published as *La chambre clare* (Paris: Éditions du Seuil, 1980).

Bartky, Sandra Lee. "Shame and Gender: Contribution to a Phenomenology of Oppression." *Center for Twentieth-Century Studies Working Papers*. Working Paper no. 7 (Fall–Winter 1989–90).

Bartram, Michael. *The Pre-Raphaelite Camera: Aspects of Victorian Photography*. Boston: Little, Brown, 1985.

Belloc, Marie A. "Interview with Mr. H. Hay Herschel Cameron." *Woman at Home* 4 (1896–97): 586.

Bradley, Laurel. "From Eden to Empire: John Everett Millais's *Cherry Ripe*." *Victorian Studies* 34, no. 2 (Winter 1991): 179–203.

Buchanan, Amy Ruth. "Death, Decay, Masks and Play: Ralph Eugene Meatyard's Family Pictures." Honors thesis, University of North Carolina, Chapel Hill, 1993.

Burke, Carolyn. "Irigaray Through the Looking Glass." *Feminist Studies* 7, no. 2 (Summer 1981): 288–306.

Calvert, Karin. *Children in the House: The Material Culture of Early Childhood.* Boston: Northeastern University Press, 1992.

Cameron, Charles Hay. *An Essay on the Sublime and Beautiful.* Unpublished MS, 1835. Bodleian and British Libraries.

Cameron, Julia Margaret. "Annals of My Glass House" (1874). London: Camera Gallery, 1889. Reprinted in *Photographic Journal* (London) (July 1927): 296–301. Also reprinted in Helmut Gernsheim, *Julia Margaret Cameron, Her Life and Photographic Work* (New York: Aperture, 1975) and Mike Weaver, *Julia Margaret Cameron, 1815–1879* (London: Herbert Press, 1984). MS source: The Royal Photographic Society of Great Britain, Bath, England.

Carroll, Lewis [C. L. Dodgson]. *Alice's Adventures in Wonderland.* In *The Annotated Alice*, introduction and notes by Martin Gardner. New York: Meridian, 1960.

———. *Through the Looking-Glass.* In *The Annotated Alice*, introduction and notes by Martin Gardner. New York: Meridian, 1960.

Certeau, Michel de. *The Writing of History.* Translated by Tom Conley. New York: Columbia University Press, 1988.

———. "The Madness of Vision." *Enclitic* 7, no. 1 (Spring 1983): 24–31.

Cixous, Hélène. "Introduction to Lewis Carroll's *Through the Looking-Glass* and *The Hunting of the Snark*." *New Literary History* 13, no. 2 (Winter 1982): 231–51.

Clément, Catherine. *The Lives and Legends of Jacques Lacan.* Translated by Arthur Goldhammer. New York: Columbia University Press, 1983.

Cohen, Morton. *Lewis Carroll, Photographer of Children: Four Nude Studies.* New York: Potter, 1978.

Cohen, Morton N., and Roger Lancelyn Green, eds. *The Letters of Lewis Carroll.* New York: Oxford University Press, 1979.

Collingwood, Stuart Dodgson. *The Life and Letters of Lewis Carroll.* London: T. F. Unwin, 1898.

Comaroff, Jean, and John Comaroff. "Medicine, Colonialism, and the Black Body." In *Ethnography and the Historical Imagination.* Boulder, Colo.: Westview Press, 1992.

Corbin, Alain. *The Foul and the Fragrant: Odor and the French Social Imagination.* Cambridge: Harvard University Press, 1986. Originally published as *Le Miasme et la jonquille: L'odorat et l'imaginaire social XVIIIe–XIXe siècles* (Paris: Aubier Montaigne, 1982).

Darwin, Charles. *Expression of the Emotions in Man and Animals.* London: John Murray, Albemarle Street, 1890.

Davidoff, Leonore. "Class and Gender in Victorian England." In *Sex and Class in Women's History,* edited by J. L. Newton, M. P. Ryan, and J. R. Walkowitz. London: Routledge and Kegan Paul, 1983.

Dawkins, Heather. "Politics of Visibility, Domestic Labour and Representation: The Diaries and Photographs (1853–74) of Hannah Cullwick." *Parallelogramme* 10, no. 4 (April–May 1985): 47–50.

——. "The Diaries and Photographs of Hannah Cullwick." *Art History* 10, no. 2 (June 1987): 154–87.

Dijkstra, Bram. *Idols of Perversity: Fantasies of Feminine Evil in Fin-de-Siècle Culture.* New York: Oxford University Press, 1986.

Duncan, J. Matthews. *Clinical Lectures on the Diseases of Women.* 4th ed. London: J. and A. Churchill, 1889.

Ellis, Havelock. *Studies in the Psychology of Sex.* 7 vols. Philadelphia: F. A. Davis, 1928.

Engen, Rodney. *Kate Greenaway.* New York: Schocken, 1981.

Foucault, Michel. *The History of Sexuality.* Translated by Robert Hurley. Pantheon: New York, 1978. Originally published as *Historie de la Sexualité,* Vol. I, *La Volenté de savoir* (Paris: Gallimard, 1976).

Freud, Sigmund. "Civilization and its Discontents." In *The Standard Edition of the Complete Psychological Works,* vol. 21. London: Hogarth Press, 1953–74.

——. "Femininity." In *The Standard Edition of the Complete Psychological Works,* vol. 22. London: Hogarth Press, 1953–74.

——. "The Sexual Life of Human Beings." In *The Standard Edition of the Complete Psychological Works,* vol. 16. London: Hogarth Press, 1953–74.

——. "Freud and Fetishism: Previously Unpublished Minutes of the Vienna Psychoanalytic Society." Edited and translated by Louis Rose. *Psychoanalytic Quarterly* 57 (1988): 147–66.

Fuss, Diana. *Essentially Speaking: Feminism, Nature and Difference.* New York: Routledge, 1989.

Gallop, Jane. *Thinking Through the Body.* New York: Columbia University Press, 1988.

Gernsheim, Helmut. *Lewis Carroll, Photographer.* New York: Dover, 1969.

——. *Julia Margaret Cameron, Her Life and Photographic Work.* New York: Aperture, 1975.

Gilbert, Sandra M., and Susan Gubar. *The Madwoman in the Attic: The Woman Writer and the Nineteenth-Century Imagination.* New Haven, Conn.: Yale University Press, 1979.

Ginsburg, Madeleine. *Victorian Dress in Photographs.* New York: Holmes and Meier, 1983.

Gitter, Elisabeth G. "The Power of Women's Hair in the Victorian Imagination." *PMLA* 99, no. 5 (October 1985): 936–54.

Gorham, Deborah. "The 'Maiden Tribute of Modern Babylon' Re-Examined: Child Prostitution and the Idea of Childhood in Late-Victorian England." *Victorian Studies* 21, no. 3 (Spring 1978): 353–79.

Greenacre, Phyllis. "The Character of Dodgson as revealed in the Writings of Carroll." In *Aspects of Alice,* edited by Robert Phillips. London: Victor Gollancz, 1972.

Grosz, Elizabeth. *Sexual Subversions, Three French Feminists.* Sydney: Allen and Unwin, 1989.

Guiliano, Edward, and James R. Kincaid, eds. *Soaring with the Dodo.* Charlottesville: University Press of Virginia, 1982.

——, ed. *Lewis Carroll: A Celebration, Essays on the Occasion of the 150th Anniversary of the Birth of Charles Lutwidge Dodgson.* New York: Clarkson N. Potter, 1982.

Hamilton, A. C., gen. ed. *The Spenser Encyclopedia.* London: Routledge, 1990.

Heath, Stephen. *The Sexual Fix.* London: Macmillan, 1982.

Hellerstein, Erna Olafson, Leslie Parker Hume, and Karen M. Offen, eds. *Victorian Women: A Documentary of Women's Lives in Nineteenth-Century England, France, and the United States.* Palo Alto, Calif.: Stanford University Press, 1981.

Hiley, Michael. *Victorian Working Women: Portraits from Life.* London: Gordon Fraser, 1979.

Hudson, Derek. *Lewis Carroll.* London: Constable, 1954.

———. *Munby: A Man of Two Worlds: The Life and Diaries of Arthur J. Munby 1828–1910.* London: Gambit, 1972.

Irigaray, Luce. *Le Langage des déments.* The Hague: Mouton, 1973.

———. *L'Oubli de l'air chez Martin Heidegger.* Paris: Les Éditions de Minuit, 1983.

———. *This Sex Which is Not One.* Translated by Catherine Porter and Carolyn Burke. Ithaca, N.Y.: Cornell University Press, 1985. Originally published as *Ce Sexe qui n'en est pas un* (Paris: Éditions de Minuit, 1977).

———. *Je, Tu, Nous.* Paris: Grasset, 1990.

———. *The Irigaray Reader.* Edited by Margaret Whitford, translated by David Macey. Oxford: Basil Blackwell, 1991.

———. *An Ethics of Sexual Difference.* Translated by Carolyn Burke and Gillian C. Gill. Ithaca, N.Y.: Cornell University Press, 1993. Originally published as *Éthique de la différence sexuelle* (Paris: Les Éditions de Minuit, 1984).

Jones, Edgar Yoxall. *Father of Art Photography: O. G. Rejlander, 1813–1875.* Greenwich: New York Graphic Society, 1973.

Kincaid, James R. "Alice's Invasion of Wonderland," *PMLA* 88, no. 1 (January 1973): 92–99.

———. *Child-Loving: The Erotic Child and Victorian Culture.* New York: Routledge, 1992.

Knight, Hardwicke. "Anne Isabella Thackeray and Julia Margaret Cameron." *History of Photography* 7, no. 3 (July–September 1983): 247–48.

Krauss, Rosalind. "Tracing Nadar." *October* 5 (Summer 1978): 29–47.

Kristeva, Julia. *Desire in Language: A Semiotic Approach to Literature and Art.* Edited by Leon S. Roudiez, translated by Thomas Gora, Alice Jardine, and Leon S. Roudiez. New York: Columbia University Press, 1980.

———. "Stabat Mater." In *The Kristeva Reader,* edited by Toril Moi. New York: Columbia University Press, 1986.

Kuykendall, Eléanor. "Toward an Ethic of Nurturance: Luce Irigaray on Mothering and Power." In *Mothering, Essays in Feminist Theory,* edited by Joyce Trebilcot. Totowa, N.J.: Rowman and Allanheld, 1984.

Lacan, Jacques. *Écrits: A Selection.* Translated by Alan Sheridan. New York: W. W. Norton, 1977. Originally published as *Écrits* (Paris: Éditions du Seuil, 1966).

———. *The Four Fundamental Concepts of Psycho-Analysis.* Edited by Jacques-Alain Miller, translated by Alan Sheridan. New York: W. W. Norton, 1977. Originally published as *Le Seminaire de Jacques Lacan, Livre XI, Les quatre concepts fondamentaux de la psychanalyse* (Paris: Éditions du Seuil, 1973).

Laqueur, Thomas, and Catherine Gallagher. *The Making of the Modern Body: Sexuality and*

Society in the Nineteenth Century. Berkeley and Los Angeles: University of California, 1987.

Levinas, Emmanuel. *Totality and Infinity.* Translated by Alphonso Lingis. Pittsburgh: Duquesne University Press, 1969.

———. *Otherwise Than Being or Beyond Existence.* Translated by Alphonso Lingis. The Hague: Martinus Nijhoff, 1981.

———. *Face to Face with Levinas.* Edited by Richard A. Cohen. Albany: State University of New York Press, 1986.

Lorimer, Douglas A. *Colour, Class and the Victorians: English Attitudes to the Negro in the Mid-Nineteenth Century.* Leicester: Leicester University Press, 1978.

Lutyens, Mary. *Effie in Venice.* London: John Murray, 1965.

Marcus, Steven. *The Other Victorians: A Study of Sexuality and Pornography in Mid-Nineteenth-Century England.* New York: Basic Books, 1964.

Marin, Louis. *Utopics: The Semiological Play of Textual Space.* Translated by Robert A. Vollrath. Atlantic Highlands, N.J.: Humanities Press International, 1990. Originally published as *Utopiques: jeux d'espaces* (Paris: Les Éditions de Minuit, 1973).

Martin, Wendy. "Anne Bradstreet's Poetry: A Study of Subversive Piety." In *Shakespeare's Sisters,* edited by Susan Gubar and Sandra M. Gilbert. Bloomington: Indiana University Press, 1979.

Mavor, Carol. "Dream Rushes: Lewis Carroll's Photographs of Girl-Children." In *The Girl's Own: A Social History of the Victorian Girl,* edited by Claudia Nelson and Lynne Vallone. Athens: University of Georgia Press, 1994.

Meinwald, Dan. *Memento Mori: Death in Nineteenth-Century Photography.* Exhibition catalog. Riverside: California Museum of Photography, University of California, 1990.

Merleau-Ponty, Maurice. *The Visible and the Invisible, Followed by Working Notes.* Edited by Claude Lefort, translated by Alphonso Lingis. Evanston, Ill.: Northwestern University Press, 1968. Originally published as *Le Visible et l'invisible* (Paris: Éditions Gallimard, 1964).

Metz, Christian. "Photography and Fetish." *October* 34 (Fall 1985): 81–90.

Miller, D. A. *Bringing Out Roland Barthes.* Berkeley and Los Angeles: University of California Press, 1992.

Nabokov, Vladimir. *The Annotated Lolita.* Edited, with preface, introduction, and notes by Alfred Appel Jr. New York: McGraw-Hill, 1970.

Nadar. "My Life as a Photographer." Translated by Thomas Repensek. *October* 5 (Summer 1978): 7–28.

Nochlin, Linda. "Morisot's *Wet Nurse:* The Construction of Work and Leisure in Painting." In *Women, Art, and Power: And Other Essays.* New York: Harper and Row, 1988.

———. "The Imaginary Orient." In *The Politics of Vision: Essays on Nineteenth-Century Art and Society.* New York: Harper and Row, 1989.

Papetti, Yolande, Françoise Valier, Bernard de Fréminville, and Serge Tisseron. *La passion des étoffes chez un neuro-psychiatre, G. G. de Clérembault (1872–1934).* Paris: Éditions Solin, 1987.

Parker, Rozsika, and Griselda Pollock. *Old Mistresses: Women, Art and Ideology.* New York: Pantheon, 1981.

Patmore, Coventry. "Mrs. Cameron's Photographs." *Macmillan Magazine* 13 (January 1866): 230.

———. *The Angel in the House.* London: George Bell and Sons, 1892.

Phelan, Peggy. *Unmarked: Politics of Performance.* New York: Routledge, 1992.

Piper, Adrian. "Passing for White, Passing For Black." *Transition* 58: 4–32.

Pollock, Griselda. *Vision and Difference: Femininity, Feminism and the Histories of Art.* London: Routledge, 1988.

Prioleau, Elizabeth. "Humbert Humbert Through the *Looking-Glass.*" *Twentieth Century Literature* 21, no. 4 (December 1975): 428–37.

Reed, Langford. *The Life of Lewis Carroll.* London: W. & G. Foyle, 1932.

Ritchie, Hester Thackeray, ed. *Thackeray and His Daughter: The Letters and Journals of Anne Thackeray, with Many Letters of William Makepeace Thackeray.* London: Harper and Brothers, 1924.

Riviere, Joan. "Womanliness as Masquerade." *International Journal of Psychoanalysis* 10 (1929): 303–13.

Schiebinger, Londa. "Skeletons in the Closet: The First Illustrations of the Female Skeleton in Eighteenth-Century Anatomy." In *The Making of the Modern Body: Sexuality and Society in the Nineteenth Century,* edited by Thomas Laqueur and Catherine Gallagher. Berkeley and Los Angeles: University of California Press, 1987.

Sedgwick, Eve Kosofsky. *Epistemology of the Closet.* Berkeley and Los Angeles: University of California Press, 1990.

———. *Tendencies.* Durham, N.C.: Duke University Press, 1993.

Showalter, Elaine. *The Female Malady: Women, Madness and English Culture, 1830–1980.* New York: Pantheon, 1985.

Silverman, Kaja. "The Fantasy of the Maternal Voice." In *The Acoustic Mirror: The Female Voice in Psychoanalysis and Cinema.* Bloomington: Indiana University Press, 1988.

Smith-Rosenberg, Carroll. *Disorderly Conduct.* New York: Oxford University Press, 1985.

Solomon-Godeau, Abigail. "The Legs of the Countess." *October* 39 (Winter 1986): 65–108.

Stallybrass, Peter, and Allon White. *The Politics and Poetics of Transgression.* Ithaca, N.Y.: Cornell University Press, 1986.

Stanley, Liz. "Biography as Microscope or Kaleidoscope?: The Case of 'Power' in Hannah Cullwick's Relationship with Arthur Munby." *Women's Studies International Forum* 10, no. 1 (1987): 19–31.

———, ed. *The Diaries of Hannah Cullwick: Victorian Maidservant.* London: Virgo, 1984.

Stern, Jeffrey. *Lewis Carroll's Library.* Charlottesville: University Press of Virginia, 1981.

Stewart, Susan. *On Longing: Narratives of the miniature, the gigantic, the souvenir, the collection.* Baltimore: John Hopkins University Press, 1984.

Suleiman, Susan Rubin. "Writing and Motherhood." In *The (M)other Tongue,* edited by Shirley Nelson Garner, Claire Kahane, and Madelon Sprengnether. Ithaca, N.Y.: Cornell University Press, 1985.

Swindells, Julia. "Liberating the Subject? Autobiography and 'Women's History': A

Reading of *The Diaries of Hannah Cullwick.*" In *Interpreting Women's Lives: Feminist Theory and Personal Narratives,* edited by Personal Narratives Group. Bloomington: Indiana University Press, 1989.

Taylor, Mark C. *Altarity.* Chicago: University of Chicago Press, 1987.

Thackeray, Anne. "A Book of Photographs." In *Toilers and Spinsters.* London: Smith, Elder, 1876.

———. *From an Island.* London, 1877.

Troubridge, Laura. *Memories and Reflections.* London: Heinemann, 1925.

Wagner, Gillian. *Barnardo.* London: Weidenfield and Nicolson, 1979.

Walkowitz, Judith. *Prostitution and Victorian Society: Women, Class and the State.* Cambridge: Cambridge University Press, 1980.

Warner, Marina. *Alone of All Her Sex: The Myth and the Cult of the Virgin Mary.* London: Weidenfield, 1976.

Weaver, Mike. *Julia Margaret Cameron, 1815–1879.* London: Herbert Press, 1984.

———. *Whisper of the Muse: The Overstone Album and Other Photographs.* Exhibition catalog for the J. Paul Getty Museum. Malibu, 1986.

Williams, Neville. *Powder and Paint.* London: Longmans, Green, 1957.

Wilsher, Ann, and Benjamin Spear. " 'A Dream of Fair Ladies': Mrs. Cameron Disguised." *History of Photography* 7, no. 2 (April–June 1983): 118–20.

Wittig, Monique. "The Category of Sex." *Feminist Issues* 2, no. 2 (Fall 1982): 64–68.

Wollen, Peter. "Fire and Ice." *Photographies* 4 (1984): 118–20.

Wood, Christopher. *Olympian Dreamers: Victorian Classical Painters, 1860–1914.* London: Constable, 1983.

Woolf, Virginia. *Freshwater: A Comedy.* Edited with a preface by Lucio P. Ruotolo. New York: Harcourt Brace Jovanovich, 1976.

Yeazell, Ruth Bernard. "Podsnappery, Sexuality, and the English Novel." *Critical Inquiry* 9 (December 1982): 339–57.

———. *Fictions of Modesty: Women and Courtship in the English Novel.* Chicago: University of Chicago Press, 1991.

Page references in italics refer to black and white illustrations (figures); all other illustrations are by plate number.

Carol Mavor is Assistant Professor of Art at the University of North Carolina at Chapel Hill.

Library of Congress Cataloging-in-Publication Data

Mavor, Carol

Pleasures taken : performances of sexuality and loss in Victorian photographs / Carol Mavor.

Includes bibliographical references and index.

ISBN 0-8223-1603-X. — ISBN 0-8223-1619-6 (pbk.)

1. Sex—England—History—19th century.   2. Sex role—England—History—19th century.

3. Photography of women—England—History—19th century.   4. Photography, Erotic.

5. Sexuality in art.   6. England—Social life and customs—19th century.   I. Title.

HQ18.G7M29   1995

306.7'0942—dc20   94-41559